SPIRIT
AND
MARTYRDOM

A Study of the Work of the Holy
Spirit in Contexts of Persecution
and Martyrdom in the New
Testament and Early Christian
Literature

William C. Weinrich

UNIVERSITY
PRESS OF
AMERICA

SPIRIT AND MARTYRDOM

A Study of the Work of the Holy Spirit in Contexts of Persecution and Martyrdom in the New Testament and Early Christian Literature

William C. Weinrich

UNIVERSITY
PRESS OF
AMERICA

Copyright © 1981 by
University Press of America, Inc.™
P.O. Box 19101, Washington, D.C. 20036

Printed in the United States of America

ISBN: 0-8191-1656-4 (Perfect)
0-8191-1655-6 (Case)

Library of Congress Number: 80-5597

IN MEMORIAM

CARL W. WEINRICH

TABLE OF CONTENTS

ABBREVIATIONS

AGG - Abhandlungen der königlichen Gesellschaft
der Wissenschaften zu Göttingen

AJT - American Journal of Theology

AnBib - Analecta Biblica

AnBoll - Analecta Bollandiana

AnGreg - Analecta Gregoriana

ASNU - Acta Seminarii Neotestamentici Upsaliensis

ATANT - Abhandlungen zur Theologie des Alten und
Neuen Testaments

BFCT - Beiträge zur Förderung christlicher
Theologie

BibScRel - Biblioteca di Scienze Religiose

BJRL - The Bulletin of the John Rylands Library

Bl-Debr - Grammatik des neutestamentlichen
Griechisch, von F. Blass, bearbeitet von
A. Debrunner

BWANT - Beiträge zur Wissenschaft vom Alten und
Neuen Testament

BZAW - Beihefte zur Zeitschrift für die
alttestamentliche Wissenschaft

BZNW - Beihefte zur Zeitschrift für die
neutestamentliche Wissenschaft

CChr - Corpus Christianorum

CNT - Commentaire du Nouveau Testament

CSEL - Corpus scriptorum ecclesiasticorum Latinorum

DACL - Dictionnaire d'archéologie chrétienne et
de liturgie

DTC - Dictionnaire de Théologie Catholique

ETL - Ephemerides Theologicae Lovanienses

EvT - Evangelische Theologie

FrThSt – Frankfurter Theologische Studien

FRLANT – Forschungen zur Religion und Literatur des Alten und Neuen Testaments

GCS – Die griechischen christlichen Schriftsteller der ersten Jahrhunderte

GiorItFil – Giornale Italiano di Filologia

HJ – Historisches Jahrbuch der Görres-Gesellschaft

HNT – Handbuch zum Neuen Testament

HTKNT – Herders Theologischer Kommentar zum Neuen Testament

HTR – The Harvard Theological Review

ICC – The International Critical Commentary of the Old and New Testament

JEH – The Journal of Ecclesiastical History

JQR – The Jewish Quarterly Review

JR – The Journal of Religion

JTS – The Journal of Theological Studies

MeyerK – Kritisch-exegetischer Kommentar über das Neue Testament

MysTh – Mystische Theologie

NGG – Nachrichten von der Gesellschaft der Wissenschaften zu Göttingen

NICNT – New International Commentary of the New Testament

NovT – Novum Testamentum

NovTSup – Novum Testamentum Supplements

NTD – Das Neue Testament Deutsch

NTS – New Testament Studies

OECT – Oxford Early Christian Texts

PG – J. Migne, Patrologia graeca

PL – J. Migne, Patrologia latina

Martyrdom was no stranger to the early Church. Jesus had promised his disciples that they would be harassed, persecuted, imprisoned and martyred. The numerous accounts of Christian martyrdom bear witness that he was telling the truth. From beginning to end the life of Jesus itself was in the shadow of threat and death. Matthew reports that the infant Jesus was targeted for murder by King Herod (Matt 2:7-18). The active ministry of Jesus evoked repeated opposition from the Jewish leaders and finally elicited plots for his removal. The Gospel narratives culminate in the recounting of Jesus' crucifixion at the hands of the Romans. The life of Jesus lay under the necessity that the Son of Man suffer many things, be rejected, and be killed (Mark 8:31).

Yet, the early Christians were certain that in Jesus of Nazareth the new age of the Messiah had dawned upon them. They perceived in Jesus the fulfillment of the promises spoken by the prophets, the fulfillment of their hopes and longings, the coming of God's Kingdom. Why was it necessary, therefore, that Jesus suffer and die? The message of a suffering Messiah and of God's Kingdom coming in the lowliness of the cross was not an easy message to accept, and the Gospels make clear that it was misunderstood, rejected, and countered even by the twelve disciples (Mark 8:32; Luke 22:49-50). However, in their certainty that Jesus had risen from the dead and in the conviction that they had received the Holy Spirit the disciples themselves entered upon a path characterized by suffering and death. Between the Peter who rebuked Jesus (Mark 8:32) and out of fear denied Jesus (Mark 14:66-72) and the Peter who fearlessly confessed Jesus before the Jewish authorities (Acts 4-5) lay the resurrection and the coming of the Holy Spirit. Jesus' saying that to be his disciple one must take up the cross became reality for the community of the Christian faithful. In the power of the Spirit the life of the believer was to be a life like that of Jesus, one of suffering and death. As Paul and Barnabas told their newlywon converts in Asia Minor, "It is necessary that we enter into the Kingdom of God through many tribulations" (Acts 14:22). In the midst of these tribulations, however, the Christians repeatedly testified that the Spirit was present exhorting, guarding, strengthening them. Tribulation became a time for rejoicing and for hope.

How is the relationship between the Holy Spirit and the suffering of the disciples of Christ to be understood? In a 1914 acticle, Karl Holl represented the viewpoint that the early and predominant view of the Christian martyr was that of an ecstatic to whom revelations were given. The martyr became a prophet by virtue of a special gift of the Spirit which enabled the martyr to view into the invisible world. In this manner the confessor and martyr became a "witness" to the resurrected Christ ("Die Vorstellung von Märtyrer und die Märtyrerakte in ihrer geschichtlichen Entwicklung," Gesammelte Aufsätze zur Kirchen-geschichte, vol. 2: Der Osten [Tübingen: J. C. B. Mohr, 1928] 68-102). The notae of the Spirit's presence in the martyr were special charismatic gifts which set the martyr off from the rest of the Christian congregation. Indeed, martyrdom was a self-contained unit within the martyr's own life and was, therefore, utterly distinct and different from the rest of his life (Holl, "Die Vorstellung von Märtyrer," 72-73). From the view that martyrdom is something qualitatively distinct and special vis-a-vis the "normal" Christian life and is therefore surrounded by a special presence and activity of the Spirit, it is a short step to the view that martyrdom is meritorious and the martyr deserving of special honor. That this step was taken early by the Christian Church is the view of Marc Lods, who generally follows the line of thinking laid down by Holl (Confesseurs et martyrs: Successeurs des prophetes dans l'eglise des trois

premiers siecles [Cahiers Theologiques 41;
Neuchatel: Delachaux & Niestle, 1958]).

It is to the credit of Holl and Lods that
they raise the question of the Spiritual nature of
Christian martyrdom in a rigorous fashion. Other
studies on early Christian concepts of martyrdom
usually rest content with the observation that the
martyr was conceived to be an especial bearer of
the Spirit. The present study wishes to examine
anew the question concerning the functions and
role of the Spirit in contexts of persecution and
Christian martyrdom. Although not intended to be
a direct confutation of the Holl-Lods viewpoint,
this study advocates the view that the early
Christians understood the relation between the
Spirit and Christian martyrdom in Christological
and ecclesiological terms. The major presupposi-
tion of all talk concerning the persecution and
martyrdom of the Christian believer was the
resurrection of Jesus and his Lordship over the
Church. The early Church understood this Lordship
of Jesus to be exercised through the Spirit who
in the power of the resurrection made the way of
the disciples of Jesus to be that of Jesus
himself.

The present work is a slightly revised
version of my dissertation which I submitted in
1977 to the faculty of the University of Basel.
Every effort has been made to take note of
pertinent research which has appeared since the
writing of my own work. In this regard, special
mention must be made of the fine book by Karin
Bommes, Weizen Gottes (1976), a study of the
theology of martyrdom of Ignatius of Antioch.

It remains to express my gratitude to those
who have been of primary assistance to me in this
study. Especially do I thank Professor Bo Reicke,
my adviser, who guided me throughout the preparation of the manuscript. His suggestions and
corrections were without exception appropriate
and beneficial to the strength of the argument.

I am also indebted to Professor Oscar Cullmann, who graciously agreed to be the second reader for my dissertation. I thank also the Lutheran World Federation whose generous fellowship enabled me to study in Basel.

Finally, I thank my wife, Barbara, whose patience and encouragement provided necessary support, and my mother and father, who early instilled in me a desire to learn and to strive after those things which do not perish. This book is dedicated to the memory of my father, who in life as well as in death exhibited the faith of the martyrs.

William C. Weinrich

Chapter 1

OLD TESTAMENT AND
INTERTESTAMENTAL LITERATURE

The Old Testament reports of two prophets who die by violent means. Jeremiah tells of the prophet Uriah whom King Jehoiakim killed by the sword (Jer 26:20-23). Better known is the murder of Zechariah ben Jehoiada by King Joash (2 Chr 24:17-22; Matt 23:35). However, that the prophet might suffer for speaking a word of judgment is clear from other stories. Obadiah hid a hundred prophets in a cave to preserve them from Jezebel's murderous desires (1 Kgs 18:4,13). The prophet Elijah fled for his life to Mount Horeb to escape from the same queen (1 Kgs 19:1-14). Jeremiah was not a stranger to beatings and imprisonments (Jer 20:2; 37:15; 38:1-6). Already in the Old Testament the view is represented that the people of Israel had repeatedly rejected God's prophets and had often killed them (Jer 7:25-26; 25:4; Lam 2:20; Neh 9:26; cf. 2 Esdr 1.32). By the time of the New Testament, martyrdom was firmly entrenched in popular stories concerning the prophets as the probable end of a prophet's career. In the collection of stories known as the Vitae Prophetarum six of the twenty-three stories end in the martyrdom of the prophet. In one witness, eight of the prophets suffer a violent death.[1]

What is assumed for all the prophets is explicitly expressed in the story of Zechariah ben Jehoiada. The words of judgment, which lead to persecution and possible death, are words spoken by the Spirit of God: Then the Spirit of God took possession of Zechariah the son of Jehoiada the priest; and he stood above the people, and said to them, "Thus says God, 'Why do you transgress the commandments of the Lord, so that you cannot prosper? Because you have forsaken the Lord, he has forsaken you'" (2 Chr 24:20; cf. Neh 9:30). The idea that the Spirit-filled prophet meets opposition has deep roots in Jewish literature.

1

Jewish literature is acquainted also with certain miraculous elements surrounding the death of a martyr. Often the martyr has visionary experiences or a heavenly voice accompanies the event of martyrdom. Such motifs, however, generally appear in later rabbinic sources, and even then these elements appear without mention of the Holy Spirit.[2]

Without question the early Church knew Jewish stories of martyrdom and was influenced by them in its own thinking concerning martyrdom. The idea that the Spirit-filled prophet might suffer for his message lived on in the Christian community (Matt 23:29-36; Mark 12:1-12; Luke 13:33-34; Acts 7:52; 1 Thess 2:15; Heb 11:36-38). The deaths of John the Baptist and of Jesus himself were at least partly understood in light of this tradition (cf. Matt 14:5; Mark 9:12-13), and it was as the Spirit-filled prophetic community that the early Church was soon to encounter violent opposition (Acts 4:3; 5:18).

Did the early Christian community receive other conceptions of the relation between the Spirit of God and persecution and martyrdom from Jewish literature? To provide an answer we investigate briefly the stories in the book of Daniel, 2 and 4 Maccabees, and the Martyrdom of Isaiah. These stories were well known and influential in the early Christian community.

1. DANIEL 3 AND 6

Central to the stories of the three young men and of Daniel is not their suffering as faithful men of God but their deliverance from any pain or suffering at all. A doubt may be voiced whether these stories even represent martyrological literature.[3] To be sure, situations are reflected in which suffering and death are distinct possibilities, but in fact suffering and martyrdom do not occur.[4] The inherent possibility of suffering and death in the situation serves only to highlight the totality and wonder of God's deliverance. The real point of the stories is that God can and will save from harm those who trust in Him (Dan 3:28; 6:23). To serve idols is futile, for, as King Nebuchadnezzar says, "There is no other god who is able to deliver in this way" (Dan 3:29).

Corresponding to the stories' message, the divine activity of which the book of Daniel speaks is not done through or to the persecuted but rather is directed against that which would inflict suffering. Dan 3:25 speaks of a fourth man "like a son of the gods" (בר אלהין) who walked with the three young men in the fiery furnace. The version of the Septuagint is more explicit: "An angel of the Lord (ἄγγελος κυρίου) entered the furnace with those around Azariah, drove the flame from the furnace and made the midst of the furnace as a damp, whistling breeze" (Dan 3:49-50 [LXX]).[5] Dan 6:23 speaks of an "angel" (מלאך) sent by God who shut the lions' mouths.

Since the persecuted are not themselves direct participants in the drama of God's intervention, there is no room for any activity of the Holy Spirit. In Dan 6:4 Daniel is described as having an "excellent spirit", or, according to the Septuagint, a "holy spirit", in him. Yet, this "spirit" has nothing to do with steadfastness or faithful confession under threat of death but is given as the reason for Daniel's superiority over other officials and for his favor before the king.

2. 2 AND 4 MACCABEES

In 2 Maccabees and 4 Maccabees martyrdom plays a dominant role.[6] For the author of 2 Maccabees the martyrdoms of Eleazar and the seven brothers and their mother are the chief examples of the "calamities" by which the people were being punished, "not for their destruction but for their chastening" (2 Macc 6:12).[7] These "calamities" have come to the people on account of their sins (2 Macc 7:18,32,36; cf. 5:17-18).[8] However, this suffering will remain only a short while, for through the righteous suffering of the martyrs God's anger will abate and He will once again be reconciled with His people (2 Macc

3

7:32-33,37-38). The deaths of the martyrs atone for the sins of the people and prepare the way for a new display of God's mercy.

It is in complete obedience to the Law, however, that their deaths possess expiatory value. The seventh brother gives up body and soul "for the laws of the fathers", calling on the Lord to show mercy to the nation soon (2 Macc 7:37). Through their steadfast refusal to transgress the commands of the Law, even on pain of death, the martyrs demonstrate their faithfulness toward God and thereby establish the necessary condition for renewed reconciliation with God. God's future acts of mercy are grounded in the obedience of the martyr.[9]

The martyr's loyalty and obedience toward the commands of the Law provide the impulse for his behavior. At the suggestion of friends that he pretend to eat the swine's flesh and so escape the penalty, Eleazar tells them to send him to Hades at once. He had made a high resolve worthy of his years and of the dignity of his age and of his grey hair acquired with honor and of his excellent life from boyhood "but especially of the holy and divinely ordained legislation" (2 Macc 6:23). Likewise, by dying in obedience to the Law's commands he will leave to the young a "noble example" of how to die "willingly and nobly for the sacred and holy laws" (2 Macc 6:28). Finally, at his last breath Eleazar comforts himself with the words, "To the Lord who has holy knowledge it is plain that, although I could have escaped death, I undergo terrible pains in my body from flogging, but in my soul I suffer these things gladly, because I fear him" (2 Macc 6:30). The phrase "in my soul" is to be understood in view of 2 Macc 1:3 where the "willing soul" (ψυχή βουλομένη) and "great heart" are the instruments by which faithful worship and an obedient life are rendered to God.

In keeping with its Stoic character, 4 Maccabees is much interested in the motivation for and execution of ethical conduct. This theme appears in the first verse. The author wishes to

4

demonstrate that "the pious Reason is sole master
of the passions" (4 Macc 1:1). When God created
man, He implanted in him his passions and
characteristics but also "enthroned" over all "the
holy, guiding mind" (τὸν ἱερὸν ἡγεμόνα νοῦν). To
this "mind" God gave the Law, and should man live
according to it, he shall rule a "moderate, just,
good and brave kingdom" (4 Macc 2:21-23). Through
the nurture and training of the Law the mind
acquires the knowledge of divine and human affairs
and in all situations chooses the life of wisdom
(4 Macc 1:15-17). To live rightly and justly,
therefore, is to be guided by the "mind" which,
being trained by the Law, guides in correspondence
to the Law.

For the author of 4 Maccabees the martyrdoms
of Eleazar and the seven brothers and their mother
are the best examples displaying the superior
power of the "pious Reason" (4 Macc 1:7-11). By
means of their "pious Reason" the martyrs withstood all the onslaughts of the passions and so
remained true to the life of wisdom, which is
embodied in the Law (4 Macc 6:31-35; 13:1-5).
When Antiochus, attempting to persuade Eleazar to
eat swine's flesh, tells Eleazar that his God will
pardon him for a transgression done under compulsion (δι' ἀνάγκην), Eleazar replies that there is
no stronger compulsion upon him than that of
"obedience to our Law" (4 Macc 5:16). In utter
contempt of the inevitable consequences, Eleazar
eloquently addresses the objects of his loyalty
and devotion: "I shall not belie you, O Law, my
Instructor (παιδευτὰ νόμε); I shall not renounce
you, O beloved Self-control (φίλη ἐγκράτεια); I
shall not put you to shame, O Reason who loves
wisdom (φιλόσοφε λόγε); I shall not deny you, O
honored Priesthood and Knowledge of the Law"
(4 Macc 5:34-35).[10] With these words Eleazar
makes known to the king that his actions will
correspond to the Law which is the ultimate source
and guide of pious living. Not even in the face
of death will he forsake the life according to the
Law. Eleazar's death is proof that "the pious
Reason" is master over the passions (4 Macc 6:31).

In his eulogy of Eleazar (4 Macc 6:31-7:23) the author says that although his body was weakened and torn, Eleazar "became a young man again in the spirit of his Reason and by his Isaac-like Reason turned the many-headed torture to impotence" (4 Macc 7:13-14).[11] Eleazar's Reason, trained by the Law, had the effect of negating all the sources of possible weakness and made Eleazar like Isaac, who by virtue of his Reason did not shrink from fear when he saw his father lift the knife against him (4 Macc 16:20).

Like Eleazar, the seven brothers and their mother defeat the passions by their "pious Reason" and in so doing remain true to the Law. Through all the torments the first brother shows that "only the sons of the Hebrews are unconquerable on behalf of virtue" (4 Macc 9:18). The "sons of the Hebrews" alone are unconquerable because only they possess the Law by which the Reason is trained for pious living (4 Macc 11:20-21). The second brother is supported and encouraged (ἐπικουφίζειν) in torment by the joys which come through the exercise of virtue (4 Macc 9:31). With eloquent metaphors and literary flourishes the author of 4 Maccabees eulogizes the force which motivated the brothers to constancy and loyalty to their religion. Brotherly love, brought about through the natural order given by the divine and all-wise Providence and especially through training in the same Law, discipline in the same virtues, and nourishment in a righteous life, produced in the brothers such mutual concord and common zeal that they encouraged each other to despise their tortures and to conquer their passions, even that of brotherly love (4 Macc 13:19-14:1). So they became as a "seven-towered Reason", which, as the towers of a harbor repulse the waves and offer calm entrance into the harbor, defended the harbor of piety and conquered the assault of the passions (4 Macc 13:6-7).

The eldest brother is called a "great-minded and Abraham-like youth" (ὁ μεγαλόφρων καὶ Ἀβραμιαῖος νεανίας) because, although his body was broken, he did not groan but bravely endured

6

the torment in silence (4 Macc 9:21-22).[12] The
word μεγαλόφρων is to be understood in view of
4 Macc 1:19 where ἡ φρόνησις is said to be the
chief of all the forms of wisdom, for through it
Reason asserts its control over the passions. In
calling the youth "Abraham-like", the passage
reflects the Jewish tradition which regarded
Abraham as the prime model of obedience to God's
commandments. Indeed, Hellenistic Judaism regarded Abraham as the realization of all the Greek
virtues (4 Macc 16:20; Wis 10:5; Philo, Abr.
52-54).[13] By silently enduring torments, the
eldest brother shows his Reason to be in control
of his passions. He is behaving in accordance
with the Law.

Some scholars have seen elements other than
the pious Reason trained by the Law as guides and
aids in the martyr's suffering. Holl believes
4 Macc 6:5-6; 7:13-14; 9:21-22 present the motif
of the dying prophet who in ecstasy speaks with
God.[14] The first of these passages says that
Eleazar was no more moved in his suffering than if
he had been tormented in a dream. Throughout the
scourging Eleazar kept his eyes raised to heaven.
There is no necessity to see ecstasy here. Indeed,
the idea of ecstasy would work against the entire
purpose of 4 Maccabees which is to show that the
"pious Reason" overcomes real passion. Reference
to "dream" does not imply ecstasy but serves
notice that the "pious Reason" in fact put to
naught the passions of Eleazar's sufferings.[15]
Surkau believes that 4 Macc 6:5-6 refers to a
vision.[16] Fischel voices the similar opinion that
a vision is "still transparent in the text" but
believes the author's strong rationalization pre-
vented him from admitting its occurrence.[17]
However, it is doubtful that a vision is implied.
Most likely the passage means simply that in his
suffering Eleazar directed himself to the source
of the Law by which the "pious Reason" is trained.

Surkau also mentions old age (2 Macc 6:18;
4 Macc 5:4; cf. Exod 20:12; Wis 4:9), large
numbers of children and fine outward appearance
(2 Macc 6:18; 4 Macc 6:2; 8:3-4) as signs of God's

special grace and favor and of special divine aid
and support enabling the martyrs to endure their
torments.[18] However, these gifts have nothing to
do with assistance in martyrdom. Their mention
simply serves to demark the martyrs as "righteous".
Similarly, the ἐξουσία to speak mentioned in
4 Macc 5:14 refers only to the permission to speak
granted by Antiochus. Divine power for confession
is not meant.[19]

3. THE MARTYRDOM OF ISAIAH

The Martyrdom of Isaiah is an example of the
popular Jewish literature concerning the prophets
of which we spoke above.[20] As such it represents
the view, present already in the Old Testament,[21]
that the Spirit-filled prophet of God suffers on
account of his message. As one whose words are
words spoken by the Spirit (<u>Mart</u>. <u>Isa</u>. 1:7),
Isaiah prophecies doom and destruction against
King Manasseh and his kingdom (<u>Mart</u>. <u>Isa</u>. 3:6-10).
As one who is Spirit-directed, Isaiah withdraws
from Jerusalem and then from Bethlehem (<u>Mart</u>. <u>Isa</u>.
2:7-8) thereby signifying in a prophetic way that
God Himself is abandoning Judah. Isaiah's words
and actions produce opposition and hatred toward
him which culminate in his martyrdom. God's
Spirit, who speaks and acts through the prophet,
meets opposition which receives concrete form in
the persecution and martyrdom of the bearer of the
Spirit.

New in the Martyrdom of Isaiah, however, is
the cosmic dimension in which the drama of persecution and martyrdom is placed. The opponent of
the Spirit is ultimately not men but Beliar, or
Satan. While it is the Spirit who speaks in
Isaiah (<u>Mart</u>. <u>Isa</u>. 1:7), it is Beliar who dwells
in the heart of Manasseh (<u>Mart</u>. <u>Isa</u>. 1:9; 2:4;
3:11). While the Spirit withdraws from Jerusalem
(<u>Mart</u>. <u>Isa</u>. 2:7-8), it is Beliar who delights in
Jerusalem (<u>Mart</u>. <u>Isa</u>. 2:4).

New as well in the Martyrdom of Isaiah are
the motifs of the martyr's vision of God (<u>Mart</u>.

Isa. 5:7) and of his speaking with the Holy Spirit during the martyrdom (Mart. Isa. 5:14). Both of these motifs are unique in Jewish Acts of the Martyrs. The parallel account of Isaiah's martyrdom in the Talmud (b. Yeb. 49a) mentions neither the vision nor the conversation with the Spirit.[22] The absence of these motifs in other Jewish Acts plus the tendency in Jewish literature at that time to transcendentalize have led Surkau to suggest that the motifs may be from a Christian hand.[23] Visions and conversation with God do appear in Christian accounts of martyrdom (Acts 7:55-56; Mart. Pol. 2:2; 5:2; Eusebius, Hist. eccl. 5.1.51,56). Without question Mart. Isa. 5:14 shares a common tradition with Mart. Pol. 2:2 and Eusebius, Hist. eccl. 5.1.51, as the close verbal correspondences show (γρύξαι, στενάξαι, ὁμιλεῖν). Yet, there is no good reason to deny that these motifs have a Jewish origin. Schoeps believes Mart. Isa. 5:2-14, which contains both elements, belongs to the original Jewish document.[24] Holl also accepts their Jewish origin.[25]

What function the vision and the conversation with the Spirit play within the Martyrdom of Isaiah is not completely clear. It is possible to understand them as special divine gifts to Isaiah as a martyr.[26] In this case, the vision and the presence of the Spirit enable Isaiah to endure the torment of being sawed asunder. Mart. Isa. 5:14 reports that Isaiah "neither cried aloud nor wept" while speaking with the Spirit. However, it is doubtful that the vision and the conversation with the Spirit may rightly be considered martyr-motifs. Since Isaiah was accused of lying because he claimed to have seen God and lived (Mart. Isa. 3:9-10), although Moses had said no one could see God and live (Exod 33:20), it is more probable that the vision is intended to verify Isaiah as a true prophet of God.[27] The account of the vision comes in the wake of a reference to the false prophets laughing and rejoicing because of Isaiah's fate and of Belchira's demand that Isaiah admit that he lied in his condemnation of King Manasseh (Mart. Isa. 5:2-6). However, as Isaiah's life as

9

a prophet had begun with a vision of God, so it
ends with a vision of God at his martyrdom.
Isaiah was a true prophet of God throughout.

A similar judgment is to be made concerning
the conversation with the Spirit. From the beginning Isaiah was in contact with the Spirit. His
prophetic speech was the speech of the Spirit
(Mart. Isa. 1:7). Although believing this to be
a martyr-motif, Holl makes the good suggestion
that the basis of Mart. Isa. 5:14 is Num 12:8[28]:
στόμα κατὰ στόμα λαλήσω αὐτῷ, ἐν εἴδει καὶ οὐ δι᾿
αἰνιγμάτων, καὶ τὴν δόξαν κυρίου εἴδεν. This
passage corresponds well to the theme of the
Martyrdom of Isaiah. As opposed to prophets who
know and speak to the Lord only in sleep and
visions (Num 12:6), Moses sees and speaks to the
Lord directly. It was the accusation against
Isaiah that he had claimed to have seen God and
lived. If Num 12:8 really was in the mind of the
author when he wrote Mart. Isa. 5:14, it would
argue strongly for the view that Isaiah's conversation with the Spirit is testimony to Isaiah as a
true prophet of God. Like the vision, the
speaking with the Spirit is a prophet-motif, not
a martyr-motif.

Mart. Isa. 5:2,6,14 make clear, however, that
the vision and the speaking with the Spirit occur
during the martyrdom itself. In this way the
martyrdom of the prophet becomes part of his
prophetic activity. Martyrdom is not just the
tragic end of the prophet but part and parcel of
his task. Thus, even while being sawn asunder,
Isaiah curses and damns his persecutors (Mart. Isa.
5:9), and as a sign of God's utter abandonment of
them, he instructs the prophets who were with him
to go to the region of Tyre and Sidon (Mart. Isa.
5:13). The order, however, is important. The
prophet becomes a martyr. The martyr is not
necessarily a prophet.

SUMMARY

The Old Testament contains several stories of
the persecution of God's Spirit-filled prophets.

10

Twice it reports of the actual murder of prophets. By the time of the New Testament, persecution and probable martyrdom of the prophet, who spoke the words of the Spirit, had become a formal element in stories about the prophets. This motif, for example, appears in the Martyrdom of Isaiah and several times in the <u>Vitae</u> <u>Prophetarum</u>. However, in pre-Christian Jewish martyrological writings the Spirit plays virtually no role. The character of the message of the stories in Daniel leaves no room for the Spirit's activity on or through the martyr. In Daniel, the message is that God shall keep His righteous followers from suffering, and therefore it precludes any activity of the Spirit on or through the martyr. 2 Maccabees knows only of the martyr's obedience to the Law as motivation for faithful suffering. 4 Maccabees attributes all the martyr's fortitude and faithfulness in suffering to the "pious Reason" and ultimately to the Law which trained and nurtured it. In 4 Maccabees, the "pious Reason" and the Law play a role which the Christians would assign to Christ or to the Holy Spirit.

The Martyrdom of Isaiah contains motifs, such as visions and speaking with the Spirit, which also appear in Christian Acts of the Martyrs. While the Martyrdom of Isaiah uses these motifs to characterize Isaiah as a prophet and not specifically as a martyr, the fact that martyrdom is incorporated into the prophet's activity gives them martyrological overtones.

When the early Christian community was faced with the necessity of reflecting upon the Spirit's activity in persecution and martyrdom, therefore, it could receive only very limited assistance from its Jewish heritage. Beyond the prophetic tradition in which the Spirit-filled prophet is often put to suffering and death by God's enemies, the Spirit plays virtually no role in contexts of persecution and martyrdom in pre-Christian Jewish literature.

1 Cf. Hans Joachim Schoeps, Die jüdischen
Prophetenmorde (SymBU 2; Uppsala: Wretmans,
1943); Theodor Schermann, Propheten- und
Apostellegenden (TU 31/3; Leipzig: J. C.
Hinrichs, 1907); also H. A. Fischel, "Martyr and
Prophet: A Study in Jewish Literature," JQR
n.s. 37 (1946/47) 270-80.

2 Fischel, "Martyr and Prophet," 364-70.

3 For the view that Daniel 3 and 6 do present
stories of martyrdom, see Curt Kuhl, Die drei
Männer im Feuer (Daniel Kapitel 3 und seine
Zusätze): Ein Beitrag zur israelitisch-jüdischen
Literaturgeschichte (BZAW 55; Giessen: Alfred
Töpelmann, 1930) 2-50.

4 This fact was not overlooked by early Christian
commentators. In answering the question why God
delivered Daniel but not the contemporary martyrs,
Hippolytus finally rests his case on the inscru-
table will of God. God saves some, such as the
figures in the book of Daniel, but He takes others
as martyrs, although He has the power to save them.
Were He to save all, there would be no martyrs to
serve as examples. Were God to take all as
martyrs, it would be said that God did not have
the power to save (Comm. Dan. 2.35 [GCS 1.108ff.]).

5 For the LXX version of Daniel 3, cf. R. H.
Charles, ed., The Apocrypha and Pseudopigrapha of
the Old Testament, vol. 1: Apocrypha (Oxford:
At the Clarendon Press, 1913) 625-37; Kuhl, Die
drei Männer im Feuer, 84-104. Early Christian
exegesis recognized the fourth man as the pre-
incarnate Logos: ὁ γὰρ λόγος ἦν σὺν ὑμῖν
(Hippolytus, Comm. Dan. 2.30 [GCS 1.100]).

6 W. H. C. Frend calls 2 Maccabees the "first
Acts of the Martyrs" (Martyrdom and Persecution in
the Early Church: A Study of a Conflict from the
Maccabees to Donatus [Oxford: Basil Blackwell,

1965] 45); Hans-Werner Surkau calls it "die
älteste Märtyrer-Erzählung in der uns erhaltenen
jüdischen Literatur" (Martyrien in jüdischer und
frühchristlicher Zeit [FRLANT 54; Göttingen:
Vandenhoeck & Ruprecht, 1938] 9).

7 Surkau, Martyrien, 9-14.

8 Surkau maintains that the purpose of suffering
according to 2 Macc 7:32,37,38 is different from
that according to 2 Macc 6:12-17, and he suggests
that we ought to see in this the work of different
authors (Martyrien, 13). Perhaps so, but in
2 Macc 7:32-33 the motifs of chastening and
punishment for sin exist in close connection.

9 Eduard Lohse, Märtyrer und Gottesknecht:
Untersuchungen zur urchristlichen Verkündigung vom
Sühntod Jesu Christi (FRLANT 64; Göttingen:
Vandenhoeck & Ruprecht, 1955) 67-68.

10 Since Antiochus offers no retort to Eleazar's
remarks, which end at 4 Macc 5:38, Surkau suggests
that he was unable to withstand Eleazar's philo-
sophical argument (Martyrien, 16; cf. 4 Macc
5:22-25). Johannes Geffcken says that Eleazar
answers "auf gut stoisch" ("Die christlichen
Martyrien," Hermes 45 [1910] 500).

11 Similar ideas are present in the Letter of the
Churches of Lyons and Vienne (Eusebius, Hist. eccl.
5.1.19,24). See below, pp. 195,197.

12 This motif recurs in Mart. Isa. 5:14; Mart.
Pol. 2:2; Eusebius, Hist. eccl. 5.1.51. Cf. below,
pp. 9,173,197.

13 See Joachim Jeremias, s.v. "Ἀβραάμ," TWNT
1 (1933) 8.

14 Karl Holl, "Die Vorstellung vom Märtyrer und
die Märtyrerakte in ihrer geschichtlichen
Entwicklung," Gesammelte Aufsätze zur Kirchengeschichte, vol. 2: Der Osten (Tübingen: J. C. B.
Mohr, 1928) 80.

15 Holl sees ecstasy as a common element in Jewish Acts of the Martyrs. Surkau correctly disputes this view (Martyrien, 32). Cf. also Adolf von Schlatter, Der Märtyrer in den Anfängen der Kirche (BFCT 19/3; Gütersloh: C. Bertelsmann, 1915) 10.

16 Surkau, Martyrien, 32.

17 Fischel, "Martyr and Prophet," 367 n. 103.

18 Surkau, Martyrien, 15-16.

19 Surkau translates "Vollmacht zu reden" (Martyrien, 15).

20 For literature, see Charles, Pseudopigrapha, 155-62; Surkau, Martyrien, 30-33.

21 See above, pp. 1-2.

22 Surkau suggests 4 Macc 6:5 as a parallel within Judaism (Martyrien, 32). To this passage Holl would add 4 Macc 7:13-14; 9:21-22 ("Die Vorstellung vom Märtyrer," 80). However, these passages contain nothing parallel to the motifs in the Martyrdom of Isaiah. See above, p. 7.

23 Surkau, Martyrien, 33.

24 Schoeps, Die jüdische Prophetenmorde, 6.

25 Holl, "Die Vorstellung vom Märtyrer," 80.

26 So Holl, "Die Vorstellung vom Märtyrer," 80; Surkau, Martyrien, 31.

27 Surkau rejects this on the grounds that it would require the vision to be seen by the persecutors as well (Martyrien, 31).

28 Holl, "Die Vorstellung vom Märtyrer," 73 n. 1.

Chapter 2

THE NEW TESTAMENT

No fact witnesses more to the essential nature of the cross of Christ in the life of the Christian than the pervasive presence of the theme of Christian suffering in the New Testament. Entire books--the Epistle to the Hebrews, 1 Peter, and the Revelation of John--were occasioned by experiences of persecution, whether official or unofficial, which Christian communities were undergoing. Paul wrote several of his epistles while under arrest and imprisonment. Common to the entire New Testament is the conviction that as the community of the Risen and Exalted Lord, the Christian community has received the Spirit which was promised it (Acts 1:8) and that therefore the way of the Christian community is the way of the Lord, the way of glory through suffering. In this chapter we discuss some New Testament passages which speak of the Spirit's presence at times of Christian suffering or of the Spiritual nature of Christian suffering.

1. SYNOPTIC GOSPELS

One of the few sayings of Jesus concerning the Holy Spirit is the promise of the Spirit's presence in times of persecution (Matt 10:17-20; Mark 13:9-11; Luke 12:11-12; cf. Luke 21:12-19). The authenticity of this saying need not be doubted.[1] However, the gospels present this word concerning the Spirit in different contexts. In Mark the saying occurs in the apocalyptic discourse of chapter 13 in which the sufferings of the disciples in the councils and synagogues and before governors and kings are presented as signs of the endtime.[2] In Matthew the saying is within the missionary discourse of chapter 10, while in Luke it is within a collection of sayings which appear to be loosely connected by means of common words or phrases.[3] Barrett believes this saying

17

had no fixed place in the tradition, and, therefore, while the saying is authentic, the contexts
are constructions of the early community.[4] However,
both the missionary discourse of Matthew 10 and
the apocalyptic discourse of Mark 13 are appropriate contexts in which Jesus could have made such a
promise. The popular tradition that prophets were
persecuted[5] and the known fate of John the Baptist
would have provided Jesus with sufficient reason
to forecast a similar fate for his disciples as
they carried out their task of mission. Similarly,
reiteration of the promise of the Spirit's activity
in times of future persecution would be appropriate
within the last address of Jesus to his disciples.

The saying in Matthew, appearing within the
missionary discourse, is most instructive for our
purposes:

> Matt 10:17-20: Beware of men. For they
> shall hand you over to councils and flog
> you in their synagogues, and you shall be
> led before governors and even kings on
> account of me, for a witness to them and
> the Gentiles (εἰς μαρτύριον αὐτοῖς καὶ τοῖς
> ἔθνεσιν). But whenever they hand you over,
> do not be anxious how you should speak or
> what you should say, for what you should
> say shall be given to you in that hour.
> For it shall not be you who speak, but
> the Spirit of your Father speaking in you
> (οὐ γὰρ ὑμεῖς ἐστε οἱ λαλοῦντες ἀλλὰ τὸ
> πνεῦμα τοῦ πατρὸς ὑμῶν τὸ λαλοῦν ἐν ὑμῖν).

The context is important. It suggests that persecution arises precisely because of the Church's
mission.[6] This is underscored by the immediately
preceding words of Jesus: "Behold, I send you out
as sheep in the midst of wolves" (Matt 10:16).
One may speak, therefore, of the inevitability of
persecution.[7] However, the inevitability of the
disciples' suffering is itself derived from the
necessity of proclamation.[8] Out of compassion for
the crowds, who were "harassed and helpless like
sheep without a shepherd", Jesus called the twelve
apostles to himself in order to send them out

(Matt 9:36-38). Similarly, the need of proclamation forces the disciples to flee from any persecution they might encounter. The shortness of
the time does not allow them to remain where
resistance is met (Matt 10:23).

This primary concern for proclamation must
not be forgotten when considering our text.
Indeed, it is in view of this concern that Jesus
promises his disciples the Holy Spirit's activity
in times of persecution. In those portentous and
difficult moments when the disciple faces the
necessity of proclamation before governors and
kings, he need not worry concerning his demeanor
or rhetorical skills or what he shall say, for the
fitting and proper word shall be given him. The
Spirit will speak through the disciple. The
advance of the proclamation will not be thwarted
through the possible weakness of the disciple.
Through the Spirit, God Himself will see to it
that the proclamation is spoken.[9] There is no
mention of a special endowment of the Spirit in
time of trouble and danger.[10] The Spirit is not
given. Rather, the gift is what (τί) is to be
said.[11] The text does not say what the content of
the given testimony is, but the context suggests
that it is either "the Kingdom of Heaven is at
hand" (Matt 10:7; cf. Matt 24:14) or a confession
of Christ (Matt 10:32).

The proper and required words shall be given
the disciples "in that hour".[12] The appearance of
the disciples before governors and kings is not
the issue of adverse fate but possesses eschatological significance. First of all, the disciples
have been led before rulers on account of Christ.
The persecution they suffer has no value in itself.
It is only because they are Christ's messengers
(Matt 10:5,16) and his servants (Matt 10:24-25)
that they suffer at all. The persecution of the
disciples is in principle persecution against
Christ himself (cf. Acts 9:4,5). Secondly, the
disciples stand before the rulers "for a witness
to them and the Gentiles" (Matt 10:18: εἰς
μαρτύριον αὐτοῖς καὶ τοῖς ἔθνεσιν; cf. Mark 13:9:
εἰς μαρτύριον αὐτοῖς; Matt 24:14: εἰς μαρτύριον

πᾶσιν τοῖς ἔθνεσιν). The meaning of this phrase
has been much discussed. Von Campenhausen argues
that μαρτύριον refers to the fact that the authorities have persecuted the disciples instead of
listening to them, which fact will provide proof
at the judgment that they are guilty.[13] It founds
the divine judgment. Others have seen in μαρτύριον
a reference to the missionary proclamation of the
disciples. It is for proclamation that the
disciples have been brought before the leaders.[14]
Von Campenhausen is surely correct in rejecting
this second view, that μαρτύριον refers to the
proclamation, and insisting on the objective
nature of the "witness".[15] The parallel passage of
Matt 24:14 makes it quite clear that μαρτύριον
does not refer to the proclamation. However, as
this same passage shows, μαρτύριον refers not to
the fact of persecution, as von Campenhausen avers,
but to the fact that the proclamation has been
made.[16]

Thirdly, the moment of persecution, when
testimony is to be given, bears with it judgment
for the disciple. All is dependent on his steadfastness in confessing Christ. The confession or
denial which he speaks under duress will be
definitively ratified at the last judgment (Matt
10:32-33; Luke 12:8-9).

Finally, the very presence of the Holy Spirit
brings eschatological decisiveness with it. It is
the Spirit who speaks the proclamation through the
disciple. Therefore, to accept or reject the
proclamation is to accept or reject the Spirit.
This is also the import of the saying concerning
blasphemy against the Holy Spirit mentioned in
Luke 12:10.[17]

Luke 21:15 presents a different form of the
saying: "For I shall give you a mouth of wisdom,
which all who oppose you will not be able to
withstand or answer" (ἐγὼ γὰρ δώσω ὑμῖν στόμα καὶ
σοφίαν, ᾗ οὐ δυνήσονται ἀντιστῆναι ἢ ἀντειπεῖν
ἅπαντες οἱ ἀντικείμενοι ὑμῖν; cf. Acts 6:10).
Unlike Matt 10:20; Mark 13:11; and Luke 12:12
where the Spirit speaks through the disciples,

here it is Jesus himself who speaks through them.[18] The disciples stand before the authorities as Jesus' representatives, as those who carry on his mission and his message.

It is with Jesus' mouth that the disciples shall speak wisdom. στόμα 'mouth' is a common Old Testament expression referring to the inspired words of the prophets, and its use here presents no difficulty.[19] The disciples will be inspired to speak as prophets. σοφία 'wisdom' in the Old Testament is often a divine gift such as a personal quality, aptitude, or virtue which is necessary for the successful execution of a given task (cf. [LXX] Exod 28:3; 31:3; 35:31,35; 36:1,2; Isa 11:2). It is possible that σοφία in Luke 21:15, therefore, refers to a certain finesse of speech or quality of presentation which promotes the success of the disciples' witness. However, if we keep in mind that in the parallel passages of Matthew and Mark the gift is what (τί) the disciples are to say, then we shall be inclined to understand σοφία as a designation for the content of the disciples' speech.

Luke twice attributes σοφία to Jesus (Luke 2:40,52). It is notable that between these two occurrences stands the story of the young Jesus sitting in the Temple with the "teachers" amazing them with his understanding (σύνεσις) and answers (Luke 2:47). At the end of Luke's gospel we find the resurrected Jesus opening the minds of the disciples "to understand (συνιέναι) the Scripture" (Luke 24:45). This "understanding" was that in "the Law of Moses, in the prophets, and in the Psalms" the suffering of the Christ and his resurrection were foretold (Luke 24:27,46-47). It is likely, therefore, that the σοφία to be given to the disciples (Luke 21:15) is an understanding of Jesus on the basis of a messianically interpreted Old Testament.[20] This interpretation well suits those occasions in Acts where Luke 21:15 is clearly reflected (Acts 4:14; 6:10).[21] Jesus once designates such a messianically interpreted Old Testament as "my words" (Luke 24:44).

Those who oppose the disciples will not "be able to withstand or answer". This cannot mean that the proclamation of the disciples bears irresistable convincing power. Rather, hatred is the more likely reaction that the disciples will receive (Luke 21:16-17). The message of the crucified and resurrected Jesus as the One promised by the Law and the prophets meets with opposition and rejection whenever it is proclaimed (cf. Acts 5:33; 7:54; 9:23). The inability to respond and answer probably refers to that imposed silence which characterizes those whose guilt is exposed by the words spoken to them. Such silence had met Jesus' own preaching (Luke 13:17; 14:6; 20:26).

Our discussion of Matt 10:17-20 para. shows that while the Holy Spirit is active at times of persecution, it is concerned with the giving of proclamation at these times and not with the situation of persecution as such. Therefore, where the Spirit is mentioned, the spoken word is accented. The Spirit guarantees that the proclamation will be made. The worst that earthly rulers can do will not frustrate God's mission. That is the promise. On the other hand, there is not the slightest hint that the Spirit leads the disciples into situations of persecution and martyrdom. Rather, the forces of evil rise to combat God's Word wherever it is proclaimed. Nor does the Spirit work in the disciples the desire for martyrdom. Rather, the disciples are to be "wise" and are to flee from persecution (Matt 10:16,23). There is no mention that the Spirit protects the disciples from harm, aids them in their legal defense, or helps them to suffer courageously. Nor does the possession of the Spirit mean that the disciples will triumph and their persecutors will be converted through their testimony. The texts mention only hate and persecution (Matt 10:21-22; Mark 13:13; Luke 21:16-17). The Spirit speaks and in its speaking the disciples make a public and candid confession.[22] The disciples, then, do not receive the Spirit because they suffer, but the Spirit dwells in them as those who are sent.[23] A strictly martyrological interpretation for these passages is excluded.

While the word of Jesus concerning the "willing spirit" (Matt 26:41; Mark 14:38) is not itself within a context of persecution and martyrdom, it is fitting that we should include it in our discussion.[24] The scene depicts Jesus as greatly distressed, troubled, and sorrowful, because he is about to confront betrayal, suffering, and death. The theme of persecution and martyrdom is very close. Furthermore, although the word concerning the "willing spirit" is directed to the disciples, who are not in immediate danger of persecution, the theme of faithful discipleship pervades the scene of Gethsemane. This theme was always significant in the Church's thinking about martyrdom.

After eating the Last Supper with his disciples, Jesus went to the Garden of Gethsemane, and there underwent a deep personal crisis in which his filial obedience was tested in the face of Satan and death. When he returned to the three disciples whom he had commanded to "wait and watch" (Mark 14:34) and found them sleeping, Jesus said to Peter:

> Simon, are you sleeping? Were you not strong enough (ἴσχυσας) to watch one hour? Watch and pray that you do not enter into temptation. The Spirit is willing, but the flesh is weak (τὸ μὲν πνεῦμα πρόθυμον ἡ δὲ σὰρξ ἀσθενής) (Mark 14:37b-38)

To what does the "willing spirit" (τὸ πνεῦμα πρόθυμον) refer? Does it refer to the spirit of man, his higher or better faculty, or to the Spirit of God, the Holy Spirit? Kuhn, to whom we owe the most intensive study of the Gethsemane story in recent years, maintains the former. The "willing spirit" refers to "das 'gute Ich' im Menschen, sein eigentliches Selbst, das das Rechte tun will."[25] According to Kuhn, the antithesis of "spirit" and "flesh" which occurs in Mark 14:38 corresponds to that found in the Qumran literature.[26] In Qumran the righteous man partakes of the "flesh", in that he is man and a sinner, and of the "spirit", in that he belongs to the elect

23

of God by divine predestination. In the constant
temptation which the righteous man faces from
Satan, the "spirit" presses him toward pious,
lawful living, but the "flesh" is the sphere of
the demonic, the domain of sin.[27] Therefore,
"flesh" is something to overcome, something over
which to gain control.[28] Mark 14:38, says Kuhn,
occurs in a similar context of Satan's temptation
and presents a similar anthropological dichotomy.[29]

Kuhn's view is not entirely convincing. Mark
14:38 gives no hint that the "flesh" must be overcome. The "flesh" is weak, not evil.[30] Furthermore, the antithesis in Mark 14:38 is not between
"spirit" and "flesh" but between "willing spirit"
and "weak flesh". Kuhn admits that the expression
"weak flesh" does not occur in the Qumran texts
and that a direct antithesis between "spirit" and
"flesh" does not occur in Qumran.[31] The term
"willing spirit" also has no parallel in Qumran.[32]

On the other hand, there are reasons for
believing that "willing spirit" refers to the
Spirit of God, the Holy Spirit.[33] First of all,
as Lohmeyer suggests, πνεῦμα πρόθυμον most likely
comes from Ps 51:14 where the term "Spirit of
willingness" (רוח נדיבה) occurs.[34] In Ps 51:14
"Spirit of willingness" clearly refers to the
Spirit of God.[35] Secondly, the Gethsemane scene
is characterized by a marked contrast between
Jesus and his disciples. While the disciples are
neither "watching" nor "praying", Jesus is uttering
repeated prayers. It is to such watching and
praying that the "spirit" is willing. Jesus, in
contrast to the disciples, has the "willing
spirit". Yet, the "spirit" which Jesus has is the
Spirit of God (Mark 1:8,10,12; 3:29). As the
Spirit was at work in the wilderness during the
temptation (Mark 1:12 para.), so now the Spirit is
at work as Jesus once again asserts his obedient
Sonship.[36] Finally, the Lukan parallel, although
it contains no mention of the Spirit, reports that
an angel from heaven appeared to Jesus and
"strengthened" him (Luke 22:43).[37] As we shall
see, the Spirit in Matt 26:41; Mark 14:38 also
"strengthened". In any case, the Lukan parallel

lends support to the view that divine activity
and not a human disposition for the good is at
work.

If, then, this saying refers to the Holy
Spirit, what is the Spirit's work? The Spirit is
described as "willing" and is contrasted to the
"flesh" which is "weak". However, to translate
πρόθυμον as 'willing' may not do full justice to
the clear antithesis (μέν . . . δέ). The usual
antinym of ἀσθενής is ἰσχυρός (1 Cor 1:25,27; 4:10;
2 Cor 10:10) or δυνατός (2 Cor 12:10; 13:3,4,9).
The Spirit is "able" or "strong". πρόθυμον,
therefore, probably connotes the idea of strengthening. The "willing Spirit" strengthens and
sustains against evil and temptation. This
interpretation receives confirmation in Mark 14:37
(Matt 26:40): "Simon, are you sleeping? Were you
not strong enough (ἴσχυσας) to watch one hour?"
The disciples, devoid of the "willing Spirit",
were unable to withstand the temptation of the
eschatological hour and therefore do not "watch"
but "sleep" (see Mark 13:35-36).[38] Jesus on the
other hand, as the one who possesses the "willing
Spirit", is in time of temptation enabled to the
faithful execution of his calling and remains the
Father's obedient Son.

2. THE GOSPEL OF JOHN

In his farewell discourse Jesus speaks of the
world's hatred for his disciples and of the witness
which the Paraclete[39] and the disciples will give
concerning him. This witness will result in the
persecution and death of the disciples (John
15:18-16:4a). This section is the logical
counterpart to the previous section (John 15:1-17)
in which Jesus spoke of his love for the disciples
and of his commandment to his disciples to love
one another. The world's hate has its root in
Jesus' "choosing" the disciples from the world
(John 15:19). As John 15:16 shows, this "choosing"
has a missionary thrust: "You did not choose me,
but I chose you and appointed you that you should
go (ὑπάγητε) and bear fruit." The word ὑπάγειν

25

along with ἀποστέλλειν refers to the mission of the seventy in Luke 10:3, and most likely it refers to the apostolic mission here as well.[40] The image of bearing fruit speaks for such an interpretation. There is thus a relationship between the mission of the disciples and their persecution and martyrdom. This relationship between mission and martyrdom is implied also in John 12:24, where Jesus combines the "dying" of a seed with its "bearing much fruit". The true disciple, he goes on to say, is the one who "hates his life" and "follows" him (John 12:25-26). Mission, discipleship, and martyrdom appear in closest connection.

John uses the verbs ἔρχεσθαι and πέμπειν to indicate Jesus' messianic mission. Jesus as the Messiah "comes" to the world (John 1:30; 4:25; 5:43; 7:31; cf. Matt 3:11; 11:3). Jesus as the Messiah is "sent" by the Father (John 4:34; 5:23, 30,37; 6:38,44; 7:16,18,28,33; 8:16,29; 12:45,49; 13:16; 14:24; 15:21). Jesus is the fully empowered ambassador from the Father. His words are not his but the Father's. His deeds are expressions of the Father's will (John 4:34; 5:30; 6:38; 7:16,18; 14:24). When, therefore, the Paraclete is said to "come" (John 15:26; 16:7,13) and to be "sent" by the Father (John 14:26) or by Jesus (John 15:26; 16:7), this means that the messianic mission of Jesus continues through the presence of the Paraclete. Likewise, as the Messiah was to "announce all things" (ἀναγγελεῖ ἅπαντα [4:25]), so the Paraclete "leads into all truth" and "announces" (ἀναγγελεῖ [16:13]) what he has received from the exalted Jesus.[41]

In that the disciples are the recipients of the Paraclete, they are the messianic community and suffer the same rejection and persecution that Jesus, the Messiah, suffered. In four conditional clauses (John 15:18,19,20) John describes the hatred which the world has for the disciples as ultimately hatred for Jesus himself. All that will happen to the disciples is because the world does not know Him who sent Jesus (John 15:21; cf. John 16:3). The disciples continue

26

the "sending" of Jesus and, therefore, persecution of them is continued persecution of Jesus and continued rejection of Jesus' mission.

The world's rejection of Jesus' messianic mission in word and deed results in judgment on the world. The hate of the world is sin (John 15:22,24). The strongly forensic nature of the context (John 15:22,24; 16:8-11) shows that the passage concerning the witness of the Paraclete and the disciples (John 15:26-27) also concerns the court process between God and the world.[42] Bultmann claims that the Paraclete is "die Kraft der Verkündigung in der Gemeinde". μαρτυρεῖν refers, therefore, to the "Wortverkündigung in der Gemeinde", although it retains its forensic connotations.[43] However, as Bultmann also recognizes, Jesus' deeds, as well as his words, "witness" to his messianic sending from the Father (John 5:36; 10:25,37; 14:11). In John 15:24 Jesus' deeds are expressly mentioned as instruments of God's judging the world. μαρτυρεῖν in John 15:26-27, therefore, includes the deeds of the believing congregation as well as its words. Through the Paraclete the words and deeds of Jesus continue, for the disciples, to whom the Paraclete is sent, say and do the words and deeds of Jesus. The "witness" of the Paraclete and the "witness" of the disciples will convict the world of sin as did the words and deeds of Jesus.

The καὶ δέ (John 15:27) appears to imply the addition of the disciples' witness to that of the Paraclete. Yet, the witness of the Paraclete and the witness of the disciples are not two separate and distinct activities but are one and the same giving of witness.[44] The disciples give witness because the Spirit is witnessing through them. The same relationship between the presence of the Spirit and the witnessing of the disciples occurs in 1 John 4:13-14: "For He has given to us from His Spirit and we have seen and witness that the Father has sent the Son as Savior of the world." Rather than implying two distinct witnesses, therefore, καὶ δέ implies a certain priority to the witness of the Paraclete. As Brown expresses

it, "the disciples' witness is simply the exteri-
orization of the Spirit's witness".[45] It is as
the Spirit-filled community, as the community to
whom the Paraclete is sent, that the disciples
witness.

The messianic task which the disciples perform
through the guidance of the Paraclete will lead to
their persecution and even to their death (John
16:2-3). The disciples will be thrown out of the
synagogues; they will become ἀποσυνάγωγοι (16:2).
This implies that the disciples will be persecuted
for their confession that Jesus is the "Christ"
(John 9:22). The Jews will even consider their
killing of Christians a positive religious service
to God.[46] This hour of persecution will be a
potential cause for a falling away from faith.
For this reason Jesus has told the disciples
"these things". The words ταῦτα λελάληκα ὑμῖν
bracket the section John 16:1-4a. In John 16:1
Jesus' telling is the basis for the disciples' not
falling away. In John 16:4a it is the basis for
the disciples' "remembering" the words in the hour
of persecution. If the disciples "remember"
Jesus' words, they will not fall away. According
to John 14:26 it is the Paraclete who "shall teach
you all things and remind you of all those things
which I have spoken to you". The Paraclete,
therefore, in bringing the disciples to remember
Jesus' words keeps them from falling away in times
of persecution. John 14:26 is similar to Luke
12:12 in that both speak of the Spirit as
"teaching" the disciples. In Luke 12:12, the
Spirit's teaching leads to the disciples' speaking
in the hour of persecution. We are probably to
understand the disciples' "remembering", or the
Spirit's "reminding", in a similar way and draw
as close a connection as possible between John
15:26-27 and John 16:1-4a--the Paraclete
"witnesses" concerning Jesus thereby "reminding"
the disciples of Jesus' words. From the perspective of the disciples, the Paraclete's "reminding"
is their "remembering" which takes active form
in their own "witness" concerning Jesus. Thus, in
actively witnessing concerning Jesus the disciples
remain secure from apostasy.

28

A relationship between John 15:26-27 and the Synoptic passages which contain the promise of the Spirit in times of persecution (Matt 10:17-20; Mark 13:9-11; Luke 12:11-12) is generally recognized.[47] Yet, certain differences have been noted. Most recently Beutler has pointed to the differences of terminology which forbid the assumption of any close connection as far as the history of traditions is concerned.[48] In the Synoptics the Spirit "speaks" (Matt 10:20; Mark 13:11) or "teaches" (Luke 12:12). In the Synoptics neither the Spirit nor the disciples "witness". Rather, the persecution becomes a "witness" that the persecutors have rejected the proclamation of the disciples (Matt 10:18; Mark 13:9). Beutler also refers to the strong Christological orientation of John which, he says, the Synoptics lack.

Nevertheless, concerning our theme a broad agreement between the Johannine and Synoptic passages may be discerned:
1) Persecution is the world's reaction against the disciples' mission. The world persecutes those whom Jesus sends (Matt 10:16; John 15:16) and who, like Jesus, bear the Spirit[49];
2) Persecution of the disciples is ultimately persecution of Jesus himself (Matt 10:18; John 15:18-24);
3) The Spirit is related closely to the proclamation (Matt 10:20; John 15:26-27);
4) The Spirit represents the cause of Jesus, not that of the disciples;
5) The Spirit works in and through the disciples (Matt 10:20; John 15:27);
6) The Spirit's presence and activity does not guarantee the disciples' safety nor bring them visible victory (Matt 10:21-23; John 16:2);
7) The Spirit's presence and activity bears the character of eschatological judgment in view of the world's rejection (Matt 10:18; John 15:22,24);
8) In so far as the Paraclete's "reminding" of the disciples keeps them from falling away, the work of the Spirit in John 15:26-16:4a may be compared with the Spirit's work implied in Mark 14:38.

29

Yet, all in all the Johannine passage is considerably richer in its associations and goes beyond the Synoptic passages in several ways:
1) In John the Spirit's connection with Jesus is tightly drawn. The Paraclete is "another Paraclete" who resembles Jesus (John 14:16). Jesus sends the Paraclete from the Father (John 15:26). In the Synoptics the Spirit is "the Spirit of the Father" (Matt 10:20) or simply the "Holy Spirit" (Matt 13:11; Luke 12:12);
2) The forensic nature of the Spirit's work is much more to the fore in John than in the Synoptic passages;
3) In both the Synoptics and in John the proclamation of the disciples brings judgment on the persecutors. However, the perspective is different. In the Synoptics the fact of proclamation will be a "witness" in the future last judgment. In John the judgment is taking place in the "witness" of the Paraclete and the disciples. The futuristic element retreats significantly within John;
4) Unlike the Synoptics where the verbal proclamation alone is mentioned (Matt 10:19-20), John presents the witness of the disciples in their works as well as in their words (John 15:24);
5) Because the disciples' works have the character of witness, the suffering and death of the disciples receives a value of its own as a witness concerning Jesus;
6) The concept of mission within John is bound to the idea of God's love for the world (cf. John 3:16). The passage concerning the world's hate for the disciples follows immediately upon a passage whose Leitmotif is Jesus' command to love one another (John 15:12-17). As in 1 John 3:13, Jesus' love, shown in his death, leads to the disciples' giving their life for the brethren. The suffering and death of the disciples, occasioned by the hate of the world, is "witness" to Jesus and therefore gives sustenance to the community of believers. This element was fundamental in the early Christian view of martyrdom and lies at the bottom of the Acts of the Martyrs

whose principal function was to exhort and encourage those who read them.[50]

3. THE ACTS OF THE APOSTLES

In Acts 4 there is the first mention of official opposition to the disciples. While Peter and John were speaking to the people, "the priests and the captain of the Temple and the Sadducees came upon them, annoyed because they were teaching the people and proclaiming in Jesus the resurrection from the dead", and they threw the disciples into prison (Acts 4:1-3).[51] After a night in prison, Peter and John were asked by the Jewish leaders "by what power or by what name" they had healed a lame man (cf. Acts 3:1-10). "Then, filled with the Holy Spirit, Peter spoke to them" (τότε Πέτρος πλησθεὶς πνεύματος ἁγίου εἶπεν πρὸς αὐτούς [Acts 4:8]). This is to be understood as fulfillment of Jesus' promise that when called upon to speak before leaders and rulers the Holy Spirit will speak through them (Luke 12:12; 21:15). The use of the aorist passive (πλησθεὶς) suggests a special moment of inspiration and serves to stress the gift character of the Spirit's presence as well as the divine origin of the following words.[52] Whether Luke intends God or Jesus as the subject of πλησθεὶς is not clear, but in view of Luke 21:15 the latter is to be preferred. The τότε makes clear that the gift of the Spirit and the Spirit-effected words are given in that moment when in answer to a query by the rulers a proper reply is necessary. Such a proper reply consists of proclamation of the crucified and resurrected Christ on the basis of a messianically interpreted Old Testament (cf. Acts 4:10-11).

The "open candor" (παρρησία) which characterized this proclamation of the disciples and the fact that such a reply came from "unlettered and common" men (Acts 4:13) caused the leaders to wonder.[53] In Acts παρρησία is closely related to verbs of speaking (Acts 4:29,31; 9:27-28; 18:25-26) and denotes that frank boldness of one who is both convinced and unafraid. However, Luke does

31

not consider παρρησία a natural gift but a result
of Spirit possession. According to Acts 4:29-31,
the congregation is filled with the Holy Spirit
and therefore receives the gift of bold speech.[54]
The imperfects (ἐθαύμαζον, ἐπεγίνωσκον [Acts 4.13])
give the impression, not of sudden wonder and
recognition, but of a wonder which marked the
leaders' reaction to the disciples' performance
throughout and of a gradual recognition of their
discipleship with Jesus.

The situation also produced a sense of
dumbfoundness in the Jewish leaders, for "they had
nothing to say in opposition" (οὐδὲν εἶχον
ἀντειπεῖν [Acts 4:14]). At first sight it appears
that it was the presence of the healed man that
produced such imposed silence (Acts 4:14a,16), but
healings, signs and wonders do not have independent
importance but are divine actions confirming the
spoken proclamation (Acts 4:29-30). Furthermore,
why would the leaders want to say anthing against
the healing of a lame man? They themselves call
the healing a "remarkable sign" (Acts 4:16).
Rather, in the word ἀντειπεῖν there is a reminder
of Jesus' promise in Luke 21:15 that in situations
of trouble he would give them "a mouth of wisdom"
against which the opponents would not be able "to
resist or speak against" (ἀντειπεῖν). As we indicated above,[55] the σοφία of which Luke 21:15
speaks is the understanding of Jesus based on a
messianically interpreted Old Testament. Hence,
it is not just the claim of Peter and John that
the healing of the lame man had been accomplished
by the name of Jesus to which the leaders could
not respond; they could not reply to the proclamation that the crucified and resurrected Jesus
was the "stone" spoken of in Ps 118. The ὑφ᾽ ὑμῶν
of Acts 4:11 does not appear in the Greek of
Ps 118:22 (117:22 [LXX]); by adding the phrase,
Peter makes Ps 118 into a word of judgment on the
Jewish leaders. The leaders cannot respond to
this word of judgment; their silence reveals
their guilt.

Resulting from this first confrontation with
the authorities was a warning to the disciples no

longer to speak or to teach in the name of Jesus (Acts 4:18).[56] However, Peter and John replied that they were "not able to remain silent concerning those things we have seen and heard" (Acts 4:20). The phrase ἃ εἴδαμεν καὶ ἠκούσαμεν is reminiscent of the disciples' special status as "witnesses" (cf. Acts 1:21-22; 10:37-41; 22:15; 26:16), and since reception of the Holy Spirit is closely related to becoming a "witness" (cf. Luke 24:48-49; Acts 1:8; 9:17), this answer of the disciples refers to the power of the Spirit which compels them to proclamation.

When they rejoin the Christian community, Peter and John report what the chief priests and elders had said to them. The Christian community responded with a prayer to God who in the words of Ps 2:1-2 had spoken "through the Holy Spirit by the mouth of our father David, Your servant". This Psalm had recently been fulfilled "in this city" when Herod and Pontius Pilate "had gathered together" (συνήχθησαν) against Jesus whom God had "anointed" (Acts 4:27). That this "gathering together" against Jesus refers to the passion is clear from the reference to "this city", meaning Jerusalem, and to Herod and Pilate (cf. Luke 23:6-16). While less explicit, the phrase ὃν ἔχρισας very likely refers to Jesus' anointing with the Holy Spirit at his baptism.[57] If so, this is evidence that the early Church associated Jesus' baptism with his passion and death.[58] In any case, it was against Jesus as the Spirit-filled that Herod and Pilate "gathered together".

However, in the situation of the Christian community Ps 2:1-2 possessed continuing fulfillment. It was the arrest of Peter and John and the consequent order not to preach that elicited the congregation's prayer and its allusion to Ps 2:1-2. In these actions on the part of the Jewish leaders the nations and rulers continue to "gather together against the Lord and His Anointed". It had been "in Jerusalem" that the rulers, elders and scribes had "gathered together" (συναχθῆναι) to question Peter and John about their activities (Acts 4:5). The early community's understanding

of its difficulties that we found in the Gospels
(Matt 10:18; John 15:21) reoccurs here as well.
In persecuting the Church one persecutes Christ
himself. This understanding is expressed clearly
in the three accounts of Paul's conversion (Acts
9:4-5; 22:7-8; 26:14-15). The early community,
therefore, understood its situation in terms of
Ps 2:1-2, but only because it understood Jesus'
passion in terms of Psalm 2. This was not regarded
as a matter of imitation, but rather of what might
be called messianic unity, for in the situation of
threat against the Church's task of preaching, it
is really "against the Lord and His Anointed" that
the authorities gather.

Von Baer emphasizes the identity of the Spirit
of Pentecost and the Spirit which rested upon
Jesus and, therefore, the parallelism between the
works of Jesus and those of his disciples.[59] As
Jesus in the Spirit had proclaimed the "good news"
and had gone about doing signs and wonders (Luke
4:18; Acts 2:22; 10:38), so also the disciples in
the Spirit proclaim the Gospel and so healings
(Acts 2:18-19; 3:7). In the same way that Jesus
as the Spirit-anointed drew hatred and was finally
killed, so also it is as the Spirit-anointed
messianic community that the Christians become the
objects of hate and persecution. The petition
that now in view of external threat God give them
the gift of "bold speech" Acts 4:29-30) is,
therefore, an act of obedience to God's will. For
in this request the congregation desired that gift,
the Holy Spirit, which, while urging the outward
expression of the Gospel, draws upon the messenger
illwill and hate. Luke informs us that "all were
filled with the Holy Spirit and spoke (imperf.)
the word of God with boldness" (Acts 4:31). Now
the whole congregation possessed that παρρησία
that earlier had characterized Peter and John.
Opposition to the Christian proclamation served
only to spread it. This motif occurs elsewhere
in Acts as well (Acts 8:1-13; 11:19; Paul's
imprisonment in Jerusalem leads to his preaching
in Rome [Acts 21-28]).

34

Acts 4:1-31 is typical of Luke's presentation of the Spirit's role in times of persecution. Other passages in Acts presenting the same kind of situation may be more briefly discussed. Acts 5:12-42 tells of an occurrence similar to that in Acts 4:1-31. Once again imprisoned and called before the authorities, the disciples recount again those things of which they are "witnesses", and they add that the Holy Spirit given by God to those who obey Him is also a "witness" (Acts 5:32). This designation of the Spirit as a "witness" implies that the "witnesses" preach in the power of the Spirit--the disciples "witness" in that the Spirit in them "witnesses".[60] The reaction of the authorities is one of rage (διεπρίοντο) and desire to kill the apostles. A similar reaction would meet Stephen (Acts 7:54), Paul (Acts 9:23,29), and Paul and Barnabas (Acts 13:46-50). The presence of the Spirit and those in whom it dwells draws opposition and hate.

Saved by the timely wisdom of Gamaliel, the disciples are released and leave the council rejoicing (χαίροντες) that they had been counted worthy to suffer dishonor for the Name (Acts 5:41). The theme of rejoicing in the midst of suffering appears elsewhere in Acts. Acts 16:25 presents Paul and Silas praying and singing hymns while imprisoned in Philippi, and Acts 13:52 tells of the disciples' being "filled with joy and the Holy Spirit" after having been driven from Antioch of Pisidia because of a persecution incited by the Jews. As the latter passage shows, such rejoicing in suffering is due to the presence of the Spirit. Yet, such joy is not a spiritualistic enthusiasm but is an expression of the Christologically grounded reality of salvation which the Christian community experiences in its historical existence. The Christian community suffers "for the Name".[61]

In his farewell address to the elders of the Church at Ephesus, Paul says that he is going to Jerusalem "bound in the Spirit" (δεδεμένος τῷ πνεύματι). He does not know what will befall him in Jerusalem, but the Spirit has told him all along the way that "chains and afflictions await" him (Acts 20:22-23). Apparently Paul is referring to prophecies given in cities he visited before reaching Ephesus (κατὰ πόλιν).[62] An account of such prophecy is given in the story of Agabus, who by means of a symbolic action likewise tells of imprisonment awaiting Paul in Jerusalem (Acts 21:10-11). Similar prophecies were told Paul in Tyre (Acts 21:4). Paul's being "bound in the Spirit" refers to his "resolve in the Spirit" to pass through Macedonia and Achaia and then go on to Jerusalem (Acts 19:21). However, it ought be remembered that suffering is explicitly mentioned as a necessary component of Paul's mission (Acts 9:15-16) and that his mission began with the gift of the Holy Spirit (Acts 9:17). Paul is "bound in the Spirit" because the Spirit given him when he became a witness for Jesus has been the director of Paul's mission (cf. Acts 16:6-7) and the impulse toward its completion. Paul's course leads to Rome my way of Jerusalem (Acts 19:21). That "chains and afflictions" await him in Jerusalem is another instance of the theme that it is through persecution that the Spirit works to spread the Gospel.

The most interesting occurrence in Acts of the Holy Spirit's presence in a context of persecution is the story of Stephen. The figure of Stephen, his position in the early community, his theology and its significance, and finally his martyrdom have exercised the learning of many a scholar.[63] For our purposes, however, it is only Stephen as one in a situation of persecution and martyrdom and the work of the Spirit on and through him which are of interest. The context of Stephen's speech (Acts 6:8-15; 7:54-8:3), therefore, forms the object of our inquiry.

Stephen appears as one of the Seven, who, in the face of some dissatisfaction within the Christian community, were especially chosen for the task of "serving tables" (Acts 6:2-6). The Seven are described as men "full of Spirit and wisdom" (Acts 6:3). The word πλήρεις denotes continuing possession, so the Spirit and wisdom are not conceived as special charismata for the

36

task of serving tables. Rather, it was the possession of these which was the prerequisite for receiving the task. "Wisdom" is not to be understood as practical wisdom, the ability to do a job correctly.[64] Such an understanding of σοφία would present too harsh a contrast to σοφία in Acts 6:10 where it very clearly does not mean practical wisdom. The Seven are rather characterized as men leading lives in obedience to the Spirit and having a view of Jesus based on a messianic understanding of the Old Testament.[65]

In the enumeration of the Seven, Stephen is especially recognized--he is a man "full of faith and the Holy Spirit" (Acts 6:5; cf. 11:24). This special characterization betrays a special interest in the person of Stephen and lends credibility to the view that the story of the Seven was meant merely to introduce Stephen.[66]

From Acts 6:8 on it is Stephen alone who occupies center stage. He is designated as "full of grace and power" and as one who "did great signs and wonders among the people" (Acts 6:8). However, the interest of the narrative is in Stephen as a preacher, for it is on account of his words that he come into conflict with the Jews (Acts 6:9-11). The Jews "could not withstand the wisdom and Spirit with which he spoke" (Acts 6:10). This is a clear allusion to Luke 21:15, except that here "Spirit" appears in the place of "mouth".[67] However, unlike Luke 21:12-15, Acts 6:10 does not refer to a context of persecution. Rather, as the imperfects (ἴσχυον, ἐλάλει) show, there was a lapse of time which was continually punctuated by disputes between Stephen and his Jewish opponents. To be sure, these disputes were not friendly ones, the "Hellenists" apparently being ready to act in extreme fashion against those with whom they disagreed (cf. Acts 9:29). Nevertheless, there is as yet no mention of a "handing over to the synagogues and prisons". It is not until Acts 6:12 that Stephen is brought into a truly juridical situation. Of course, the text wishes us to understand that Stephen continued to speak "with wisdom and the Spirit" before the Council; the long speech of Stephen in Acts 7 makes that obvious. Yet, it is not because Stephen is persecuted that he speaks. It was Luke's view that all Christian proclamation was Spirit-motivated and pointed to Jesus as the ful- fillment of Old Testament promises. Such procla- mation often was made in situations of threat and persecution, for hatred was a common reaction to it (cf. Acts 5:33), but persecution was not the only context in which proclamation was made.

Luke is interested in Stephen, therefore, not because Stephen was a martyr but because it was Stephen's proclamation which precipitated the crisis which led to the spread of the Gospel from Jerusalem (cf. Acts 1:8; 8:1). Were Stephen of interest to Luke only as a martyr, it would be difficult to understand why the martyrdom of James, one of Jesus' disciples, receives only passing notice (Acts 12:1-2). It is a mistake, therefore, to treat the story of Stephen as a story of martyrdom with a long speech inserted into it.[68] This must be remembered when evaluating those features of the Stephen narrative which at first glance appear as typical martyr-motifs.

The first such feature is that of Stephen's face appearing as an angel's (Acts 6:15). According to Holl, Acts 6:15 prepares the way for Acts 7:55-56 and signifies that the glory of God which the martyr sees afterward already shines on his face.[69] Acts 6:15, along with Acts 7:55-56, characterizes Stephen's speech as one given out of direct visionary experience.[70] Such an inter- pretation goes hand in hand with the view that the transfiguration of Stephen's face is a sign of his Spirit-possession which enables him to make the following speech.[71] However, such an understanding of Acts 6:15 is not satisfying. Of course Stephen's speech is Spirit-inspired. As Acts 6:10 makes plain, his preaching was always in the power of the Spirit. But had Luke wished to stress the Spirit-inspired nature of Stephen's speech before the Sanhedrin, he would most likely have intro- duced Stephen's speech with a formula such as πλησθεὶς πνεύματος ἁγίου, as he did elsewhere

(Acts 2:4; 4:8,31; 13:9). Also, there is not the slightest reason to suppose that Stephen's speech was visionary. It is clear from Acts 6:10 (ἐλάλει; imperf.) that Stephen spoke repeatedly. His speech before the Council was but an example of the kind of preachment made by Stephen. Of course, the circumstances of that speech were more ominous.

Another explanation of Acts 6:15 is that it is a typical martyr-motif.[72] Having the face of an angel, the martyr is shown to be under the protection of God,[73] or to manifest the glory of God in a way reserved for the Righteous who participate in judgment,[74] or already to possess heavenly characteristics.[75] Mundle, for example, mentions 4 Macc 6:2 and Berakoth 9a as Jewish parallels and Mart. Pol. 2:3; 12:1; Eusebius, Hist. eccl. 5.1.35 as Christian parallels.[76] An examination of these passages, however, shows that they have little, if any, relevance here. With the exception of 4 Macc 6:2, all are late witnesses. 4 Macc 6:2 itself is really no parallel. There is no mention of Eleazar's outward countenance changing in a way visible to others. Although disrobed, Eleazar is said to be ἐγκοσμούμενον τῇ περὶ τὴν εὐσέβειαν εὐσχημοσύνῃ. But this simply says that Eleazar's real decoration was his piety rather than his clothes (cf. 1 Pet 3:3-4; 1 Tim 2:9-10). Similarly, the Christian sources mentioned above do not really provide parallels to Acts 6:15. Mart. Pol. 2:3 speaks of the martyrs as already being angels, but there is no suggestion of an outward change of countenance.[77] Mart. Pol. 12:1 says that Polycarp's face was "filled with grace". Yet, this need not imply that Polycarp's face shone or possessed heavenly characteristics. More likely Polycarp's poise and self-composure in the face of the proconsul's threats is meant (Mart. Pol. 11). On the other hand, Eusebius, Hist. eccl. 5.1.35 does speak of the martyrs' faces being filled with the future glory.[78] Yet, there is no mention of any similarity to an angel. Berakoth 9a may be a parallel, but it is quite late, probably third century.[79] In conclusion, therefore, Acts 6:15

is not to be understood in terms of martyrological motifs. Its meaning lies elsewhere.

A close look reveals that Acts 6:15 is a statement not so much concerning Stephen as it is concerning the Jewish leaders. All the members of the Council saw Stephen's face shine as an angel's. By placing such a notice before Stephen's speech, Luke sets in the sharpest relief the Jew's rejection of Stephen's message and their murder of him. Even though the clearest sign was given them that they were hearing a prophet of God, yet they rejected and killed him. That his face was as an angel's shows Stephen to be a prophet and his speech that of a prophet.[80] There is, then, much to be said for Glombitza's suggestion that Acts 6:15 be understood in terms of Acts 7:53.[81] Angels had brought the Law to Israel,[82], but Israel had not kept the Law but had instead always resisted the Holy Spirit (Acts 7:51) and killed those who "announced beforehand the coming of the Righteous One" (Acts 7:52). Now Stephen stands as an angel before Israel to present to it the correct understanding of its history. But again Israel rejects God's messenger who speaks by the Holy Spirit.

It is a more difficult task to evaluate the vision of Stephen:

> Being full of the Holy Spirit, he gazed into heaven and saw the glory of God (δόξα θεοῦ) and Jesus standing at the right hand of God, and he said, "Behold, I see the heavens opened and the Son of Man standing at the right hand of God" (Acts 7:55-56).

Appearing as it does in the closest connection with Stephen's martyrdom, the vision can very easily be regarded as a special Spirit-effected experience given to the martyr.[83] As such, it is regarded as a typical feature of stories of martyrdom. As we have seen, the prophet Isaiah had a vision at the moment of his martyrdom (Mart. Isa. 5:7), and accounts of visions occur with some regularity in early Christian Acts of the Martyrs (Mart. Pol. 5:2; Pass. Perp. 4; 7:4-8;

8; 10; 11-13; <u>Pass</u>. <u>Fruct</u>. 5). Nevertheless, the importance of visions in martyr-literature may be overly emphasized,[84] and it would be unwise to accept this view of Stephen's vision too hastily.

The language of Acts 7:55 does not suggest a special gift of the Spirit to Stephen because of his situation, that is, it does not suggest a special revelation for the martyr. The present tense (ὑπάρχων) and the adjectival form πλήρης suggest rather an abiding condition in which Stephen exists. Stephen possesses the Spirit not because he is persecuted and about to suffer martyrdom but because he is a member of the Christian community which has received the Spirit. Therefore, while certainly Spirit-effected, Stephen's vision is not given because he is to be martyred.

Furthermore, an examination of alleged parallels within early Christian Acts of the Martyrs shows that they do not parallel Stephen's vision as closely as has been suggested. First of all, the vision of a martyr often concerns the martyr himself. The martyr receives prophetic foreknowledge of his martyrdom (<u>Mart</u>. <u>Pol</u>. 5:2; <u>Pass</u>. <u>Perp</u>. 4; 10)[85] or of experiences which are to occur to him after death (<u>Pass</u>. <u>Perp</u>. 11-13; <u>Pass</u>. <u>Fruct</u>. 5). A vision may occur concerning someone who needs the martyr's aid (<u>Pass</u>. <u>Perp</u>. 7:4-8; 8). In addition, almost all martyr-visions occur when the martyr is dreaming or in a state of trance, ecstasy, or the like. According to <u>Mart</u>. <u>Pol</u>. 5:2, Polycarp received his vision ἐν ὀπτασίᾳ. Similarly, Perpetua and Sanctus had their visions during states from which they "awoke" (experrectus sum [<u>Pass</u>. <u>Perp</u>. 4:10; 7:9; 8:4; 10:14; 13:8]). Apparently experrectus sum means in these passages, "I awoke from sleep" (cf. <u>Pass</u>. <u>Perp</u>. 4:2: crastina die tibi renuntiabo; 7:3: ipsa nocte). The Greek text translates with ἐξυπνίσθην. Isaiah was apparently in ecstasy during his vision, for <u>Mart</u>. <u>Isa</u>. 5:7 reports that he did not see those around him, although his eyes were open.

At first sight Acta Carpi 39 seems to offer a parallel to Stephen's vision. Upon being nailed to a stake, Carpus smiled because he saw "the glory of the Lord" (εἶδον τὴν δόξαν κυρίου καὶ ἐχάρην). Likewise Acta Carpi 42 reports that Agathonike, who was standing by as an onlooker, saw "the glory of the Lord" and recognized it as a heavenly call to offer herself in martyrdom. However, the "glory of the Lord" which Carpus and Agathonike saw does not refer to a vision of the exalted Christ in heaven but to the martyrdoms which they were witnessing. The "glory of the Lord" which Carpus saw was the martyrdom of Papylus; the "glory of the Lord" which Agathonike saw was the martyrdom of Carpus. For this reason Agathonike could call her own martyrdom a "glorious repast" (τὸ ἔνδοξον ἄριστον [Acta Carpi 42]). The sufferings of the martyr were often regarded as manifestations of Christ's glory.[86]

The story of Stephen bears no similarity with these early Christian martyr-texts. There is no indication that Stephen was in a trance or ecstasy. He was conscious enough to relate on the spot his vision to his hearers. Furthermore, the vision of Stephen was not for his own benefit--it did not reveal the future fate of the martyr--but it was for the benefit of the Jewish leaders. It is the climax of Stephen's proclamation before the Council. The vision is primarily of the "Son of Man standing at the right hand of God". Whatever the significance of "standing" may be,[87] Jesus is definitely seen to be exalted. Scharlemann has noted that Stephen's recital of Israel's history follows the pattern of the rejection and exaltation of central figures.[88] Thus, Joseph was rejected by his brothers but exalted by God (Acts 7:9-10), and Moses was rejected by Israel but exalted by God (Acts 7:27-28,35). Likewise, the Righteous One rejected by the Jews is now seen in the vision to be exalted to the right hand of God. As in Acts 5:30-33, it is reference to the exaltation of him whom the Jews killed that elicited murderous hatred.[89]

42

In conclusion, then, Luke did not report the story of Stephen out of any martyrological interest and did not understand the features of Stephen's transfiguration and vision as martyr-motifs. While the Holy Spirit is present and active throughout the narrative, there is no idea of Stephen's possessing the Spirit because of his situation as martyr. Rather, it is as a member of the messianic community that Stephen possesses the Spirit, and in accordance with the Lukan conception, the Spirit is active primarily in the Christian proclamation.[90]

If the vision is not given to Stephen as martyr, why then was such a vision given only to Stephen? If the vision of the exalted Jesus was only the climax to Stephen's proclamation, why could not the climax be verbal as it is in Acts 5:31? We have noted that opposition to the Christian message served only to spread it further. This was especially true in Stephen's case. Until he appeared, opposition had stopped short of the actual killing of the Christian proclaimer. But with Stephen opposition resulted in the Church's first martyr and the persecution which followed resulted in the spread of the Gospel to Judaea and Samaria. It was Stephen and his preaching which proved to be pivotal in the Gospel's advance from Jerusalem to the ends of the earth (Acts 1:8).[91] It is perhaps not surprising that such a momentous event was accompanied by divine signs which served not only to confirm the verity of the message but also the extent of Israel's continuing rejection of the Holy Spirit.

4. THE EPISTLES OF PAUL

To Paul, no less than to other early Christian writers, it was obvious that persecution was the lot of the Christian (Rom 8:36; 1 Thess 3:3-4; 2 Tim 3:12). However, whenever Paul reflects on Christian suffering, it is his own suffering as an apostle of Christ that occupies center stage (1 Cor 4:8-13; 2 Cor 4:7-15; 6:3-10;

43

11:1-12:10; Phil 1:12-26; 1 Thess 2:1-12.[92]
Nowhere does Paul speak at any length about the
suffering of Christians in general.[93] Corresponding to this difference in accent, passages in
which Paul discusses his apostolic suffering will
be treated first and then passages in which Paul
remarks about Christian suffering in general.

According to the report of Acts 9:16, the
risen Lord told Ananias that it was necessary for
Paul to suffer much for the Name (δεῖ παθεῖν). It
is clear that this suffering is not only to take
place within the context of Paul's mission but
also that this suffering belongs to the esse of
Paul's apostleship. To be an apostle of the risen
Lord was to be a suffering apostle. In other
words, it was in Paul's suffering that the Lord,
who sent, was at work.[94] To what the report of
Acts only alludes, Paul himself stresses again
and again.

Paul speaks of his suffering most extensively
in 2 Corinthians. In Corinth Paul faced an opposition of "superlative apostles" (2 Cor 11:5;
12:11), who saw in their skilled speech (2 Cor
11:5-6), their wonders and signs (2 Cor 12:11-12),
and their ecstasies and visions (2 Cor 5:12-13;
12:1-10) proofs of their own Spirit possession.
On the other hand, these opponents denied that
Paul possessed the Spirit. They claimed that Paul
walked κατα σάρκα, that is, in the absence of the
Spirit (2 Cor 10:2) and doubted that Christ spoke
through Paul (2 Cor 13:3). The form of Paul's
ministry--characterized as it was by humility
(ταπεινός [2 Cor 10:1]), weakness (ασθένεια [2 Cor
10:10]), meekness (πραΰτης) and gentleness
(ἐπιείκεια [2 Cor 10:1])--spoke against its
pneumatic nature in the eyes of these opponents.[95]
In the face of such opposition, Paul argued that
it was precisely his sufferings which showed the
pneumatic nature of his apostolate.

We begin with 2 Cor 5:18-6:10, which prog-
resses from God's reconciling work in Christ to
Paul's apostolic suffering. It is his suffering
that shows Paul to be a "servant of God" (διάκονος

44

θεοῦ [2 Cor 6:3-10]). Some scholars have found Paul's reference to his sufferings sudden and unexplainable here. Finding neither a syntactical nor a substantive connection to the prior material, Windisch suggests that an "Übergangspassus" has fallen out. While in 2 Cor 6:1-2 Paul is directly exercising his office, in 2 Cor 6:3-10 he speaks about "seine Bewährung im Kampf des Lebens . . . , aber ohne Betonung des Predigtdienstes".[96] Lietzmann finds the connection between 2 Cor 6:2 and 2 Cor 6:3 "völlig abrupt".[97] However, Güttgemanns has recently shown that 2 Cor 6:3-10 is polemically formulated.[98] The terms for Paul's suffering (ὑπομονή, θλῖψις, ἀνάγκαι, etc.) play an important role in Paul's defense of his apostolate elsewhere in 2 Corinthians. 2 Cor 6:3-10, therefore, does not have merely a general significance but speaks directly to the issue of the legitimacy of Paul's apostolate. One is to assume the closest relationship between 2 Cor 6:3-10 and the foregoing verses.

In 2 Cor 5:18 Paul describes God as He "who reconciled us to Himself through Christ and gave to us the ministry of reconciliation" (τοῦ καταλλάξαντος ἡμᾶς ἑαυτῷ διὰ χριστοῦ καὶ δόντος ἡμῖν τὴν διακονίαν τῆς καταλλαγῆς). To whom do ἡμᾶς and ἡμῖν refer, and do they refer to the same persons? Bultmann argues that ἡμᾶς refers to all Christians, and while he admits that ἡμῖν may refer to Paul or the apostles, he prefers, in analogy to 2 Cor 5:19c (ἐν ἡμῖν), to refer ἡμῖν to the congregation.[99] Windisch and Lietzmann argue similarly.[100] However, "ministry" (διακονία) surely means the apostolate as it does in 2 Cor 3:8,9; 4:1; 6:3, and τίθεσθαί τι ἐν τινί (2 Cor 5:19c) virtually possesses the technical meaning "to commission someone with something" (cf. Ps 104:27 [LXX]).[101] These considerations plus the apologetic nature of this section lead to the conclusion that both ἡμῖν (2 Cor 5:18) and ἐν ἡμῖν (2 Cor 5:19c) refer to the apostles, and very likely to Paul alone, and that 2 Cor 5:18b and 2 Cor 5:19c refer to the commissioning of Paul, or the apostles, with the ministry of reconciliation. What then about ἡμᾶς (2 Cor 5:18)? Although it is clear from 2 Cor 5:19a that God's reconciliation comprehends the "world" (κόσμος), ἡμᾶς most likely refers to the apostles. This interpretation avoids a sudden change of person between ἡμᾶς and ἡμῖν in 2 Cor 5:18 and does credit to the strong apologetic character of this section.[102]

We must now ask what relationship God's act of reconciliation in Christ has with his institution of the apostolic office. Are they two closely related, but yet distinct, acts of God, or are they two elements of one and the same divine action? Windisch represents the first alternative and speaks of "zwei Einrichtungen", "die Stiftung der Versöhnung in dem Tode Christi und der Dienst zur Kundgebung des Geschehenen an die Welt".[103] In this view the apostle is he whose task it is to make known that which has already occurred. However, since in 2 Cor 5:18 both καταλλάξαντος and δόντος are governed by the same definite article (τοῦ), and since in 2 Cor 5:19 both μὴ λογιζόμενος and θέμενος introduce explanatory clauses of the main verb (ἦν . . . καταλλάσσων), the second alternative--that God's act of reconciliation and the institution of the apostolic office are elements of one divine action--is to be preferred.[104] In 2 Cor 5:20 Paul draws the necessary conclusion about the execution of the apostolic office (οὖν): because God's act of reconciliation in Christ is at the same time the institution of the ministry of reconciliation, the apostolic proclamation is the instrument of God's reconciliation.[105] As God's ambassador (πρεσβεύομεν) the apostle is "in the place of Christ" (ὑπὲρ χριστοῦ) and thus God works through the apostle (ὡς τοῦ θεοῦ παρακαλοῦντος δι᾽ ἡμῶν [2 Cor 5:20]). The verb παρακαλεῖν is to be given full salvific significance as is shown by the analogous expression καταλλάγητε τῷ θεῷ in 2 Cor 5:20b. In the Septuagint παρακαλεῖν is used several times to denote the effecting of salvation. In Ps 70:20-21 παρακαλεῖν is parallel to ζωοποιεῖν; in Ps 85:17 and Isa 49:8-10, from which Paul quotes (2 Cor 6:2),

46

παρακαλεῖν parallels βοηθεῖν. According to Isa 51:3,12 God Himself will comfort His people at the time of salvation (cf. Isa 40:3). The double occurrence of νῦν in 2 Cor 6:2 expresses the fact that the apostolic ministry of Paul is the time and the <u>locus</u> in which God is effecting His salvation, which He accomplished in Christ. Paul, then, rightly says that he "works (with God)" (2 Cor 6:1),[106] for the apostolic παράκλησις (παρακαλοῦμεν [2 Cor 6:1]) is God's παράκλησις δι᾽ ἡμῶν (2 Cor 5:20).

However, the apostle in no way replaces Christ. The ὑπὲρ χριστοῦ does not imply that Christ is absent but rather the contrary, that in the apostle Christ is present and, indeed, as he through whom God decisively acted, as the Crucified One. Only in this way can God be working through the apostle. For this reason Paul's apostolate in every way carries the imprint of the cross, for the cross of Christ was the one salvific act of God and to this salvific act the apostolic existence belongs.[107] Therefore, the preaching of Paul has "Christ crucified" as its sole content (1 Cor 1:23), and the apostolic life is characterized by θλῖψις, ἀνάγκαι, etc. (2 Cor 6:3-10).

Hence, it is clear that 2 Cor 6:3-10 is not in any way unexplainable but that it necessarily follows the foregoing verses. It is also clear why here, precisely in view of his sufferings, Paul calls himself a "servant of God" (διάκονος θεοῦ).[108] As God's minister, he must work in ὑπομονή, θλῖψις, ἀνάγκαι, for his διακονία itself is founded in God's reconciling activity which occurred in the cross of Christ. Paul's apostolic suffering is pneumatic because God is working in it. His suffering is the cross of Christ manifested in the life of the apostle.

It is from this perspective that 2 Cor 12:7-10 is best understood. Paul is given a "thorn in the flesh", and upon his request that it be removed is told by God: "My grace (χάρις) is sufficient for you, for (my) power is perfected in weakness (ἀσθένεια)." The paradox that in weakness the

47

power of Christ is perfected has often been
regarded as a general "divine law". Windisch
speaks of a "Gesetz, dem das Göttliche folgt", and
Plummer refers to God's providence: "Where it is
manifest that man was powerless, God's power
becomes, not more real, but more evident."[109]
However, the polemical character of the context of
2 Cor 12:7-10 is unmistakeable, and what Paul says
here is in defense of the legitimacy and efficacy
of his apostolate.

2 Cor 12:7-10 stands at the end of the section 2 Cor 11:1-12:10, which is dominated by the
notion of boasting (2 Cor 11:10,12,16,17,18,30;
12:1,5,6,9; cf. 2 Cor 10:13,15,16,17). The major
difference between Paul and his opponents appears
to have been over the manner in which one shows
himself to be a "servant of Christ". The opponents
boasted of what they thought was an advantage of
race. They were Hebrews, Israelites, the seed of
Abraham (2 Cor 11:22). According to Paul, such a
boast was κατὰ σάρκα (2 Cor 11:18), ἀφροσύνη
(2 Cor 11:21). Paul could also boast of these
same things (κἀγώ [2 Cor 11:18]). However, there
the likeness between Paul and his opponents ended.
Paul, rather than his opponents, was a true
"servant of Christ" (ὑπὲρ ἐγώ [2 Cor 11:23]).[110]

To demonstrate that he is a "servant of
Christ", Paul lists his experiences of suffering
and persecution. For this purpose Paul adopts the
style of oriental royal inscriptions and the res
gestae of Roman emperors that tell of the great
deeds of the hero.[111] In keeping with the need
for boasting (2 Cor 11:30), therefore, Paul uses a
form in which men made self-praise. For Paul,
however, his great deeds were precisely his
sufferings, those things which show his weakness
(τὰ τῆς ἀσθενείας [2 Cor 11:30]). In these he
will boast. Why this is so he explains in 2 Cor
12:1-10.

Among the accusations against Paul was that
he lacked ecstatic experiences. This proved to
Paul's opponents that no divine power was at work
in Paul. Faced with such opposition, Paul,

48

apparently against his will, refers to a previous
ecstatic experience of his own. However, in so
doing Paul speaks in the third person. He objec-
tifies his visionary experience. The effect of
using such an objectivizing style is that even in
referring to his own ecstasies Paul rejects their
validity for answering the question at hand,
namely, what manner of existence characterizes a
"servant of Christ". Not the visions of that man
mark him as an apostle of Christ, although the
visions were those of Paul himself. Rather, the
"weakness" which characterizes Paul's existence,
that which one sees in him and hears from him
(2 Cor 12:6),[112] demonstrates that Paul is a true
apostle of Christ. Therefore, it is not quite
true when Cambier asserts that 2 Cor 12:6-7
contains a comparison between two criteria of
judging an apostle, charismatic gifts and external
weakness, and that while not rejecting the
apostolic character of charismatic gifts, Paul
argues only that that is not the criterion by
which to judge him.[113] It is precisely Paul's
argument that visions and the like do not necessarily bear apostolic character. Therefore, Paul
can deny the apostleship of those who base themselves solely on such experiences. Paul bases his
own apostleship on some other ground, namely, on
his apostolic weakness. In his weakness Christ is
at work.

This central perception of his apostolic
existence Paul gained from an experience which he
describes in 2 Cor 12:7-9a. A "thorn for the
flesh" (σκόλοψ τῇ σαρκί), an "angel of Satan"
(ἄγγελος σατανᾶ), was given him by the Lord in
order that it might "beat" (κολαφίζῃ) him.[114]
Many scholars see in the "thorn" a reference to an
illness under which Paul suffered.[115] However,
the use of the verb κολαφίζεσθαι elsewhere in the
New Testament indicates rather that Paul has in
mind physical mistreatment caused by external
enemies. In Matt 26:67 (Mark 14:65) it refers to
the blows Jesus received from the soldiers. In
1 Pet 2:20 it is parallel to πάσχειν and refers to
the general social harassment which the Christians

in Asia Minor faced. Paul uses the verb one other
time, in 1 Cor 4:11, where along with such words
as ἀσθενεῖς, ἄτιμοι, λοιδορεῖσθαι, and διωκοῦσθαι
it denotes Paul's apostolic sufferings. Paul's
"thorn", therefore, most likely was his sufferings
as an apostle.[116]

Three times Paul asked the Lord to remove
this "thorn". But the answer was "my grace is
sufficient for you, for (my) power is perfected in
weakness" (ἀρκεῖ σοι ἡ χάρις μου. ἡ γὰρ δύναμις
ἐν ἀσθενείᾳ τελεῖται [2 Cor 12:9a]). The word
χάρις may be variously interpreted. It may refer
to the undeserved salvific activity of God toward
man (Rom 3:24; 4:4; 5:15; 6:14; 11:6; 2 Cor 8:9;
9:14; Gal 1:6,15; 5:4; Eph 1:7; 2:5). In this
case the answer, which Paul received, would imply
that Paul ought not ask for more than was necessary, the grace of Christ. However, Paul often
calls his apostolic office a χάρις (Rom 1:5; 12:3;
15:15; 1 Cor 3:10; 15:10; Gal 2:9; Eph 3:8), and
this is probably what is meant here.[117] The γάρ
shows that the second sentence is explanatory of
the first. That means that χάρις is closely
related to the words "in weakness" (ἐν ἀσθενείᾳ).
It was the weakness of his appearance which was at
issue between Paul and his opponents concerning
the apostolic ministry. The exalted Lord says
that it is precisely "in weakness" that his power
"is perfected", that is, finds its most perfect
expression. Paul's sufferings, therefore, are not
merely the "Vorbedingung der Kraft",[118] nor the
"Unterpfand des Gegenwärtigseins der
Christuskraft",[119] but they are the very way in
which the cross of Christ, the power of God
(1 Cor 1:24), is shown forth in the apostolic life
of Paul.[120] For this reason, Paul's boast is in
his weakness, and for this reason Paul must boast
in his weakness, for only in his weakness does the
power of Christ "rest upon" (ἐπισκηνοῦν) him. The
Christological foundation for Paul's suffering
here becomes evident. As it was in the cross that
Christ worked in power, so now in the suffering of
his apostle the Crucified One is revealed as the
κύριος who is now present and active.

In a similar way, 2 Cor 4:7-15 speaks of the suffering apostle as the instrument through which the living Lord works. In 2 Cor 3:7-18 Paul had described his ministry as one characterized by "glory" (δόξα). His ministry was one of the Spirit (διακονία τοῦ πνεύματος), one of righteousness (διακονία τῆς δικαιοσύνης [2 Cor 3:8-9]). However, Paul's opponents could not perceive "glory" in the reality of Paul's sufferings. "The god of this world" had blinded them so that they could not see "the light of the God of the glory of Christ" (2 Cor 4:4). However, Paul argues, it is precisely in the bodies of the suffering apostles (ἐν ὀστρακίνοις σκεύεσιν)[121] that the glory of Christ ("the light of the Gospel"), here called a "treasure", resides. Only God, therefore, may be seen as the source of power which works through the apostles (2 Cor 4:7).

In 2 Cor 4:10 Paul calls his sufferings "the death of Jesus" (ἡ νέκρωσις τοῦ Ἰησοῦ). The parallel expression in 2 Cor 4:11a would suggest that νέκρωσις signifies a process of ever-repeated experiences of suffering and persecution (ἀεί; cf. 2 Cor 4:8-9).[122] However, elsewhere νέκρωσις refers to a situation or condition (Mark 3:5 [D]; Rom 4:19; Hermas, Sim. 9.16.2-3), and the verb περιφέρειν implies the same thing. Furthermore, the phrase "in the body" (ἐν τῷ σώματι), which must be understood locally, also insists on this latter interpretation. Paul's life is therefore described as a continual situation of death. The following ἵνα clause presents the purpose of this situation, that "the life of Jesus might be manifested in our bodies" (ἡ ζωὴ τοῦ Ἰησοῦ ἐν τῷ σώματι ἡμῶν φανερωθῇ). The local expression ἐν τῷ σώματι prevents any reference to 2 Cor 4:8-9 and thereby excludes understanding "the life of Jesus" as the power which preserves the apostle from destruction.[123] Paul's sufferings are not something from which he must be freed. Rather, in them, and to be sure, there where they become concrete, in the body which is characterized by death (ἐν τῇ θνητῇ σαρκὶ ἡμῶν [2 Cor 4:11]), the life of Jesus is revealed. The apostle's suffering, therefore, is "die paradoxe Epiphanie der ζωή".[124] The apostle's suffering reveals that the Crucified One lives as κύριος.

2 Cor 4:11 adds nothing new to the argument of 2 Cor 4:10 but, as Güttgemanns has observed, views the same situation from a different perspective. While 2 Cor 4:10a views the apostle's sufferings sub specie Christi, 2 Cor 4:11a, along with 2 Cor 4:8-9, describes what actually happened to the apostle.[125] 2 Cor 4:8-9 presents as it were a chronicle of Paul's revelatory experiences.[126] In that the apostle is always being given over into death, the Crucified One is shown to be continually alive.

The suffering of the apostle serves to found the Church. The apostle suffers, but the congregation has life (2 Cor 4:12). It is completely to misread the text to understand 2 Cor 4:12 as a reference to a vicarious dying of Paul which brings life to the congregation.[127] It is not Paul's sufferings which give life to the congregation, but, as the context shows, Jesus' life which is present and manifest in Paul's suffering. The Crucified One as κύριος founds his congregation and is active in it, not in deeds of power and glory but "in der mühseligen Arbeit der Missionäre".[128]

This proclaiming and congregation-founding character of Paul's apostolic suffering appears elsewhere is Paul's writings. Two passages will serve the discussion. The first is Paul's words to the Philippian Christians that his imprisonment had resulted in a progress (εἰς προκοπήν) of the Gospel (Phil 1:12). In a ὥστε clause Paul gives two examples of this advance: 1) "my chains have become visible in Christ among the whole praetorium and all the rest" (τοὺς δεσμούς μου φανεροὺς ἐν χριστῷ γενέσθαι ἐν ὅλῳ τῷ πραιτωρίῳ καὶ τοῖς λοιποῖς πᾶσιν [Phil 1:13]); 2) "most of the brethren in the Lord, having confidence in my chains, more readily dare fearlessly to speak the word of God" (τοὺς πλείονας τῶν ἀδελφῶν ἐν κυρίῳ πεποιθότας τοῖς δεσμοῖς μου περισσοτέρως τολμᾶν

ἀφόβως τὸν λόγον τοῦ λαλεῖν [Phil 1:14]). Both
statements present difficulties. Lohmeyer's
attempt to interpret Phil 1:13 in a strictly
martyrological sense is well known. Paul, being a
martyr, suffers "in Christ" and is in a special
way the bearer of Christ's revelation. This
thought is combined with that of witness and confession before the highest public.[129] This view,
however, does not do justice to Paul's pointed
reference to his chains which is reminiscent of
his repeated references to his apostolic suffering
elsewhere in his epistles. These sufferings were
not incidental to his mission but integral to it,
for in them Jesus the Crucified was made visible.
Christ crucified was met in the suffering apostle.
This same thought recurs here in the epistle to
the Philippians. Paul's imprisonment did not
simply give opportunity to preach to the
praetorium and the others. Paul's imprisonment
itself was a proper correlative of Paul's proclamation. In the prisoner Paul, Christ crucified
is present and manifested (φανεροὺς γενέσθαι).[130]

The major problem in Phil 1:14 is whether
πεποιθότας is to be taken with ἐν κυρίῳ or τοῖς
δεσμοῖς μου. Paul combines πεποιθέναι with ἐν
κυρίῳ elsewhere (Gal 5:10; Phil 2:24; 2 Thess 3:4;
cf. Rom 14:14), and this has led some scholars to
opt for this alternative.[131] Yet, the latter
alternative appears to do more justice to the
context. It was Paul's chains which were central
in spreading the Gospel to the praetorium. Most
likely the chains are viewed here as instrumental
in increasing the boldness of the Christian
brethren to speak. Our previous conclusions help
us to understand how this could be. In the
suffering apostle the brethren recognized the
presence of the crucified Christ and were thereby
emboldened to speak. In a similar fashion Paul
exhorts Timothy: "Do not be ashamed of the witness
of our Lord nor of me (its) prisoner" (2 Tim 1:8).
The prisoner Paul places himself alongside the
proclamation of the Gospel. In Paul's suffering
the content of the proclamation, the crucified
Christ, is seen to be present. This same theme

appears later in early Christian Acts of the Martyrs. For example, when Blandina is hung in the shape of the cross, the Christians see "him who was crucified for them" and receive "great eagerness" (Eusebius, Hist. eccl. 5.1.41).

The second passage is 1 Thess 1:5; 2:1-12. Paul knows that the brethren at Thessalonica are God's chosen, "for our Gospel was not among you in word only but also in power and in the Holy Spirit and with much fruitfulness" (ἀλλὰ καὶ ἐν δυνάμει καὶ ἐν πνεύματι ἁγίῳ καὶ πληροφορίᾳ πολλῇ [1 Thess 1:5]). Some scholars have understood ἐν δυνάμει καὶ ἐν πνεύματι ἁγίῳ (hendiadys) to refer to wonders accompanying Paul's preaching.[132] Yet, it seems more likely that these words refer to the apostolic presence among the Christians in Thessalonica, for Paul interjects a statement concerning the manner of his sojourn among them ("for you know what kind of men we were among you for your sake" [1 Thess 1:5]). The manner of his sojourn becomes plain in 1 Thess 2:1-12. Paul spoke the word of God boldly (ἐπαρρησιασάμεθα) in the midst of much struggle (1 Thess 2:2),[133] and his behavior was characterized by the gentleness of a nurse toward her children (1 Thess 2:7) and the kindness of a father with his children (1 Thess 2:11). The Gospel, therefore, was among the Christians of Thessalonica "in power and in the Holy Spirit", that is, in proclamation and in the lowly manner of the apostle's life.

The apostle's existence among them was on their behalf (1 Thess 1:5), that is, it intended to create a Christian community. That this occurred was proof of their election. This is the significance of the words πληροφορίᾳ πολλῇ, which here mean "great abundance" or "great fruitfulness" not "full conviction".[134] The congregation at Thessalonica is the "fruit" of Paul's activity. The point is negatively expressed in 1 Thess 2:1 where Paul says that his stay was "not in vain" (cf. 1 Cor 15:10,18; 2 Cor 6:1; Gal 2:2; 1 Thess 3:5). Christ crucified, preached by Paul and visible in his apostolic life, brings the Church into existence. That is simply to say that Paul's apostolic ministry is a function of the Spirit.

Before turning to a discussion of texts which
speak of the suffering of the Christian community,
one more text in which Paul mentions the Holy
Spirit within the context of his own suffering
must be considered. The text is Phil 1:19-20.
Paul writes that while the brethren were emboldened to speak the word of God, some spoke out of
"good will" and "love" and others spoke from
"envy" and "rivalry" (Phil 1:15-17). In both
cases, however, Christ was proclaimed, and in that
Paul rejoices. Then Paul continues: "And I shall
rejoice, for I know that this shall become salvation for me through your prayers and the support
of the Spirit of Jesus Christ" (άλλὰ καὶ χαρήσομαι·
οἶδα γὰρ ὅτι τοῦτό μοι ἀποβήσεται εἰς σωτηρίαν
διὰ τῆς ὑμῶν δεήσεως καὶ ἐπιχορηγίας τοῦ πνεύματος
Ἰησοῦ χριστοῦ [Phil 1:19]). Paul looks forward
to a moment of rejoicing in the future[135] when he
shall receive his "salvation". Does σωτηρία mean
Paul's release from prison, or does it have a more
religious connotation? One can answer this
question only when the meaning of τοῦτο is
discerned.

Some scholars understand τοῦτο to mean the
situation of imprisonment in which Paul finds
himself.[136] This would mean that Paul's imprisonment was expected to end either in release, which
would be cause for joy, or in his death, which
would bring eternal joy. τοῦτο could conceivably
refer also to the concern that the Philippians
felt for Paul, although there is nothing in the
text to suggest this. However, if it is recalled
that Paul rejoiced in the fact that Christ was
preached, the possibility that Paul had in mind a
future proclamation of Christ and that τοῦτο
refers to this future proclamation becomes an
attractive option. Paul's quotation of Job 13:16
[LXX] shows that this is in fact the way τοῦτο
is to be understood. In the Septuagint context,
τοῦτο refers to the fact that Job is going to
speak and plead his cause before God even though
he may be in great danger in doing so. Job shall
thereby appear just before God, and this will be

55

his σωτηρία (Job 13:18). In quoting this passage Paul refers to the future proclamation which he will make before the authorities, which proclamation will show him to be faithfully executing his apostolic mission.[137] Paul's σωτηρία will consist in God's favorable judgment given at the completion of the apostolic task faithfully done. This will give him cause for rejoicing.[138]

In this task of the faithful execution of the apostolic mission, Paul will be aided "through your prayers and the support of the Spirit" (δια τῆς ὑμῶν δεήσεως και ἐπιχορηγίας τοῦ πνεύματος). The significance of the καί is difficult to determine. It may be a coordinate combining two objects. In this case, Paul lists two sources of aid, the prayers of the congregation and the aid of the Spirit. Yet, were such the case, a second τῆς before ἐπιχορηγίας would be expected. It is better, therefore, to take τῆς ὑμῶν with both δεήσεως and ἐπιχορηγίας and take τοῦ πνεύματος as an objective genitive. In the sense of a hendiadys, καί introduces the content of the congregation's prayer. This interpretation gives content both to δέησις and to ἐπιχορηγία: the congregation prays that Paul be aided with the gift of the Holy Spirit. Paul is so assured that the prayer will be answered that he attributes to the prayer itself that which the Spirit will do, assist him to proclaim Christ when he is before the rulers. Paul knows himself to be a recipient of the promise spoken by Jesus (Matt 10:17-20), but here he conceives the congregation in prayer as the supporting context within which this promise will be effected.

As we have noted, Paul's apostolic sufferings have Church-building character because in them the Crucified One as the living Lord is at work. The life at work in the congregation is the life of the crucified Christ, and that means that what was true of Christ is, through the proclamation and the suffering of the apostle, true also of the Christian congregation.[139] The congregation suffers, but therein the Crucified One as the living Lord is present, at work, and made visible.

That is to say, their suffering is of the Spirit.
With caustic irony, Paul compares his sufferings
to the glorified view the Corinthians had of their
Christian existence (1 Cor 4:8-13). They thought
themselves "wise", "strong", "in glory". Rather,
they should "imitate" the apostle, for he is their
"father" (1 Cor 4:14-16).

In this respect the Thessalonian congregation
had become a model to all the believers in
Macedonia and Achaia (1 Thess 1:7). They had
become imitators of the apostle and of the Lord,
"having received the Word in great tribulation
with the joy of the Holy Spirit" (δεξάμενοι τὸν
λόγον ἐν θλίψει πολλῇ μετὰ χαρᾶς πνεύματος ἁγίου
[1 Thess 1:6]). The reception of the Word cannot
itself be the point of imitation, for there would
be no analogous occurrence in the life of Jesus.
Rather, they were imitators in that their acceptance of the Christian message took place within
the same paradox of θλῖψις and χαρά that characterized the apostle's existence, and that of the
Lord.[140] This χαρά is of the Holy Spirit (cf.
Acts 13:52). It denotes that eschatological
rejoicing which the presence of the Spirit gives
and which is here conceived to characterize not
only the proclamation of the Word in the midst
of affliction, as in Acts, but also the reception
of the Word in the midst of affliction.

The Word of God, preached and accepted in the
midst of struggle, continues to work within the
Christian community and to elicit opposition. The
congregation at Thessalonica stands within a
persecuted communion with the apostles, the
prophets, the congregation in Judaea, and the Lord
Jesus himself (1 Thess 2:14-15). All of these
were killed or persecuted because the Word of God
worked in them, and the same was true among the
Christians of Thessalonica (λόγον θεοῦ, ὅς καὶ
ἐνεργεῖται ἐν ὑμῖν τοῖς πιστεύουσιν [1 Thess 2:13]).
This resulted in their becoming imitators (μιμηταὶ
ἐγενήθητε) of the churches in Judaea, for they
suffered at the hands of their countrymen as the
Judaean Christians had at the hands of their
(1 Thess 2:14).[141] Michaelis argues that this

imitation is a passive one. The Christians at
Thessalonica did not seek to be imitators but
became imitators in that they suffered.[142] Lately
de Boer has taken issue with this view. He argues
that the Thessalonians were more or less consciously imitating the pattern of faithful
suffering which the Judaean Christians had
given.[143] These Christians were "not helpless and
unwilling victims" but had "decided to remain
steadfast in their chosen way and to endure the
suffering . . . and at every moment of the
suffering they had to reaffirm their choice."[144]
As true as this may be, yet this is not the thrust
and interest of the text. The only active agent
of which the text speaks is the Word of God. This
Word draws opposition, not by giving impulse
toward martyrdom, but by effecting that change in
one's life which implies judgment on a former way
of life (1 Thess 1:9-10).

On occasion Paul's exhortation to his fellow
workers is grounded in the necessary cruciform
character of the apostle's own ministry, which,
although unique, gives form and content to all
Christian proclamation. Therefore, Paul reminds
Timothy that his attitude toward the suffering
apostle is not unrelated to his task as a protector
of the Gospel (2 Tim 1:7-14). God has given
Timothy, as He has Paul, a "Spirit, not of
timidity, but of power, love, and self-control"
(οὐ γὰρ ἔδωκεν ἡμῖν ὁ θεὸς πνεῦμα δειλίας, ἀλλὰ
δυνάμεως καὶ ἀγάπης καὶ σωφρονισμοῦ [2 Tim 1:7]).
This Spirit does not work shame toward the Gospel
nor toward the suffering apostle but rather brings
one to suffer for the Gospel. This Paul knows
full well, for he suffers imprisonment precisely
because he is in the service of the Gospel (2 Tim
1:11-12). Therefore, he exhorts Timothy: "suffer
(with me) for the Gospel according to the power of
God" (συγκακοπάθησον τῷ εὐαγγελίῳ κατὰ δύναμιν
θεοῦ [2 Tim 1:8]). If Timothy is to serve the
Lord, he will join Paul in suffering, and his
suffering, like Paul's, will serve the Gospel.
Such suffering will serve the Gospel because it
is "according to the power of God". In 2 Tim

1:9-10, θεοῦ is modified by a hymn-like account of God's gracious salvific call given and revealed in the appearance of the Savior, who destroyed death and brought life and incorruptibility. Timothy is called to suffer, for as the power of God was in the crucified Christ destroying death and bringing life, so in the suffering of Timothy God is working through the Spirit of power which He gave. It is in this context that Paul writes about preserving "the trust", which must mean the message of the Gospel entrusted to Paul and then to Timothy. In 2 Tim 1:12, Paul relates his suffering with his confidence that God is "able to guard my trust until that day". Paul does not mean by this that he trusts in God's power despite the fact that he is suffering. Rather, Paul is not ashamed of his suffering, because he knows tnat the God in whom he trusts is He who in the crucified Christ worked in power. The exhortation to Timothy to "guard the trust", therefore, will not be unrelated to the exhortation to "suffer with me for the Gospel". Both exhortations rest on the fact that the Spirit which dwells in Timothy is of power and not of timidity.

The ministry of reconciliation which Paul executes as the suffering apostle is rooted in the reconciling work of God in Jesus Christ (2 Cor 5:18-6:2). His ministry, which has the character of the cross, has congregation-building power, for in it the life of the Crucified One as Lord is present. A congregation, therefore, comes into being when the crucified Christ--presented in the proclamation of Christ crucified and present in the suffering apostle--is accepted as Lord. In this acceptance the congregation itself enters into an existence characterized by the paradox of suffering and joy. This whole complex of ideas is pithily expressed by Paul in the opening verses of his second letter to the Corinthian Church (2 Cor 1:3-7).

Paul is concerned that his sufferings will be misunderstood (2 Cor 1:8), and he wishes to make it clear that they play a necessary mediatorial role between God's reconciling activity and the

existence of the Corinthian congregation as a
Christian community.[145] Paul speaks of affliction
and suffering (θλῖψις, θλίβεσθαι; παθήματα,
πάσχειν) and of consolation (παράκλησις,
παρακαλεῖν). It is the wont of some scholars to
conceive this antithesis in such a way as to
psychologize and sentimentalize these verses.
Thus Plummer writes: "In missionary work sympathy
is the great condition of success." παράκλησις
refers not necessarily to deliverance from
suffering but deliverance from the anxiety which
suffering brings.[146] According to Windisch, at
the bottom of 2 Cor 1:3-7 lies the general human
experience that only he can help others in need
who himself has been helped in similar fashion.[147]
Schneider expressly abandons any attempt to give
a theological interpretation to this passage:
"Die begrifflich-philologische Analyse ruht also
auf der psychologischen Analyse."[148] From the
Pauline mysticism perspective, Schmitz writes:
"So wird aus der Leidensgemeinschaft zwischen dem
Apostel und der Gemeinde eine Trostgemeinschaft."[149]
Common to all these views is the understanding of
παράκλησις as something (sympathy, an encouraging
word) which serves to relieve or counteract
suffering or its effects. Yet, what can it
possibly mean when Paul speaks of the παράκλησις
which he gives as that which he himself is being
given by God (διὰ τῆς παρακλήσεως ἧς παρακαλούμεθα
αὐτοι ὑπὸ τοῦ θεοῦ [2 Cor 1:4])? The present
tense (παρακαλούμεθα) rules out any idea that Paul
passes on what he had once received. It must mean
that in the apostle's giving of παράκλησις God
Himself is active in παράκλησις. The "comfort"
which Paul gives is the "comfort" God is giving.
But does Paul conceive God as the author of
sympathetic consolation, as the hidden speaker of
encouraging words? Such a thought is so unlike
Paul that Windisch, who believes that is exactly
what Paul is saying, is forced to conclude that
the idea of God as the ultimate source of
παράκλησις is purely subordinate.[150] However,
Paul's argument is utterly theocentric. All
follows from who God is (2 Cor 1:3). A different
significance for παράκλησις must be sought.

60

Paul begins with a blessing to "the God and
Father of our Lord Jesus Christ, the Father of
mercies and the God of all consolation" (ὁ θεὸς
καὶ πατὴρ τοῦ κυρίου ἡμῶν 'Ιησοῦ χριστοῦ ὁ πατὴρ
τῶν οἰκτιρμῶν καὶ θεὸς πάσης παρακλήσεως [2 Cor
1:3]). The chiastic pattern is to be observed.
Both πατὴρ τῶν οἰκτιρμῶν and θεὸς πάσης παρακλήσεως
refer to Him who saves, redeems, helps and gives
life.[151] Through the use of chiasm, Paul affirms
that Jesus Christ is the content of God's
"mercies" and His "every consolation". For God to
work in παράκλησις, then, is for Him to work in
Jesus Christ, and this, as we have seen in the
discussion of 2 Cor 5:20, God does in the ministry
of reconciliation which Paul as the suffering
apostle performs. 2 Cor 1:4, therefore, speaks
of the reconciling activity of God in Christ
which is present precisely in the ministry of the
suffering apostle and which through the ministry
of the suffering apostle is extended to others.
As there is only one salvific activity of God,
Paul can and must speak of the παράκλησις which he
gives as that which God gives.

2 Cor 1:5, introduced by ὅτι, is explanatory
of 2 Cor 1:4a. The "affliction" (θλῖψις) which
Paul undergoes (2 Cor 1:4a) is here Christologically interpreted as "sufferings of Christ"
(παθήματα τοῦ χριστοῦ), and as elsewhere, this is
to be understood to mean that in Paul's sufferings
the Crucified One is present as the living Lord.
The correlation (καθὼς-οὕτως) becomes clear. The
abundance of sufferings which Paul undergoes
corresponds to the abundance of God's salvific
activity which the apostle receives and mediates.
2 Cor 1:6, which is explanatory of 2 Cor 1:4b, is
sometimes regarded as evidence that Paul perceived
his suffering as atoning. Our discussion shows
this to be mistaken. Through Paul's ministry,
which is characterized by suffering, God works in
παράκλησις, that is to say, God saves (παράκλησις
καὶ σωτηρία),[152] because Paul's ministry is rooted
in God's reconciling work in Jesus Christ. Therefore, whether Paul is "afflicted" or "comforted",
which are two sides of the same coin, the congre-

gation receives God's παράκλησις. As 2 Cor 1:3 shows, this means in the final analysis that they receive Jesus Christ, the Crucified One. The result is that the congregation itself receives the form of Christ. As in the apostle, God effects in the congregation the patient endurance of suffering. Paul can write, therefore, that the Corinthians undergo "the same sufferings" as he himself suffers, for the sufferings of both the apostle and the congregation are understood to be the sufferings of Christ (2 Cor 1:6). In both, the Crucified One is present as the living Lord.

Yet, with the possible exception of 1 Thess 1:7-10, Paul does not attribute to the suffering of the congregation the same proclamatory significance as he does to his own suffering. Rather, Christian suffering provides the context for a life which in faith and hope holds fast to the promise of God. Only there where there can be no thought of merit does the grace of God work (Rom 4:4). Only there where all trust and expectation is directed to God alone is there peace with God (Rom 4:5; 5:1). Paul, therefore, holds up Abraham as the great man of faith (Rom 4:16-22). Even in view of the utter impotency of his own body (τὸ ἑαυτοῦ σῶμα νενεκρωμένον) and the impotency of Sarah (τὴν νέκρωσιν τῆς μήτρας Σάρρας), in hope he still believed in the God "who makes the dead alive and brings into being that which does not exist" (Rom 4:17). It is with this model of the life of faith in mind that Paul speaks of Christian suffering in Rom 5:3-5.

Such suffering becomes the very object of Christian boasting (Rom 5:2,3), for in it God works that "endurance" (ὑπομονή), "approved character" (δοκιμή), and "hope" (ἐλπίς) which with certainty bring the Christian to final victory. Paul writes: "Affliction works patience" (ἡ θλῖψις ὑπομονὴν κατεργάζεται [Rom 5:3]). This cannot mean that affliction in itself has the power to effect endurance. Perhaps κατεργάζεται should be given a passive thrust so that we should translate, "affliction is made to work endurance". Be this

62

as it may, the implied subject of κατεργάζεται
is God, whose love is given through the Holy
Spirit (Rom 5:5), and the statement asserts that
in affliction the Christian's faith in God's
promises takes the form of endurance.[153] With
ὑπομονή comes δοκιμή, for in that faithful endurance rests also one's tested character. And with
δοκιμή comes ἐλπίς, for remaining steadfast in
affliction--that is, ever being a δοκιμαζόμενος--
is itself a taste of that eschatological victory
which awaits all believers at the end.[154] It
shows that God indeed continues to raise the dead,
to bring forth hope where there is no hope. For
this reason hope "is not put to shame". It is the
foretaste of victory.[155]

Why hope is not put to shame, why it is a
taste of victory, is given in Rom 5:5b: "For the
love of God is poured out into our hearts through
the Holy Spirit which is given to us." This is
the final and ultimate source of the Christian's
faith, his endurance, his tested quality, and his
hope. God's eschatological salvific act in
Christ, His love (Rom 5:8),[156] is the creative and
thus victorious reality at work in the Christian
who suffers affliction. This reality is given to
the Christian by the Spirit who is itself this
reality.[157] With the presence of the Spirit the
victory which God wrought for us in Christ becomes
the reality of the Christian life in the midst of
affliction. This victory is shown in the
Christian's ὑπομονή, δοκιμή, and ἐλπίς.

5. THE FIRST EPISTLE OF PETER

The Holy Spirit is closely bound to the theme
of Christian suffering in 1 Pet 4:14: "If you are
abused for the Name of Christ, (you are) blessed,
for that which is of the Glory and the Spirit of
God rests upon you" (εἰ ὀνειδίζεσθε ἐν ὀνόματι
χριστοῦ, μακάριοι, ὅτι τὸ τῆς δόξης καὶ τὸ τοῦ
θεοῦ πνεῦμα ἐφ᾽ ὑμᾶς ἀναπαύεται).[158] The phrase
τὸ τῆς δόξης καὶ τὸ τοῦ θεοῦ πνεῦμα is cumbersome
and notoriously difficult to interpret. The text
early underwent changes and interpolations.[159]

The addition of καὶ (τῆς) δυνάμεως is well-attested and may represent the original reading.[160] However, after a long discussion, A. García del Moral concludes that καὶ (τῆς) δυνάμεως is not original but was added due to the affinity between δύναμις and πνεῦμα in the New Testament and perhaps as well to clarify the reference to Isa 11:12 which speaks of the πνεῦμα ἰσχύος (גְבוּרָה הרוּחַ).[161] The deletion of καὶ τό also has wide support, but this change is obviously an attempt to escape the difficulty of the repeated article. The text as given above, therefore, forms the basis for interpretation.

Does τὸ τῆς δόξης καὶ τὸ τοῦ θεοῦ πνεῦμα refer to one or to two subject? The answer to this question is not easy. If one subject is intended, then either the καί is explicative ("the Spirit of glory, that is, the Spirit of God") or τό is repeated for emphasis ("the Spirit of glory, indeed, the Spirit of God").[162] In this case the δόξα of 1 Pet 4:14 is the same as that of 1 Pet 4:13--by virtue of the presence of the Spirit of glory, the Christian sufferer already participates in the future glory that will be revealed.[163] In support of this interpretation is 1 Pet 5:1 where the author, "a witness of the sufferings of Christ", says clearly that he is also a "partaker in the glory that is to be revealed". Against this view, however, remains the repetition of the article which usually distinguishes two concepts.[164] Further, the expression "Spirit of glory" is not known elsewhere in the New Testament, and even if its occurrence here were accepted, it is not clear why it would be necessary to clarify the "Spirit of glory" as the "Spirit of God" to Christian readers.

The second alternative is that two subjects are meant. In this case, the δόξα of 1 Pet 4:14 is not that of 1 Pet 4:13, but some other δόξα. This does raise the difficulty of two meanings of δόξα within the immediate context. Yet, the abrupt manner in which δόξα is introduced in 1 Pet 4:14 (τὸ τῆς δόξης) perhaps points in this direction.[165] Favoring this alternative is the fact that elsewhere in 1 Peter glory pertains to Christ and not to the Spirit (1 Pet 1:21; 4:11,13; 5:1) and the Christian's anticipatory possession of the future glory is bound more to his firm hope than to his suffering (1 Pet 1:3-5,13; 3:15).[166] Furthermore, the mention of the Spirit is a reference to Isa 11:2 where δόξα does not appear and where the gifts of the Spirit are not future realities proleptically present in the activity of the recipient.

All in all, the arguments in favor of two subjects and against one subject seem stronger. The construction of an article followed by a genitive is not unknown in Biblical Greek (cf. Lev 7:7; 1 Sam 6:4; Matt 21:21; Jas 4:14; 2 Pet 2:22). In such constructions the unexpressed subject is internal to or belongs to that expressed by the genitive. Therefore, τὸ τῆς δόξης means "that relative to glory" or "that which concerns glory".[167] Wohlenberg suggests that τὸ τῆς δόξης refers to the sign of glory, that which founds and assures the Christian of the future glory, that is, to baptism. "The Spirit of God", then, refers to the Spirit given at baptism.[168] A better solution, however, is to see in τὸ τῆς δόξης a reference to the Shekinah or presence of God.[169]

When Christians suffer for the Name, the glory of God, or Shekinah, rests upon them. The Shekinah was understood by the Jews as God's presence among them. However, God had special abodes. The glory of God reposed (שכן) in the form of a cloud in the tent in the wilderness (Exod 40:34-35; Num 9:15-22) and was especially believed to rest in the Temple (2 Chr 5:11; 6:1-2, 40-42). The prophet Ezekiel repeatedly speaks of the presence of God's glory in the Temple (Ezek 10:18-22; 11:22-25; 43:1-9). In 1 Pet 2:5, the author had exhorted his readers, who were in some situation of threat and opposition,[170] to be built up as "living stones" into a "spiritual house". 1 Pet 4:14, then, says that whenever the Christians are abused for the Name, they are in fact that "spiritual house" upon which the

Shekinah reposes as it once reposed upon the Israelites, the Tabernacle, and the Temple. The persecuted community is the residence of God, His Temple.

The Spirit of God also rests upon the persecuted community. Here 1 Peter refers to Isa 11:2 where the Messiah from Jesse is promised. Upon the Messiah shall rest "a Spirit of God, a Spirit of wisdom and understanding, of counsel and strength, of knowledge and godliness and of the fear of God". The Septuagint does not have an article before πνεῦμα, and García del Moral may be correct in suggesting that by adding the article before πνεῦμα in 1 Pet 4:14, the author gave πνεῦμα the more concrete meaning, "that Spirit of God of which the prophet Isaiah spoke".[171] The Messiah promised by Isaiah was to be God's agent for establishing on earth the reign of God. Through him God was to judge with truth and righteousness and set up His Kingdom of peace (Isa 11:3-10). This the Messiah would do through the Spirit of God who in "resting" upon the Messiah worked for the execution of this divine plan. What is occurring in and through the persecuted Christian community, says the author, is the messianic work of establishing God's reign here and now. This is being accomplished in the power of the Spirit.

The persecuted community is the house in which God dwells and through which God in His Spirit effects His reign. Suffering, therefore, is not a special, tragic situation which comes upon the Christian unawares and unwanted and against which the Spirit strives by instilling in the sufferer the necessary attitudes to endure. Rather, suffering is the very matrix of the Christian life through which the Christian does God's will.[172] God does not call the Christian to suffering as such but to the "doing of good" (ἀγαθοποιεῖν) in suffering (1 Pet 2:20-21; 3:9,17; 4:19).[173] For this reason the suffering of Jesus is used to ground the exhortatory sections of 1 Peter (1 Pet 1:18-21; 2:21-25; 3:18-4:1,13).

Jesus is the great pattern (ὑπογραμμός [1 Pet 2:21]) which the Christian is to follow when he is abused and mistreated. Even while suffering abuse and contumely Jesus did not return like for like but worked humbly for the other (1 Pet 2:21-25). Likewise, the Christian is to persevere in the doing of good even though he be persecuted (εἰ ἀγαθοποιοῦντες καὶ πάσχοντες ὑπομενεῖτε [1 Pet 2:20]). The two present participles ἀγαθοποιοῦντες and πάσχοντες show that the "doing of good" and the "suffering" are two contemporary situations. They should not be translated as though the one were the cause of or the result of the other, as is often done.[174] Rather, as the example of Jesus shows, revilement gives no cause for the Christian to cease from the doing of good but gives occasion for the positive working for the good of the other. For to this positive working for good, even in situations of unjust suffering, God has called the believer (εἰς τοῦτο ἐκλήθητε [1 Pet 2:21; 3:9]).

1 Pet 4:19 presents this same complex of ideas as a summary of the section 1 Pet 4:12-19: "And so in conclusion, let those who are suffering according to God's will commend their souls to a faithful Creator in the doing of good." The words παρατιθέσθωσαν τὰς ψυχάς are reminiscent of Ps 31:5 from which Jesus quoted while upon the cross (Luke 23:46). As in 1 Pet 2:21-23; 3:18-22, Jesus in his passion is both the form and the content of the Christian's behavior. The Christian's "commending himself" to God consists in his actively working for his neighbor's good (ἀγαθοποιΐα).

The Christian assumed the passion of Jesus as the pattern for his life in his baptism. The allusion to Isa 11:2 in 1 Pet 4:14 may itself include a veiled reference to the Christian's baptism, for the influence of Isa 11:2 upon the accounts of Jesus' baptism is likely.[175] Be that as it may, the idea of Christian existence as the daily realization of the covenant made with God in baptism is presented in the first verses of

67

the epistle. The Christian is "sanctified by the
Spirit for obedience and the sprinkling of the
blood of Jesus Christ" (ἐν ἁγιασμῷ πνεύματος, εἰς
ὑπακοὴν καὶ ῥαντισμὸν αἵματος Ἰησοῦ χριστοῦ
[1 Pet 1:2]). In view of the following final
clause (εἰς) ἐν is to be interpreted instrumen-
tally. "By the sanctification of the Spirit" the
election of the Father is effected. This is a
reference to the baptism of the Christian.
However, since ἁγιασμός is a <u>nomen actionis</u>,
baptism is not construed as an act which recedes
into the past as a dead act, but as an act which
is being realized ever anew by the Spirit. The
"sanctification" of the Spirit in baptism becomes
the form of Christian existence and behavior.

This interpretation is strengthened by the
εἰς clause, which, although it expresses the goal
and effect of the Spirit's sanctifying activity,
expresses this goal and effect in words based on
the scene of the sealing of the covenant reported
in Exod 24:3-8. The εἰς makes it unlikely that a
second allusion to baptism is intended, but the
thought is of the continual renewal of the
baptismal covenant in the Christian life through
behavior which is continually characterized by
obedience and the sprinkling of Jesus' blood.
What is the meaning of ῥαντισμὸς αἵματος Ἰησοῦ
χριστοῦ? The εἰς and the fact that ῥαντισμός
also is a <u>nomen actionis</u> rule out the possibility
that the once for all act of Jesus' death is
meant. Rather, the death of Jesus appears as
having a continuing function in the life of the
Christian. As part of the εἰς clause, the
"sprinkling of the blood of Jesus" is understood
as a <u>characteristicum</u> of the Christian's life.
Here, then, as elsewhere in 1 Peter, the passion
of Jesus is the pattern of Christian existence.
"Sprinkling of the blood of Jesus Christ" is a
pictorial expression to designate that behavior
which is founded upon and patterned after the
passion of Jesus. It is that behavior to which
1 Peter repeatedly exhorts. In this case, the
καί between ὑπακοήν and ῥαντισμόν has a certain

epexegetical thrust: "to obedience, that is, to behavior patterned upon Christ's passion."

This conception of baptism appears again in 1 Pet 3:21 where baptism is described as a συνειδήσεως ἀγαθῆς ἐπερώτημα εἰς θεόν. The words συνείδησις ἀγαθή signify one's positive and loyal disposition toward something, in this case toward God's commandments.[176] ἐπερώτημα is a technical term for the making of a contract.[177] Baptism, then, is the act of initiation whereby God's election is realized and in which the Christian enters upon a contractual arrangement with God to act faithfully according to God's will.

The Christians of whom 1 Pet 4:14 speaks are living according to Jesus' passion, that is, after the pattern which they assumed in their baptism. They suffer "as Christians". This statement is not a historical one as though it referred to a legal attitude of the Roman government toward the Church. Opposed as χριστιανός is to φονεύς, κλέπτης, κακοποιός, and ἀλλοτριεπίσκοπος in 1 Pet 4:15, it seems to be equivalent to ἀγαθοποιός, which designates the believer as one doing good according to the pattern of Jesus, and especially within times of persecution. As 1 Pet 4:14 tells us, whenever this occurs, the believing community is shown to be the House of God where His Shekinah reposes and the community in which the Spirit is working for the fulfilling of God's plan.

6. THE EPISTLE TO THE HEBREWS

The Epistle to the Hebrews was written for a situation in which external pressure of some sort was having a stultifying effect upon the life of the Christian community (Heb 6:11-12; 10:25; 12:12-17; 13:1-10) and was even threatening to produce apostasy (Heb 3:12; 6:6; 10:29). The purpose of the epistle is not to remind the readers of the Spiritual nature of their sufferings but to prevent their leaving the Christian community. One argument of the author is the serious nature of the sin of apostasy.

69

Certain judgment awaits the apostate (Heb 2:2-3; 3:12-19; 6:4-8; 10:35-39; 12:15-17,25), for he has "trampled on the Son of God, disdained the blood of the covenant by which he was sanctified, and contemptuously handled the Spirit of grace" (ὁ τὸν υἱὸν τοῦ θεοῦ καταπατήσας καὶ τὸ αἷμα τῆς διαθήκης κοινὸν ἡγησάμενος ἐν ᾧ ἡγιάσθη, καὶ τὸ πνεῦμα τῆς χάριτος ἐνυβρίσας [Heb 10:29]).

Heb 10:22 describes the Christians as those whose "hearts have been sprinkled clean from an evil disposition and whose bodies have been washed with pure water (ῥεραντισμένοι τὰς καρδίας ἀπο συνειδήσεως πονηρᾶς καὶ λελουσμένοι τὸ σῶμα ὕδατι καθαρῷ). Both statements refer to the purification the Christian received at his baptism and his assumption of the obligation to follow God's commands. Behind this passage stands especially the promise of Ezek 36:25-27: "I will sprinkle clean water upon you. . . . A new heart I will give you, and a new Spirit I will put within you; and I will take out of your flesh the heart of stone and give you a heart of flesh. And I will put my Spirit within you, and cause you to walk in my statutes and be careful to observe my ordinances" (cf. Ezek 11:19-20). Through the gift of the Spirit in their baptism (cf. Heb 6:4-5) the Christians have become a community of faith and obedience. They are unlike the wilderness generation which was characterized by "hardness of heart" (cf. Acts 7:51). Qumran knows of ritual washings which are bound to the gift of the "Spirit" for obedient living (1QS 3:6-9; 4:20-22). In Heb 10:22, as in 1 Peter, συνείδησις denotes one's disposition or attitude toward God's commandments (Heb 9:14).

However, in contradistinction to obedient living, the apostate "sins deliberately" (ἑκουσίως ἁμαρτάνειν [Heb 10:26]). The Old Testament speaks often of ἀκουσίως ἁμαρτάνειν which means to transgress God's commandments unwillingly or unknowingly. Such a sin could be forgiven (Num 15:22-31; Lev 4:2,13,22,27; 5:15; cf. Ps 19:12-13). This concept lies behind Jesus' prayer for his

persecutors, "Father, forgive them, for they know
not what they do" (Luke 23:34; cf. Acts 3:17;
7:60). Opposed to this was the deliberate or
knowing transgression of God's commandments which
excluded one from God's people, thus giving the
sinner over to judgment. This was "to sin with a
high hand" (רמה ביד; ποιεῖν ἐν χειρὶ ὑπερηφανίας).
This concept is known in the Old Testament (Num
15:30), appears quite often in Qumran (1QS 5:12;
8:17,21ff.; 9:1; CD 8:8; 10:3; 19:21),[178] and
appears here in Heb 10:26 (ἐκουσίως ἁμαρτάνειν).

In Heb 10:29 one who rejects God's commandments by apostasizing is said to have "trampled
on the Son of God and to have disdained the blood
of the covenant", for it was through the sacrifice
of God's Son that the believer first had been
brought into the covenant with God. An apostate
also "abused the Spirit of grace". T. Judah 24:2
offers a good parallel to the thought of Heb 10:29.
In the days of the Messiah "the Spirit of grace"
will be poured out, "and you shall be to Him sons
in truth, and you shall walk in his commandments
first and last". This is very similar to Ezek
36:25-27 which speaks of the Spirit's causing the
people of God to walk in God's statutes. To abuse
the Spirit of grace, then, is to disregard or
actively to reject his promptings to obey God's
commands and his aid to be faithful to the
covenant with God. This the apostate does who
abandons the Christian community in the face of
threat and slander.

The Epistle to the Hebrews does not present
the Spirit as active in the Christian's suffering.
He is rather among the gifts of salvation which
one at times of persecution can impugn and
affront or whose workings one can ignore or
reject.

7. THE FIRST EPISTLE OF JOHN

In 1 John the Spirit and blood appear together in the wellknown passage concerning the
three witnesses (1 John 5:5-8). According to

John's Gospel, the disciples will continue the mission of Jesus in word and deed through the Paraclete. As the community of the Messiah, the disciples are a messianic community. John's Gospel is explicit that this will include persecution and martyrdom (John 15:18-16:4a; 21:18-19). 1 John 5:5-8 allows for the same view.

1 John 5:5 describes the messianic community as that community which believes that Jesus is the Son of God, that is, the Messiah. As the messianic community, the Christian community exhibits the same features which characterized the mission of Jesus. 1 John 5:6 presents those events which showed Jesus to be the Messiah: "this is he who came through water and blood, Jesus Christ". It is generally agreed that "water" and "blood" refer to the baptism and death of Jesus (already Tertullian, De bapt. 16:1), those events which marked the beginning and the end of Jesus' messianic activity.[179] Since he faced heretics who denied the messianic character of Jesus' death, John emphasizes that element: "not in water only, but in water and in blood".[180]

The Spirit assures by its witness (καὶ τὸ πνεῦμα ἐστιν τὸ μαρτυροῦν) that Jesus is the Messiah who "came" through water and blood (1 John 5:6). While the presence of the Spirit at Jesus' baptism and death certainly lies in the background (cf. John 1:29-34), the present participle (μαρτυροῦν) shows that the author is now speaking of the messianic community.

As the messianic community, the Christians exhibit the same messianic signs as did Jesus who was the Messiah: "there are three who witness, the Spirit, the water, and the blood, and these three are in accord" (ὅτι τρεῖς εἰσιν οἱ μαρτυροῦντες, τὸ πνεῦμα καὶ τὸ ὕδωρ καὶ τὸ αἷμα, καὶ οἱ τρεῖς εἰς τὸ ἕν εἰσιν [1 John 5:7-8]). To what realities in the life of the community these witnesses refer remains an object of much scholarly discussion. The suggestion of Manson that the order reflects the Syrian practice of anointing, water baptism, and first communion

following the Jewish order of initiation--circum-
cision, proselyte baptism, sacrifice--is
wellknown.[181] However, a stricter adherence to
the parallel between the Messiah (Jesus) and the
messianic community is advisable. For Jesus it
was his baptism and his death which showed forth
his messiahship.

"Water" must refer to the Christian's baptism
by which he begins his membership in the messianic
community (cf. John 3:5). Strict adherence to the
parallel with Jesus would demand that "blood"
refer to the Christian's death and, indeed, to his
martyrdom. It must be admitted that the language
and thought of 1 John 5:6-8 fully allow for this
interpretation. It is within the conceptual
purview of this passage that the martyrdom of a
Christian is a sign of the true messianic
community, through which sign the Spirit witnesses
to Jesus, the Messiah. Yet, although martyrdom
is included within the conceptual purview of this
passage, it is not primary. "Blood" may very well
signify the eucharist (cf. John 6:48-58,63).[182]
However, 1 John also speaks elsewhere of Jesus'
death, once mentioning "the blood of Jesus which
cleanses us from all sin" (1 John 1:7) and once
mentioning Jesus' laying down his life for us
(1 John 3:16). The first passage is especially
worthy of note, for there the αἷμα has present
significance (καθαρίζει) and is closely related
to the community's life (κοινωνίαν ἔχομεν μετ'
ἀλλήλων), especially to the confession of sins
(1 John 1:8-9). 1 John 1:8 also places us into
the polemical situation of the letter as does
1 John 5:6-8. The second passage relates Jesus'
death and active love among the brethren. It may
be through the community's confession of sin and
its active love that the Spirit presents the
witness of the blood of Jesus.[183]

8. THE REVELATION OF JOHN

The Revelation of John has justly been called
a martyrological document.[184] Throughout there is

reference to the persecuted and the martyred dead
(Rev 1:9; 2:10,13; 6:9; 11:7; 12:11,17; 13:7,10,15;
14:12,13; 16:6; 17:6; 18:24; 19:2; 20:4,9). This
is in keeping with the Revelation's understanding
of Christian existence as a partaking in the
eschatological war in which Satan is the true
enemy (Rev 2:10,13; 12:10,17; 20:8-9; cf. 13:7,15).
Of interest is the close relationship which the
word group μαρτ- has with suffering and death.
Without exception those called μάρτυς 'witness'
die a violent death (Rev 2:13; 11:3; 17:6).[185]
Twice the phrase "to have the witness of Jesus"
(ἔχειν τὴν μαρτυρίαν ᾽Ιησοῦ) appears in martyrological contexts (Rev 6:9; 12:17), while the
phrase "on account of the word of God and the
witness of Jesus" (διὰ τὸν λόγον θεοῦ καὶ τὴν
μαρτυρίαν ᾽Ιησοῦ) appears in three such contexts
(Rev 1:9; 6:9; 20:4). Twice the giving of witness
immediately precedes suffering and death (Rev
11:7; 12:11).

The frequent appearance of the phrase "the
witness of Jesus" (ἡ μαρτυρία ᾽Ιησοῦ) in martyrological contexts raises the question concerning
its meaning. In Rev 19:10c, "the witness of
Jesus" is identified with "the Spirit of prophecy"
(τὸ πνεῦμα τῆς προφητείας). This statement has
been held to be a gloss because of its alleged
awkward position. Charles believes Rev 19:10c
should have preceded τῷ θεῷ προσκύνησον.[186] In
this case, the γάρ is explanatory and Rev 19:10c
serves to identify "those who have the witness of
Jesus" as prophets.[187] However, a parallel
passage (Rev 22:9) replaces "those who have the
witness of Jesus" with "the prophets and those who
keep the words of this book". "To have the
witness of Jesus", therefore, characterizes the
entire Christian community--both those who give
prophecy and those who receive it. However, since
the prophets were in some way distinguished from
the regular faithful (Rev 11:18; 16:6; 18:20,24;
22:9), [188] Rev 19:10c cannot serve the purpose of
identification this interpretation gives to it.

Rev 19:10c is to be understood in relation to
the angel's imperative, "worship God". John is

not to worship the angel, for the revelation John receives is not from the angel but from God (cf. Rev 1:1). However, the exhortation to proskynesis refers us also to God's kingly dignity (cf. Rev 4:10; 7:11; 11:16; 19:4) and allows us to say more. God's rule is exercised in "the witness of Jesus" which itself is expressed through "the Spirit of prophecy". John ought worship God, for the very revelation he receives is an expression of God's rule over him.

"The witness of Jesus" is, therefore, an active, dynamic concept. It has the character of event. This is already intimated in its identity with "the Spirit of prophecy". The genitive 'Ιησοῦ must be understood as a subjective genitive so that ἡ μαρτυρία 'Ιησοῦ means "the witness which Jesus gives".[189] The view that the genitive is objective, however, recently acquired a competent proponent in T. Holtz,[190] and before going on we must respond to his arguments. These may be summarized in the following way. 1) μαρτυρία 'Ιησοῦ never speaks of an activity of Jesus but always of an activity of the congregation or one of its members. According to Holtz, this is clear from the meaning of μαρτυρία which, while not a technical term for martyrdom in the Revelation, contains in itself the notion of suffering and death.[191] 2) The simple name "Jesus" is used where the congregation is the active subject. Where John sees Christ as the active agent, however, other titles, determined by tradition, are used. Therefore, "Jesus" does not occur in the introductory or concluding portions of the Revelation but is always accompanied by either χριστός (Rev 1:1,2,5) or κύριος (Rev 22:20,21).

Holtz's second argument rests on pure oversight. In his treatment of the name "Jesus", Holtz does not mention Rev 22:16 which directly contradicts his argument. Here the simple name "Jesus" appears in a framework-passage of the Revelation and, indeed, as the active agent: "I Jesus sent my angel to witness to you these things for the churches." Important for the present argument is that Jesus sends his angel to "witness". "Jesus", therefore, may be the subject of witness.

Concerning the first point of Holtz, Brox has correctly argued that in the Revelation the word group μαρτ- itself has nothing to do with suffering and death.[192] Nowhere does μαρτυρεῖν appear in a martyrological context. Since the two witnesses are killed after their μαρτυρία is ended (Rev 11:7), μαρτυρία does not necessarily have a martyrological connotation. On the three occasions where those called μάρτυς suffer martyrdom (Rev 2:13; 11:7; 17:6) words to that effect are expressly added. This would not have been necessary had the term itself included the notion of violent death.[193]

On the other hand, there are positive reasons for believing the genitive ᾿Ιησοῦ to be subjective. Three times ἡ μαρτυρία ᾿Ιησοῦ is accompanied by ὁ λόγος τοῦ θεοῦ where τοῦ θεοῦ most likely is subjective (Rev 1:2,9; 20:4). Once it is accompanied by αἱ ἐντολαὶ τοῦ θεοῦ (Rev 12:17) where τοῦ θεοῦ is certainly subjective. Also where a genitive appears elsewhere with μαρτυρία the genitive is subjective (Rev 11:7; 12:11). More important, however, is the use of the other members of the μαρτ- word group, μάρτυς and μαρτυρεῖν, in relation to Christ.

We have asserted that ἡ μαρτυρία ᾿Ιησοῦ, the witness which Jesus gives, indicates the exercise of Christ's (God's) rule. This is confirmed by those passages where Christ is called μάρτυς and where he is said to "witness". E. Schussler Fiorenza has argued that all these passages speak of the relation of the exalted Lord to his congregation.[194] In these passages Christ's function as "witness" gives expression to Christ's rule over his congregation and, indeed, as the Messiah-King who is coming at the Parusia. In Rev 22:16 Jesus is mentioned as the source of the prophetic word directed to the churches, and he is called "the root and offspring of David", which refers to his kingly dignity. Most likely the title, "the bright morning star" (Rev 22:16), also refers to the Lordship of Jesus.[195] Jesus exercises his rule as king in that he speaks to the churches through the prophets, or through the words of "this book" (cf. Rev 1:3; 22:6,18).[196] In Rev 22:20, ὁ μαρτυρῶν ταῦτα is he who is coming soon, that is, at the Parusia. That he who rules the Christian community through the prophetic word is the coming Messiah-King is shown by other factors as well. The expression "faithful and true" occurs four times. Twice it characterizes the prophetic word (Rev 21:5; 22:6), once him who comes at the Parusia (Rev 19:11), and once Christ, who as "the faithful and true witness" speaks to the Church at Laodicea (Rev 3:14). Also, Christ is said to have the sword of judgment (Rev 1:16; 2:12,16; 19:15). "Der μάρτυς und der zur Parusie kommende Messiaskönig sind ein und derselbe. Wie der Messiaskönig zum Gericht über die Welt erscheint, so übt der μάρτυς jetzt schon das Gericht über die Gemeinde durch sein mahnendes und tadelndes prophetisches Wort aus."[197]

Therefore, the entire Christian community, both those who speak and those who receive prophecy, is governed by the exalted Lord in that he "witnesses" to the community through the Spirit of prophecy. This government, to be sure, expresses itself in exhortation, warning, and promise to the Christian community. But more than that is involved. The community not only receives "the witness of Jesus", but as those who "have the witness of Jesus" the Christians themselves witness to the world. This is not a second witness but the same witness, as is shown by the expression "my witnesses" (Rev 2:14; 11:3; 17:6). As "the witness of Jesus" gives expression to the Lordship of Jesus, the witness of the congregation gives expression to the Lordship of Jesus over it. Such witness brings the witnessing, worshipping community into conflict with Satan and with those who express his will, for, as Schnackenburg has written, this witness is "die Ansage ihrer (the anti-Christ forces) Niederlage und des über sie ergehenden Gerichtes".[198] It belongs also to the

revelation which Jesus gives to his community
that through the believers' steadfast "holding" to
the Name of Jesus and the refusal to deny the
faith of Jesus (Rev 2:13), through the refusal to
worship the beast (Rev 20:4), through the "word of
their witness" (Rev 12:11), the defeat of Satan
becomes manifest and is further realized.[199] This
latter is clearly expressed in Rev 17:14: "the
Lamb shall conquer them (those arranged against
the Lamb) for he is the Lord of Lords and King of
Kings and those with him are called and chosen and
faithful." For this reason the war which Satan
wages is with "the saints" (Rev 12:17; 13:7) or
with the Lamb and those who follow him wherever he
goes (Rev 14:1-5). That Christians are persecuted
and killed "on account of the witness which Jesus
gives" (διὰ τὴν μαρτυρίαν ᾽Ιησοῦ) means, therefore,
that Christians are persecuted because they live
under the rule of Jesus.[200] As such, they are
the natural enemies of Satan.

The persecution and deaths of the saints show
the absolute rejection of Christ's rule by his
enemies. Although the word does not appear in the
Revelation, the blood of the saints is a μαρτύριον
against Satan and his followers (cf. Rev 6:9-11;
16:6; 17:6; 18:24; 19:2) and, therefore, sets the
stage for their final judgment and destruction.
The Revelation stands in the same tradition as
Matt 10:18; Mark 13:9 which also speak of the
appearance of Christ's apostles and their proclamation before kings and councils as a μαρτύριον
against the persecutors.

SUMMARY

The New Testament witness to the Spirit's
role and presence in Christian suffering is a
varied, multifaceted witness. The pervasiveness
of the theme throughout the New Testament reflects
not only a hortatory reaction to opposition and
persecution which happened to occur, but also--
and foremost--an analytical affirmation concerning
the Christian existence. Christians suffer

78

because they follow the crucified Christ, who is now the exalted Lord. To be a disciple of the Lord is to be guided by the Spirit.

Therefore, the Spirit's connection with Christian suffering is always bound up with ideas of proclamation, obedience, sonship, steadfastness, judgment and the like. Ecstasy, visions, the speaking in tongues either do not occur, or they serve other interests than the martyrological interest, or they are expressly deemphasized. In the story of Stephen, for example, certain "supernatural" elements are related. Yet, these have virtually no relation to Stephen as a martyr but serve to show Stephen to be a prophet from God and to support and climax his proclamation. Paul expressly distinguishes his visionary experiences from the significance of his suffering as an apostle.

The Christological character which the Spirit gives to Christian suffering is most strikingly portrayed in Paul's view of his apostolic suffering. The Spiritual nature of his apostleship is shown precisely in the weakness and suffering he experiences, for in his weakness and suffering the crucified Christ is seen to be Lord. Indeed, the Crucified One is met in his suffering apostle. John's conception of the Christian community continuing the messianic mission of Jesus in word and deed through the Paraclete, and Peter's idea of the Christian community following the pattern of Jesus in passion, whereby it shows itself to be God's dwelling place and the locus of God's reign, display a pronounced Christological perspective as well.

Throughout the New Testament the Lordship of Jesus forms the background of the Spirit's work in contexts of persecution and martyrdom. The disciples suffer "for the Name", "on account of Jesus", "because of the witness of Jesus". Striking is the frequent connection between persecution, Christian suffering and mission. Because the disciples are "sent", they are persecuted (Synoptics, Acts, Revelation, Paul, John).

This motif continues the Old Testament and Jewish notion of the Spirit-filled prophet who is persecuted, hated, and finally killed. Such persecution and suffering is viewed under a dual perspective. It either brings judgment upon the persecutors (John, Revelation) or it serves to extend the proclamation (Acts, Stephen, Paul).

The Spirit effects the faithful execution of the Christian's task even at times of persecution and suffering. The Spirit is "willing" to lend aid for loyal sonship (Mark 14:38); it enables the constant "doing of good" in a situation of unjust suffering (1 Peter); it enables a suitable proclamation to be made (Matt 10:18-20; Acts; Phil 1:20-21).

The Spirit's presence in suffering brings forth signs of Christ's victory. The eschatological joy which characterizes the disciples in suffering (Acts 5:41; 16:25; 13:52) is such a sign. Likewise, the steadfast faith in God's promises even within a seemingly hopeless situation witnesses to the victory which Christ has already won and which shall be revealed (Rom 5:3-5).

NOTES TO CHAPTER TWO

1   C. K Barrett, The Holy Spirit and the Gospel
Tradition (London: SPCK, 1947) 130.

2   So also Luke 21:15, except that here it is
Jesus who speaks through the disciples and not the
Holy Spirit. The Matthean parallel (Matt 24:9-14)
contains no mention of divine assistance.

3   Barrett, The Holy Spirit and the Gospel
Tradition, 130.

4   Barrett, The Holy Spirit and the Gospel
Tradition, 131. Cf. Bo Reicke, "Den primära
israelsmissionen och hednamissionen enligt
synoptikerna," SvTK 26 (1950) 92-97.

5   Matt 23:29-37; Mark 9:12-13; 12:1-12; Acts
7:52; Rom 11:3; 1 Thess 2:15; Heb 11:36-37. See
above, p. 1.

6   Unlike Matthew, the context of Mark 13 does
not imply that persecution is a result of mission.
However, Mark 13:10 implies that persecution
arises within the context of the mission.

7   O. Michel goes beyond the evidence when he
speaks of a "Notwendigkeit des Martyriums"
(Prophet und Märtyrer [BFCT 37/2; Gütersloh:
C. Bertelsmann, 1932] 25). The future tense of
the verbs in Matt 10:17,18,21,22 also point to
the inevitability of persecution.

8   H. von Campenhausen, Die Idee des Martyriums
in der alten Kirche, 2nd ed. (Göttingen:
Vandenhoeck & Ruprecht, 1964) 6. Cf. Mark 13:10:
δεῖ κηρυχϑῆναι τὸ εὐαγγέλιον.

9   There is no sentimentality in the words μὴ
μεριμνήσητε (Matt 10:19). They do not intend to
convey the idea that everything will be all right
or to relieve the disciples of hard preparatory
reflection (cf. 1 Pet 1:13; 3:15). Rather, they

81

help convey the note of promise that the march of God's Kingdom through proclamation is assured because God Himself works to assure it. Against G. Haufe, "Form und Funktion des Pneuma-Motivs in der frühchristlichen Paränese," StEv 5 (Berlin: Akademie, 1968) 77: "Das Pneuma-Motiv erscheint lediglich in Gestalt eines Trostmotivs."

10 F. Büchsel (Der Geist Gottes im Neuen Testament [Gütersloh: C. Bertelsmann, 1926] 187) and G. R. Beasley-Murray (A Commentary on Mark Thirteen [London: Macmillan, 1957] 47-48; "Jesus and the Spirit," Mélanges Bibliques en hommage au R. P. Béda Rigaux [Gembloux: Duculot, 1970] 473) correctly stress this fact. Otherwise, V. Taylor, The Gospel According to St. Mark (London: Macmillan, 1952) 509.

11 The idea of testimony as something given also occurs in the Old Testament (Exod 4:10-17; Num 22:35; Jer 1:9).

12 The "hour" is closely connected with the "handing over" of the disciples. Note the same connection in the story of Jesus' arrest (Matt 26:45; Mark 14:41).

13 Von Campenhausen, Die Idee des Martyriums, 24-26.

14 So Taylor, Mark, 507; Beasley-Murray, Commentary on Mark Thirteen, 40; Douglas R. A. Hare, The Theme of Jewish Persecution of Christians in the Gospel According to St Matthew (SNTSMS 6; Cambridge: At the University Press, 1967) 106-7; A. A. Trites, The New Testament Concept of Witness (SNTSMS 31; Cambridge: Cambridge University, 1977) 70. A. Schlatter speaks of both the disciples' testimony and their suffering (Der Märtyrer in den Anfängen der Kirche [BFCT 19/3; Gütersloh: C. Bertelsmann, 1915] 22).

15 For an objective understanding of εἰς μαρτύριον, cf. Mark 6:11; Luke 9:5 (ἐπ᾽ αὐτούς);

also Deut 31:26; Barn. 8:3,4; Ign. Trall. 12:3;
Ign. Phld. 6:3.

16 The fact that the proclamation has been made
"throughout the whole world" (Matt 24:14),
therefore, founds the divine judgment of the whole
world. So also E. Peterson, Zeuge der Wahrheit
(Leipzig: J. Hegner, 1937) 16; N. Brox, Zeuge
und Märtyrer: Untersuchungen zur frühchristlichen
Zeugnis-Terminologie (SANT 5; München: Kösel,
1961) 28,30.

17 Some scholars believe that the phrase τῷ δὲ
εἰς τὸ ἅγιον πνεῦμα βλασφημήσαντι (Luke 12:10b)
refers to the disciples, who are warned by Jesus
that refusal to heed the promptings of the Spirit
before kings and rulers means nothing less than
blasphemy against the Spirit. So H. von Baer,
Der Heilige Geist in den Lukasschriften (BWANT 39;
Stuttgart: W. Kohlhammer, 1926) 145; A. Schlatter,
Das Evangelium des Lukas (Stuttgart: Calwer,
1931; 2nd ed. 1960) 529-30; Barrett, The Holy
Spirit and the Gospel Tradition, 106-7; G. W. H.
Lampe, "St. Peter's Denial," BJRL 55 (1972/73) 356.
Yet, Luke 12:11-12 envisions the confession being
made, and the δεῖ (12:12) implies that it must be
made according to the divine plan. Luke 12:10
contains, therefore, a promise that a suitable
witness, demanded by the divine plan and given
under the tutelage of the Spirit, will be
addressed by the disciples before their tormentors.
In view of this promise, it is most likely that
Luke 12:10b refers, not to the disciples, but to
those before whom the disciples stand, the leaders
of the synagogues, the rulers (cf. Acts 13:45
where the Jews ἀντέλεγον τοῖς ὑπὸ Παύλου
λαλουμένοις βλασφημοῦντες; cf. S. Brown, Apostasy
and Perseverance in the Theology of Luke [AnBib 36;
Rome: Pontifical Biblical Institute, 1969] 107-9;
Brown speaks of a "functional identity" between
the Spirit and the disciples). Luke 12:10a may
refer to the rejection suffered by Jesus during
his ministry. The preaching of the disciples in
the power of the Spirit (12:10b), therefore, would

give a new opportunity for repentance and faith
(So W. Grundmann, Das Evangelium nach Lukas,
2nd ed. [THKNT 3; Berlin: Evangelische
Verlagsanstalt, 1961] 255; Brown, Apostasy and
Perseverance, 108).

18 According to Luke 21:13, persecution shall
come upon the disciples for witness (ἀποβήσεται
ὑμῖν εἰς μαρτύριον). Here εἰς μαρτύριον refers to
the positive witness which the disciples are to
give. This corresponds with the specifically
Lukan use of witness terminology (cf. H.
Strathmann, s.v. "μάρτυς," TWNT 4 [1942] 510;
Brox, Zeuge und Märtyrer, 28-29).

19 Cf. Exod 4:15; Deut 18:18; Isa 34:16; 40:5;
58:14; 62:2; Jer 1:9; Ezek 3:17,27; 33:7; Hos 6:5;
Mic 4:4.

20 A summary statement similar to that concerning
Jesus (Luke 2:40) is made in Acts 9:22 concerning
Paul: Jesus grew in strength (ἐκραταιοῦτο) being
filled with wisdom, while Paul also grew in
strength (ἐνεδυναμοῦτο). It is significant that
Paul's growth in strength is shown in his
confounding the Jews in Damascus by "proving that
he (Jesus) is the Christ".

21 See below, pp. 32,37.

22 This is not to be understood as involving
ecstasy, glossalalia, or revelatory visions. "Es
ist nichts als das rechte Wort am rechten Platz
für einen Jünger Jesu, der um seines Glaubens
willen, angeklagt ist" (Büchsel, Der Geist Gottes,
186). Mark 13:11 especially maintains the
integrity of the disciples: "Whatever is given
to you in that hour, that speak." The imperative
(λαλεῖτε) implies that the possibility of
resisting the Spirit's aid exists.

23 Von Campenhausen correctly stresses that
there is no emphasis on physical suffering and
death nor any distinction made between the

"martyr" and other Christians (<u>Die Idee des</u>
<u>Martyriums</u>, 9).

24 The Church early used Matt 26:41; Mark 14:38
in martyrological contexts (Eusebius, <u>Hist</u>. <u>eccl</u>.
5.1.29; Irenaeus, <u>Adv</u>. <u>haer</u>. 5.9.2 [see below,
pp. 193-94]; Tertullian, <u>Ad</u> <u>mart</u>. 4:1; <u>De</u> <u>fuga</u>
8:1-3; <u>De</u> <u>pat</u>. 13:7-8 [see below, pp. 258-59,261]).

25 H. G. Kuhn, "Jesus in Gethsemane," <u>EvT</u>
12 (1952/53) 275. He compares "spirit" with the
νοῦς (Rom 7:23,25), ὁ ἔσω ἄνθρωπος (Rom 7:22), or
the ἐγω ὁ θελων ποιεῖν το καλον (το ἀγαθον)(Rom
7:19,21). E. Lohmeyer also holds that "spirit"
refers to the spirit of man (<u>Das</u> <u>Evangelium</u> <u>des</u>
<u>Markus</u> [MeyerK; Göttingen: Vandenhoeck &
Ruprecht, 1937] 317-18).

26 K. G. Kuhn, "Πειρασμος--ἁμαρτια--σαρξ im Neuen
Testament und die damit zusammenhängenden
Vorstellungen," <u>ZTK</u> 49 (1952) 200-222; Kuhn,
"Jesus in Gethsemane," 279-85. Cf. H. Braun,
<u>Qumran</u> <u>und</u> <u>das</u> <u>Neuen</u> <u>Testament</u>, 2 vols. (Tübingen:
J. C. B. Mohr, 1966), 1:54-55; 2:256.

27 Kuhn, "Πειρασμος--ἁμαρτια--σαρξ," 209-11.

28 Kuhn, "Jesus in Gethsemane," 277.

29 Kuhn, "Jesus in Gethsemane," 276: there is a
"Widerstreit im Menschen zwischen Wollen und Tun";
Lohmeyer, <u>Markus</u>, 318: "So ist der Mensch ein
gespaltenes Wesen."

30 Braun also stresses that the בשר of Qumran is
more closely related to sin than is the σαρξ of
Mark 14:38 (<u>Qumran</u> <u>und</u> <u>das</u> <u>Neue</u> <u>Testament</u>, 1:55).

31 Kuhn, "Jesus in Gethsemane," 282.

32 Kuhn suggests "broken spirit" (רוח נשברה
[1QS 8:3; 11:1]) as a corresponding term
("Πειρασμος--ἁμαρτια--σαρξ," 214). "Broken
spirit" comes from Ps 51:19.

33   So Büchsel, Der Geist Gottes, 180-83;   E.
Schweizer, s.v. "πνεῦμα," TWNT 6 (1959) 394;   J.
Schniewind, Das Evangelium nach Markus (NTD 1;
Göttingen: Vandenhoeck & Ruprecht, 1963) 153:
spirit as "die unmittelbare Gegenwart Gottes".

34   Lohmeyer, Markus, 317-18;   also Schweizer,
s.v. "πνεῦμα," 394. The LXX translation of
"spirit of willingness" (LXX Ps 50:14) is
πνεύματι ἡγεμονικῷ. However, the LXX does give
πρόθυμος for נדב in 1 Chr 28:21; 2 Chr 29:31.

35   Note the parallelism with the רוח קדשׁ (LXX:
τὸ πνεῦμα τὸ ἅγιον) of Ps 51:13. Kuhn agrees that
Mark 14:38 reflects Ps 51:14 and that Ps 51:14
speaks of God's Spirit ("Jesus in Gethsamane," 277).

36   Note that Jesus prays ἀββα ὁ πατήρ which in
Gal 4:6 is the cry of "the Spirit of His Son" and
in Rom 8:15 is the cry of the Christians through
the "Spirit of sonship".

37   Luke 22:43-44 is missing in several manuscripts. Nevertheless, these verses bear Lukan
characteristics (see K. H. Rengstorf, Das
Evangelium nach Lukas [NTD 1; Göttingen:
Vandenhoeck & Ruprecht, 1963] 250-51). Kuhn
believes Luke omitted this saying because it
refers to the spirit of man and therefore does not
correspond to the Christian understanding of
spirit as the Spirit of God ("Jesus in Gethsemane,"
284). But if that is so, why did Matthew and
Mark include it?

38   For a discussion of the theme of spiritual
wakefulness in the New Testament, see Evald
Lövestam, Spiritual Wakefulness in the New
Testament (Lunds Universitets Arsskrift N.F. 55/3;
Lund: C.W.K. Gleerup, 1963).

39   A discussion of the problems presented by the
figure of the Paraclete is beyond the purview of
this study. A useful bibliography of modern
research may be found in Raymond E. Brown, The

Gospel According to John, 2 vols. (Garden City, New York: Doubleday, 1970), 2:1143-44. There is no sufficient reason to deny that the identification of the Paraclete with the Holy Spirit is originally Johannine (see Raymond E. Brown, "The Paraclete in the Fourth Gospel," NTS 13 [1966/67] 125,126-32).

40 So C. K. Barrett, The Gospel According to St. John (London: SPCK, 1955) 399; Brown, John, 2:665; against R. Bultmann, Das Evangelium des Johannes (MeyerK; Göttingen: Vandenhoeck & Ruprecht, 1957) 420 n. 2; H. Strathmann, Das Evangelium nach Johannes (NTD 2; Göttingen: Vandenhoeck & Ruprecht, 1963) 212.

41 For the resemblances between the Paraclete and Jesus, see Brown, John, 2:1140-41. That the Spirit is called ἄλλος παράκλητος (John 14:16) implies that Jesus himself had acted as Paraclete.

42 J. Beutler, Martyria: Traditionsgeschichtliche Untersuchungen zum Zeugnisthema bei Johannes (FrThSt 10; Frankfurt: J. Knecht, 1972) 275: "Damit ist sein Zeugnis Teil des 'grossen Prozesses' zwischen Jesus und der 'Welt'."

43 Bultmann, Evangelium des Johannes, 426.

44 The sense requires that a περὶ ἐμοῦ after μαρτυρεῖτε be assumed (15:27). μαρτυρεῖτε is present indicative but future in thrust. Cf. Beutler, Martyria, 275.

45 Brown, John, 2:690; Beutler, Martyria, 275: "das Zeugnis des Geistes verwirklicht sich vielmehr im Christuszeugnis der Jünger". In Acts 5:32 both the disciples and the Holy Spirit appears as "witnesses". Despite the similarity between Acts 5:32 and John 15:26-27, in both passages the Lukan and Johannine notions of "witness" retain their distinctive character (cf. Brox, Zeuge und Märtyrer, 78-79; Beutler, Martyria, 303-4).

46 Cf. Num. Rab. 21:3: "If a man sheds the blood of the wicked, it is as though he had offered a sacrifice" (quoted in Str-B, 2:565). For the persecution of Christians by Jews, see Josephus, Ant. 20.9.1; Acts 7:58; 12:1-5; Justin, Dial. 95:4; 133:6; Mart. Pol. 13:1.

47 Brown gives a chart showing the parallels (John, 2:694). Bultmann denies that any connection exists between the Johannine passage and the Synoptic passages (Evangelium des Johannes, 426 n. 5).

48 Beutler, Martyria, 303.

49 As Jesus' reception of the Spirit inaugurated his mission as Messiah (John 1:29-34), so the disciples' reception of the Spirit inaugurates their mission as the messianic community: "As the Father has sent me, even so I send you" (John 20:21).

50 Cf. Mart. Pol. 1:1; 2:2; 20:1; Pass. Perp. 1:1-6; Mart. Apoll. 47; Mart. Pion. 1:1; 22:4. This theme may already appear in the post-resurrection encounter between Christ and Peter (John 21:15-19). Jesus asks Peter on three occasions whether he loves him, and each time Peter replies in the affirmative. To Peter's replies, Jesus responds respectively, βόσκε τὰ ἀρνία μου (John 21:15), ποίμαινε τὰ πρόβατά μου (John 21:16), and βόσκε τὰ πρόβατά μου (John 21:17) (For a discussion of the terminology in John 21:15-17, see Brown, John, 2:1102-6). Thereupon, in a doubly solemn pronouncement (ἀμην ἀμην), Jesus foretells of Peter's martyrdom (John 21:18). The command, "feed my sheep", is often interpreted in terms of missionary preaching or of Peter's position of authority within the early community (For a discussion of the various interpretations, see Brown, John, 2:1112-17). Certainly, the preceding section, which speaks of the "catching of fish" (John 21:4-14), has a mission thrust, and the figure of shepherd is often used in the Old

Testament for one with authority (2 Sam 5:2; 1 Chr 17:6). Nevertheless, John 21:14 appears to conclude the section John 21:4-14, and the words ὅτε οὖν ἠρίστησαν appear to begin a new scene. Jesus' command to feed the sheep is connected, it would rather seem, with his prediction of Peter's martyrdom. The figure of the good shepherd as he who lays down his life for the sheep (John 10:11-18) precludes any necessity for appealing to Old Testament imagery. In telling Peter to "feed the sheep", Jesus is telling him to be a good shepherd. As Jesus is the Good Shepherd who gave his life for the sheep (John 10:11,14), so now Peter, as Jesus' disciple (ἀκολούθει μου [John 21:19]), is to be a good shepherd who feeds the sheep, that is, who gives his life in martyrdom. The three-fold question of Jesus is usually understood in the light of Peter's three-fold denial. It may be that in his denial Peter was a "hireling who is no shepherd" and when faced with danger flees, allowing the sheep to scatter (John 10:12-13). However, in his martyrdom Peter will confess Jesus and "feed the sheep". In his martyrdom Peter will show himself to be a good shepherd who did not flee in the face of danger. The implication is that Peter's martyrdom keeps the sheep together (cf. John 10:16). This would be wholly in keeping with the view that Jesus' death had "gathering" power (cf. John 12:32).

51 This scene resembles that of Jesus' arrest in Gethsemane (Luke 22:52). At the arrest of Jesus, however, it was the "chief priests" (ἀρχιερεῖς), the "captains of the Temple" (στρατηγοί), and the "elders" (πρεσβύτεροι). For the use of ἐπέστησαν, cf. Luke 20:1; Acts 6:12.

52 The use of the aorist passive of πίμπλημι to describe a special moment of inspiration is common in Luke-Acts (Luke 1:15,41,67; Acts 2:4; 4:8,31; 9:17; 13:9). It is to be distinguished from the adjective πλήρης which denotes more the abiding character of the Spirit's presence (cf. Luke 4:1; Acts 6:3,5; 11:24).

53 The words ἀγράμματοι . . . καὶ ἰδιῶται refer
to the disciples' lack of training in Biblical
interpretation (cf. John 7:15). The words appear
in the papyri in the sense "illiterate", "unedu-
cated". But according to Luke an understanding
of Jesus' death and resurrection based on the Old
Testament was a necessary prerequisite for the
mission of the disciples (cf. Luke 24:45-46). It
is likely, then, that it is in view of such a
Biblical argument that the leaders wondered.

54 Cf. H. Schlier, who points out that in Acts
the meaning of παρρησία is determined by the
situation of confessing before a hostile public
(s.v. "παρρησία," TWNT 5 [1954] 880-81).

55 See above, p. 21.

56 It is exaggerated to call Acts 4:1-22 "die
erste Christenverfolgung", as does G. Stählin
(Die Apostelgeschichte [NTD 2; Göttingen:
Vandenhoeck & Ruprecht, 1963] 71). As Acts 4:7
implies, this first arrest was more the result of
an errand of factfinding than of an active attempt
at repression. This begins at Acts 4:17.

57 Cf. Acts 10:38: ἔχρισεν αὐτὸν ὁ θεός πνεύματι
ἀγίῳ καὶ δυνάμει. Psalm 2 is quoted in Acts 4:27
and at the descent of the Spirit at Jesus' baptism
(Luke 3:22). This also indicates that ὃν ἔχρισας
refers to Jesus' anointing with the Spirit at his
baptism.

58 It has been plausibly asserted that such an
association originated with Jesus himself (Mark
10:38; Luke 12:50); see O. Cullmann, Die
Tauflehre des Neuen Testaments, 2nd ed. (ATANT 12;
Zürich: Zwingli, 1958) 14-15; G. W. H. Lampe,
The Seal of the Spirit, 2nd ed. (London: SPCK,
1967) 39.

59 Von Baer, Der Heilige Geist in den
Lukasschriften, 17ff.

60 This mention of the Spirit as "witness" is parallel to the reference to Scripture in Acts 4:11. The Spirit-filled "witness" proclaimed Jesus in the light of a messianically interpreted Old Testament.

61 Cf. Matt 5:11-12; Luke 6:22-23; 1 Thess 1:6; 1 Pet 1:6; 4:13-14; Jas 1:2,12. For a discussion of the theme of joy in suffering, see W. Hauck, "Freude im Leiden: zum Problem einer urchristlichen Verfolgungstradition," ZNW 46 (1955) 68-80.

62 The formula λέγον ὅτι (Acts 20:23) may introduce words which faithfully reproduce the actual words of prophecy.

63 In addition to the commentaries, the following studies may be mentioned: W. Foerster, "Stephanus und die Urgemeinde," Dienst unter dem Wort (Gütersloh: C. Bertelsmann, 1953) 9ff.; Bo Reicke, Glaube und Leben der Urgemeinde: Bemerkungen zu Apg 1-7 (ATANT 32; Zürich: Zwingli, 1957); M. Simon, St. Stephen and the Hellenists in the Primitive Church (London: Longmans, Green, 1958); J. Bihler, Die Stephanusgeschichte im Zusammenhang der Apostelgeschichte (Münchener Theologische Studien; München: M. Hueber, 1963); M. Scharlemann, Stephen: A Singular Saint (AnBib 34; Rome: Pontifical Biblical Institute, 1968).

64 So E. Haenchen, Die Apostelgeschichte (MeyerK; Göttingen: Vandenhoeck & Ruprecht, 1959) 216: "praktische Lebensklugheit"; F. F. Bruce, Commentary on the Book of the Acts (NICNT; Grand Rapids, Michigan: Wm. B. Eerdmans, 1973) 128: "competent in administration".

65 See above, pp. 21,32. Cf. O. Glombitza, "Zur Charakterisierung des Stephanus in Act 6 und 7," ZNW 53 (1962) 238-44.

66 M. Dibelius, "Die Reden der Apostelgeschichte und die antike Geschichtsschreibung," Aufsätze zur

Apostelgeschichte, 4th ed. (FRLANT n.s. 42;
Göttingen: Vandenhoeck & Ruprecht, 1961) 155.

67 See above, pp. 20-21.

68 Against H.-W. Surkau, _Martyrien in jüdischer
und frühchristlicher Zeit_ (FRLANT 54; Göttingen:
Vandenhoeck & Ruprecht, 1938) 109: "Die
Stephanus-Rede gehört nicht zum Martyrium"; H.
Conzelmann, _Die Apostelgeschichte_ (HNT 7; Tübingen:
J. C. B. Mohr, 1963) 45: "Die Rede ist in das
(erweiterte) Martyrium von Lk eingeschoben."

69 K. Holl, "Die Vorstellung vom Märtyrer und die
Märtyrerakte in ihrer geschichtlichen Entwicklung,"
Gesammelte Aufsätze zur Kirchgeschichte, vol. 2:
Der Osten (Tübingen: J. C. B. Mohr, 1928) 71.

70 Holl, "Die Vorstellung vom Märtyrer," 71;
also Bihler, _Die Stephanusgeschichte_, 30-31:
"Stephanus hält also die Rede als Visionär. . . .
Was Stephanus sagt, sagt er auf Grund einer
höheren Erkenntnis."

71 So Haenchen, _Die Apostelgeschichte_, 225;
Bihler, _Die Stephanusgeschichte_, 30.

72 Conzelmann, _Die Apostelgeschichte_, 45: "Der
Vers zeigt die christliche Märtyreridee in statu
nascendi."

73 Schlatter, _Der Märtyrer in den Anfängen der
Kirche_, 36.

74 W. H. C. Frend, _Martyrdom and Persecution in
the Early Church: A Study of a Conflict from the
Maccabees to Donatus_ (Oxford: Basil Blackwell,
1965) 85.

75 W. Mundle, "Die Stephanusrede Apg. 7: eine
Märtyrerapologie," _ZNW_ 20 (1921) 137. André
Grabar writes that in early Christian iconography
the martyr was imagined as in his posthumous state
in paradise which was shown by a change on his

countenance (*Martyrium: Recherches sur le culte des reliques et l'art Chretien antique*, 2 vols. [Paris: College de France, 1943-46], 2:42-43). Concerning Acts 6:15, Grabar writes: "la grâce divine qui réside dans le martyr au Paradis devra se refléter sur son visage".

76 Mundle, "Die Stephanusrede Apg. 7: eine Märtyrerapologie," 137.

77 See below, pp. 173-74.

78 See below, p. 197.

79 See Str-B, 2:666.

80 Here we may cite a parallel, *Num. Rab.* 10:5: "When the prophets went on an errand of the Holy One, blessed be He, the Holy Spirit which rested upon them gave them an awe-inspiring appearance in the eyes of those that saw them, so that all were afraid of them, for they looked like angel" (quoted in Str-B, 2:666). Cf. H. Kraft, "Zur Entstehung des altchristlichen Märthrertitels," *Ecclesia und Res Publica* (Göttingen: Vandenhoeck & Ruprecht, 1961) 69-71.

81 Glombitza, "Zur Charakterisierung des Stephanus in Act 6 und 7," 244.

82 Unlike Paul (Gal 3:19), Stephen refers to the mediation of the Law by angels to underline the importance of the Law (cf. Scharlemann, *Stephen: A Singular Saint*, 130).

83 So Holl, "Die Vorstellung vom Märtyrer," 71-72; Mundle, "Die Stephanusrede Apg 7: eine Märtyrerapologie," 137; H. A. Fischel, "Martyr and Prophet: A Study in Jewish Literature," *JQR* 37 (1946/47) 364-66; M. Lods, *Confesseurs et martyrs: Successeurs des prophètes dans l'eglise des trois premiers siècles* (Cahiers théologiques 41; Neuchâtel: Delachaux et Niestlè, 1958) 29.

84   See H. Delehaye, Sanctus: Essai sur le culte
des saints dans l'antiquite (Subsidia hagiographica 17; Bruxelles: Societe des Bollandistes,
1927) 102-3;   Brox, Zeuge und Märtyrer, 63.

85   Isaiah (Mart. Isa. 1:7) and Pionius (Acta
Pionii 2:2) also knew beforehand of their martyrdoms, but no visions are connected with their
receiving this knowledge.

86   See below, pp. 189,190,191,195,196-97.

87   Usually the Son of Man "sits" at God's right
hand.   For a review of interpretations, cf. C. K.
Barrett, "Stephen and the Son of Man," Apophoreta
(BZNW 30; Berlin: Alfred Töpelmann, 1964) 32-38.
In view of the strong Samaritan influence in
Stephen's speech, Scharlemann suggests that the
Samaritan view of Moses as God's Man lies behind
Stephen's language.   As God's Man, Moses rules
the world and intercedes with God for the faithful
during what the Samaritans called "the standing"
(Stephen: A Singular Saint, 15-16).

88   Scharlemann, Stephen: A Singular Saint, 39,80.

89   The idea that in the exalted Jesus Stephen has
the assurance of his own exaltation is certainly
not foreign to the text and would be included in
any view of Christian discipleship.   But this is
not the purpose of Stephen's vision, which was
given for the sake of the hearers of Stephen's
message, not for the sake of the martyr.

90   Von Baer, Der Heilige Geist in den
Lukasschriften, 103:   "Eine Eigenart der
Lukasschriften, im speziellen aber der
Apostelgeschichte ist, dass alle beschriebenen
Geisteswirkungen mittelbar oder unmittelbar zur
Verkündigung der frohen Botschaft in Beziehung
stehen."

91   Von Campenhausen, Die Idee des Martyriums, 86:
"Sein Tod bildet in der Apostelgeschichte den

Markstein für die beginnende Ausbreitung des Evangeliums zu allen Völkern, über den anfänglichen jüdisch-palästinensischen Rahmen hinaus."

92   J. Schneider, Die Passionsmystik des Paulus: ihr Wesen, ihr Hintergrund und ihr Nachwirkungen (UNT 15; Leipzig: J. C. Hinrichs, 1929) 14: "Wer sein Leben als Apostel Jesu Christi beschreiben will, muss die Geschichte seiner Leiden schreiben." For this theme, see especially E. Güttgemanns, Der leidende Apostel und sein Herr: Studien zur paulinischen Christologie (FRLANT 90; Göttingen: Vandenhoeck & Ruprecht, 1966).

93   According to Güttgemanns, Paul speaks of the suffering of the congregation in Rom 5:3; 8:17-18, 35-36; 12:12; 1 Cor 12:26; 2 Cor 1:4-7; 8:2,13; Gal 6:12; Phil 1:29; 3:10; 4:14; 1 Thess 1:6; 2:14; 3:4; 2 Thess 1:4-7 (Der leidende Apostel, 323 n. 1).

94   What is said of Paul in Acts 9:15-16 is said of the Ebed Jahwe, who as God's messenger of salvation to the nations (Isa 42:1; 49:6) is brought into suffering (Isa 50:4-6). Paul, precisely as an apostle of Christ, suffers in the accomplishment of God's purposes.

95   The exact identity of Paul's Corinthian opponents is the object of a lively scholarly debate. The vast consensus of scholarly opinion, however, agrees that the opponents perceived their Spirit-possession in certain displays of power, while they denied Paul's Spirit-possession in view of his lowly character. See D. Georgi, Die Gegner des Paulus im 2. Korintherbrief: Studien zur religiösen Propaganda in der Spätantike (WMANT 11; Neukirchen: Neukirchener Verlag, 1964); W. Schmithals, Die Gnosis in Korinth: Eine Untersuchung zu den Korintherbriefen (FRLANT 66; Göttingen: Vandenhoeck & Ruprecht, 1965); E. Käsemann, "Die Legitimität des Apostels: Eine Untersuchung zu II Korintherbrief 10-13," ZNW 41 (1942) 33-71; G. Friedrich, "Die Gegner des

Paulus im 2. Korintherbrief," Abraham Unser Vater. Festschrift für O. Michel (Arbeiten zur Geschichte des Spätjudentums und Urchristentums 5; Leiden: E. J. Brill, 1963) 181-215; J. Cambier, "Le critère paulinienne de l'apostolat en 2 Cor. 12.6s," Biblica 43 (1962) 483-88; Güttgemanns, Der leidende Apostel, 94-97,154-56,282-304; D. W. Oostendorp, Another Jesus: A Gospel of Jewish-Christian Superiority in II Corinthians (Kampen: J. H. Kok, 1967); J. H. Schütz, Paul and the Anatomy of Apostolic Authority (SNTSMS 26; Cambridge: Cambridge University, 1975) 165-86.

96 H. Windisch, Der zweite Korintherbrief, 9th ed. (MeyerK; Göttingen: Vandenhoeck & Ruprecht, 1924; repr. 1970) 201-2.

97 H. Lietzmann, An die Korinth I/II, 4th ed. by W. G. Kümmel (HNT 9; Tübingen: J. C. B. Mohr, 1949) 127.

98 Güttgemanns, Der leidende Apostel, 303-4. In the interpretation of the 2 Corinthian passages, I have largely followed the exegesis of Güttgemanns, which seems to me convincing.

99 R. Bultmann, Exegetische Probleme des zweiten Korintherbriefes: Zu 2. Kor 5.1-5; 5.11-6.10; 10-13; 12.21 (SymBU 9; Uppsala: Wretman, 1947; repr. Darmstadt: Wissenschaftliche Buchgesellschaft, 1963) 16.

100 Windisch, Korintherbrief, 193-94; Lietzmann, Korinther II, 126.

101 Güttgemanns, Der leidende Apostel, 313 n. 222.

102 A. Plummer, A Critical and Exegetical Commentary on the Second Epistle of St. Paul to the Corinthians (ICC; Edinburgh: T. & T. Clark, 1915; repr. 1956) 182; Güttgemanns, Der leidende Apostel, 313.

103 Windisch, Korintherbrief, 190-91.

104 So G. Bornkamm, s.v. "πρεσβεύω," TWNT
6 (1959) 682; Güttgemanns, Der leidende Apostel,
315.

105 Cf. Bornkamm, s.v. "πρεσβεύω," TWNT 6 (1959)
682: "Die Verkündigung ist also nicht nur eine
nachträgliche Mitteilung das Heilsgeschehens,
sondern gehört zu ihm wesensmässig hinzu." Ingo
Hermann speaks of a "Funktionsidentität of Christ
and the apostle (Kyrios und Pneuma: Studien zur
Christologie der paulinischen Hauptbriefe [SANT 2;
München: Kösel, 1961] 23). See also the remarks
of J.-F. Collange, Enigmes de la deuxieme Épître
de Paul aux Corinthiens: Étude exegetique de
2 Cor. 2:14-7:4 (SNTSMS 18; Cambridge: Cambridge
University, 1972) 274.

106 A τῷ θεῷ is to be understood (so Windisch,
Korintherbrief, 199; Plummer, Second Corinthians,
189).

107 See especially Güttgemanns, Der leidende
Apostel, 315-17.

108 Only here does Paul call himself a διάκονος
θεοῦ. In Rom 13:4 the one in authority is called
διάκονος θεοῦ, and in 1 Thess 3:2 (v.l.) Timothy
is called διάκονος τοῦ θεοῦ. However, in the
latter case the reading συνεργός is to be
preferred (cf. 2 Cor 6:1).

109 Plummer, Second Corinthians, 354; Windisch,
Korintherbrief, 391. Similarly, W. Grundmann,
Der Begriff der Kraft in der neutestamentlichen
Gedankenwelt (BWANT 60; Stuttgart: W. Kohlhammer,
1932) 104.

110 One cannot be sure whether ὑπὲρ ἐγώ presents
a comparison or a contrast. In view of 2 Cor
11:13ff. where Paul terms his opponents "false
apostles, deceitful workers who disguise themselves as apostles of Christ" and "servants of
Satan", it is improbable that Paul would have
allowed them the title διάκονοι χριστοῦ, even to

a degree. ὑπὲρ ἐγώ probably implies a contrast.
Plummer translates: "I have a better claim to be
called a διάκονος χριστοῦ than they have" (Second
Corinthians, 322).

111   See A. Fridrichsen, "Zum Stil des paulinischen
Peristasenkatalogs 2 Cor. 11.23ff.," Symbolae
Osloensis 7 (1928) 25-29; "Peristasenkatalog und
res gestae. Nachtrag zu 2 Cor. 11.23ff.," Symbolae
Osloensis 8 (1929) 78-82.

112   The verbs βλέπειν and ἀκούειν are to be
strictly understood as the senses of seeing and of
hearing (cf. Cambier, "Le critère paulinien,"
498-505; Schütz, Anatomy of Apostolic Authority,
236-38).

113   Cambier, "Le critère paulinien," 495.

114   The logical subject of ἐδόθη is the κύριος of
2 Cor 12:8. The difficulty of Paul's calling
something given him by Christ an "angel of Satan"
disappears if one accepts Güttgemanns suggestion
that Paul uses an expression used against him by
his Corinthian opponents (Der leidende Apostel,
164-65).

115   For discussion of the possible nature of this
illness, see Plummer, Second Corinthians, 349-51;
Windisch, Korintherbrief, 385-88; K. L. Schmidt,
s.v. "κολαφίζω," TWNT 3 (1938) 820-21; E.-B. Allo,
Saint Paul. Seconde Epître aux Corinthiens (Études
Bibliques; Paris: J. Gabalda, 1956) 313-23. See
also Philippe H. Menoud, "The Thorn in the Flesh
and Satan's Angel (2 Cor. 12.7)," Jesus Christ and
the Faith: A Collection of Studies (Pittsburgh
Theological Monograph Series 18; Pittsburgh:
Pickwick, 1978) 19-30. Menoud believes the thorn
is the psychological and theological suffering
Paul had because he could not convert the Jews to
the Gospel.

116   So Cambier, "Le critère paulinien," 495-96;
Güttgemanns, Der leidende Apostel, 165.

117 So Käsemann, "Die Legitimität des Apostels,"
53; Cambier, "Le critère paulinien," 492 n. 1;
498 n. 1; Güttgemanns, Der leidende Apostel, 166.

118 Windisch, Korintherbrief, 393; Lietzmann,
Korinther II, 156.

119 Grundmann, Begriff der Kraft, 104.

120 Cf. Käsemann, "Die Legitimität des Apostels,"
54: "ihre Offenbarungsart, ihr Medium, und
notwendiges Korrelat"; also Güttgemanns, Der
leidende Apostel, 168; D. Lührmann, Das
Offenbarungsverständnis bei Paulus und in
paulinischen Gemeinden (WMANT 16; Neukirchen:
Neukirchener Verlag, 1965) 60.

121 Plummer argues that the "earthen vessels"
must refer to the whole personality of the
apostles to prevent a too limited interpretation
(Second Corinthians, 126-27). However, it is
clear from 2 Cor 4:10,11 that the bodies of the
apostles are meant.

122 So Windisch, Korintherbrief, 144-45;
Plummer, Second Corinthians, 130: "The Apostle's
life, like the Lord's, was a perpetual martyrdom."

123 So Windisch, Korintherbrief, 146; Plummer,
Second Corinthians, 129-30.

124 Güttgemanns, Der leidende Apostel, 123;
cf. Schütz, Anatomy of Apostolic Authority, 243-44.

125 Güttgemanns, Der leidende Apostel, 121-22.
Cf. Collange, Enigmes, 151-60.

126 Lührmann, Offenbarungsverständnis, 61. The
four participles introduced by ἀλλ' οὐκ (2 Cor
4:8-9), therefore, do not imply rescue or deliverance from Paul's sufferings but, on the
contrary, his continuation in suffering. Because
Paul is not "crushed" he will continue to be
"afflicted". Cf. Collange, Enigmes, 148-51.

127 As does Windisch, Korintherbrief, 147.

128 G. Bertram, "Paulus Christophorus: ein anthropologisches Problem des Neuen Testaments," Stromata (Leipzig: J. C. Hinrichs, 1930) 35; cf. Schütz, Anatomy of Apostolic Authority, 246.

129 E. Lohmeyer, Der Brief an die Philipper, 12th ed. (MeyerK; Göttingen: Vandenhoeck & Ruprecht, 1961) 39-41.

130 See Lohmeyer, Philipperbrief, 40 n. 1.

131 So J. Gnilka, Der Philipperbrief (HTKNT 10/3; Freiburg: Herder, 1968) 59 n. 29; P. Bonnard, L'Épitre de Saint Paul aux Philippiens (CNT 10; Neuchâtel: Delachaux et Niestlè, 1950) 23.

132 Grundmann, Begriff der Kraft, 98; D. M. Stanley speaks of an outpouring of charismatic gifts ("'Become Imitators of Me': The Pauline Conception of Apostolic Tradition," Biblica 40 [1959] 864).

133 This implies experiences similar to those suffered in Philippi (προπαθόντες, ὑβρισθέντες [1 Thess 2:2]). Cf. Acts 17:1-9.

134 See Willis P. de Boer, The Imitation of Paul: An Exegetical Study (Kampen: J. H. Kok, 1962) 110-11.

135 ἀλλὰ καί intensifies the previous phrase: "And I shall in the future especially rejoice."

136 Lohmeyer, Philipperbrief, 51 n. 2: "die persönliche Lage des Pls"; so also Gnilka, Philipperbrief, 66; G. Friedrich, Der Brief an die Philipper (NTD 3; Göttingen: Vandenhoeck & Ruprecht, 1963) 103.

137 τοῦτο may even be understood in the broader sense of Paul's faithful execution of his apostolic mission as a whole, τοῦτο being equal

το ἐν πάσῃ παρρησίᾳ μεγαλυνθήσεται χριστὸς ἐν τῷ σώματί μου (Phil 1:20b). Note the phrase ὡς πάντοτε καὶ νῦν. Paul hopes faithfully to execute his task as he always has.

138 Bonnard, Philippiens, 27: "On voit que Paul ne peut pas séparer son salut personnel de l'accomplissement de son ministére de témoin de Jesus-Christ."

139 Grundmann, Begriff der Kraft, 118: "Für die Gemeinde gilt dasselbe, was wir am Christus, am Evangelium, am Apostel wahrgenommen hatten: Sie hat Anteil an der Knechtstalt des Christus." Güttgemanns speaks of "eine expansive Tendenz" of the revelation of Christ crucified in the apostolic existence which wishes to create in the existence of the congregation its "Ort" (Der leidende Apostel, 189-91).

140 de Boer, Imitation of Paul, 115; A. Schulz, Nachfolgen und Nachahmen: Studien über das Verhältnis der neutestamentlichen Jüngerschaft zur urchristlichen Vorbildethik (SANT 6; München: Kösel, 1962) 286-87.

141 The γάρ introduces the proof for 1 Thess 2:13c. The Christians at Thessalonica were not like the people of the parable who received the word with joy (μετὰ χαρᾶς) but in time of persecution apostacized (Luke 8:13; cf. Mark 4:17).

142 W. Michaelis, s.v. "μιμέομαι," TWNT 4 (1942) 668-69. He refers to the passive construction, ἐπάθετε ὑπό. Cf. Schulz, Nachfolge und Nachahmen, 315. For μιμηταὶ ἐγενήθητε the Vulgate translates facti estis.

143 de Boer, Imitation of Paul, 99-108.

144 de Boer, Imitation of Paul, 100-1.

145 This role as mediator has often been noticed, especially in connection with Paul's repeated

exhortation to be his imitators (see E. Kamlah, "Wie Beurteilt Paulus sein Leiden? Ein Beitrag zur Untersuchung seiner Denkstruktur," ZNW 54 [1963] 225; Güttgemanns, Der leidende Apostel, 325-27). Concerning 1 Cor 10:31-11:1, Stanley writes: "His own mediatorial rôle is highly necessary. He is not merely a mouthpiece through which the Gospel is handed on mechanically to other men. Not only what he says, but how he says it, as well as what he is, have a part to play in the Christian formation of those he evangelizes ("'Be Imitators of Me'," 874).

146 Plummer, Second Corinthians, 10-11.

147 Windisch, Korintherbrief, 39.

148 Schneider, Passionsmystik des Paulus, 49-50.

149 O. Schmitz, s.v. "παρακαλέω, παράκλησις," TWNT 5 (1954) 796.

150 Windisch, Korintherbrief, 38-39: "Die Getrösteten werden Trostbringer für andere, und-- dies freilich nur ein Nebengedanke--wenn die Ap. andere trösten, so kommt dieser Segen nicht aus ihnen, sondern von Gott, der wirklich 'Gott allen Trostes' ist."

151 For παρακαλεῖν, see above, pp. 46-47. οἰκτίρειν and οἰκτιρμοί are commonly associated with the saving activity of God: οἰκτίρειν (LXX: Pss 66:1-2; 101:14; 102:13; 122:2; Isa 27:11; Jer 13:14; 21:7); οἰκτιρμοί (LXX: Pss 24:6; 68:16; 78:8; 102:4; 118:77,156). οἰκτιρμοί corresponds to the Hebrew רחמים which was a frequent characteristic of God in Judaism (cf. R. Bultmann, s.v. "οἰκτίρω," TWNT 5 [1954] 162).

152 The καί is epexegetical. Cf. 2 Cor 5:20-6:2 where God working in παράκλησις through Paul leads to Paul's announcement that the "day of salvation" is at hand.

153 O. Michel, Der Brief an die Römer (MeyerK; Göttingen: Vandenhoeck & Ruprecht, 1963) 132: "Der Glaube nimmt in der Anfechtung die Form des Ausharren, die Standhaftigkeit." E. Käsemann is right when he writes of θλῖψις: "Es spiegelt vielmehr den Schatten des Kreuzes, in welchem Gottes eschatologische Macht allein wirksam werden will" (An die Römer [HNT 8a; Tübingen: J. C. B. Mohr, 1973] 125).

154 This chain (ὑπομονή-δοκιμή-ἐλπίς), therefore, does not imply different steps of faith, but with the one the other is given.

155 Cf. Pss 21:6; 24:20 where οὐ καταισχυνθῆναι parallels σωθῆναι and ἐρρυσθῆναι.

156 ἡ ἀγάπη τοῦ θεοῦ (Rom 5:5) is not our love for God (Augustine) but God's love for us.

157 The picture of God's love "being outpoured" implies that the Spirit is not merely the bringer of God's love but itself the present reality of God's love. ἐκχύειν is often used of the Spirit (Joel 3:1; Acts 2:17; 10:45). The perfect form ἐκκέχυται shows that God's love (i.e. Spirit) is not a possession but is given ever anew.

158 For the Old and New Testament background of such a beatitude for those who suffer, see Helmut Millauer, Leiden als Gnade: Eine traditions-geschichtliche Untersuchung zur Leidenstheologie des ersten Petrusbriefes (Europäische Hochschulschriften, Reihe 23, Theologie 56; Bern: Herbert Lang, 1976) 156-64.

159 For a survey of the variants, see A. García del Moral, "Critica textual de I Ptr. 4.14," Estudios Biblicos 20 (1961) 45-48.

160 F. W. Beare, The First Epistle of Peter, 2nd ed. (Oxford: Basil Blackwell, 1958) 166: "The evidence for καὶ (τῆς) δυνάμεως seems too strong and too widely represented for us to reject

it;   it is equally hard to account for its loss
if it be genuine, and for its insertion it it be
false."

161   García del Moral, "Critica textual," 54-67.

162   So, for example, J. N. D. Kelly, The Epistles
of Peter and of Jude (Harper New Testament
Commentaries; New York: Harper & Row, 1969) 187.
The translation of the RSV, "the Spirit of glory
and of God", is unlikely because of the repeated
τό.

163   So G. Kittel, s.v. "δοκέω, δόξα," TWNT
2 (1935) 254;   R. Knopf, Die Briefe Petri und Juda
(MeyerK; Göttingen: Vandenhoeck & Ruprecht, 1912)
180;   K. H. Schelkle, Die Petrusbriefe (HTKNT 13/2;
Freiburg: Herder, 1961) 124;   Kelly, First Peter,
186-87.

164   García del Moral, "Critica textual," 51;
Bl-Debr §269.6.

165   A. García del Moral, "Sentido trinitario de
la expresion 'Espiritu de Yave' de Is. XI.2 en
I Pdr. IV.14," Estudios Biblicos 20 (1961) 195-96.

166   García del Moral, "Critica textual," 52;
"Sentido trinitario," 195.

167   So G. Wohlenberg, Der erste und zweite
Petrusbrief und der Judasbrief, 3rd ed. (Kommentar
zum Neuen Testament 15; Leipzig: A. Deichert, 1923)
137;   E. G. Selwyn, The First Epistle of St. Peter
(London: Macmillan, 1949) 222;   García del Moral,
"Critica textual," 51.

168   Wohlenberg, Der erste Petrusbrief, 137.

169   So also Selwyn, First Peter, 222-24;   García
del Moral, "Critica textual," 52;   "Sentido
trinitario," 196-200.

170 1 Peter presupposes throughout an actual
situation of persecution. The language, however,
does not allow us to postulate more than a situation of social abuse. πύρωσις (1 Pet 4:12) merely
reintroduces a metaphor used already in 1 Pet 1:7,
and ὀνειδίζειν (1 Pet 4:14) need mean nothing more
than verbal abuse (cf. Pss 43:16; 54:12; Matt
27:44; Mark 15:32). That martyrdom is not
envisioned is clear from 1 Pet 4:19: those
suffering are to continue in good works.

171 García del Moral, "Critica textual," 52-53.

172 We cannot speak, therefore, of a special gift
of the Spirit during times of suffering, as do
Kelly, First Peter, 187: "special anointing";
Beare, First Peter, 192: "occasional visitation";
Büchsel, Der Geist Gottes, 460: "Leiden für
Christus bringt Geistbesitz ein."

173 See Wilhelm Brandt, "Wandel als Zeugniw nach
dem 1. Petrusbrief," Verbum Dei Manet in Aeternum.
Festschrift für Otto Schmitz (Witten: Luther-
Verlag, 1953) 10-25.

174 RSV: "But if when you do right and suffer
for it"; NEB: "If when you have behaved well and
suffer for it".

175 García del Moral, "Sentido trinitario,"
175-76.

176 See Bo Reicke, The Disobedient Spirits and
Christian Baptism: A Study of I Pet iii.19 and
its Context (ASNU 13; København: Ejnar Munksgaard,
1946) 174-82.

177 Reicke, Disobedient Spirits, 182-86.

178 Cf. also 1QS 2:11-18; 7:22-25; CD 7:20-8:1;
19:33-35; 20:3-15,25-27. The concept was general
throughout Judaism (cf. Str-B, 2:264; 3:689-90).

179   See P. W. Keppler, "Geist, Wasser und Blut:
Zur Erklärung von I Joh. 5.6-13 (ev. Joh. 19.34),"
Theologische Quartelschrift 68 (1886) 7-10;   A.
Klöpper, "I Joh. 5.6-12," Zeitschrift für
wissenschaftliche Theologie 43 (1900) 383,388;
Beutler, Martyria, 276;   R. Schnackenburg, Die
Johannesbriefe (HTKNT 13/3; Freiburg: Herder,
1953) 230;   R. Bultmann, Die drei Johannesbriefe
(MeyerK; Göttingen: Vandenhoeck & Ruprecht, 1967)
82.   It is unlikely that 1 John 5:6 implicitly
refers to John 19:34.   John 19:34 has an inverse
order (αἷμα καὶ ὕδωρ) and the prepositions διά
and ἐν would hardly be appropriate to describe
that which flowed out of Jesus' wound.

180   The change of preposition from διά to ἐν
causes no basic shift of meaning, although there
may be the nuance in ἐν that the "water" and the
"blood" have present significance.   However, in
1 John 5:6a and 1 John 5:6b ὕδωρ and αἷμα have
the same referents, the baptism and death of
Jesus.

181   T. W. Manson, "Entry into Membership of the
Early Church," JTS 48 (1947) 25-33.

182   So Schnackenburg, Johannesbriefe, 234;
Bultmann, Johannesbriefe, 83.

183   This interpretation does not exclude that
which sees a reference to the eucharist.   Very
likely the confession of sins would have a
liturgical setting (plur., ἐαν ὁμολογῶμεν τὰς
ἀμαρτίας ἡμῶν) and such a confession was very
early part of the eucharistic celebration (cf.
Did. 14:1: κλάσατε ἄρτον καὶ εὐχαριστήσατε,
προεξομολογησάμενοι τὰ παραπτώματα ὑμῶν).   The
early community's charity was also bound to the
eucharistic celebration (see Justin, 1 Apol. 67).
It is also possible that both ὕδωρ and αἷμα refer
to baptism.   The use of both water and blood
figures to represent baptism occurs elsewhere in
the New Testament (cf. Heb 10:22; 1 Pet 1:2).
Also, in the baptism scene of John's Gospel

(John 1:29-34) the Baptist recognizes Jesus as "the Lamb of God who takes away the sins of the world". The idea of the shedding of blood is thereby introduced into the baptismal scene. Similarly, it may be that in John 19:34 baptismal imagery is introduced into a scene of the shedding of blood.

184 E. Lohmeyer, "Die Idee des Martyriums in Judentum und Urchristentum," ZST 5 (1928) 247; von Campenhausen, Die Idee des Martyriums, 42; A. Brekelmanns, Martyrerkranz: Eine symbolgeschichtliche Untersuchung im frühchristlichen Schriftum (AnGreg 150; Rome: Universita Gregoriana, 1965) 21.

185 Christ is twice called "witness" (Rev 1:5; 3:14), but as we shall argue below, the term does not denote or imply his death.

186 R. H. Charles, A Critical and Exegetical Commentary on the Revelation of St. John (ICC; Edinburgh: T. & T. Clark, 1920), 2:130-31.

187 Charles, Revelation, 2:130; H. Strathmann, s.v. "μάρτυς," TWNT 4 (1942) 506.

188 See W. Huss, Die Gemeinde der Apocalypse des Johannes (Diss. München, 1967) 85; D. Hill, "Prophecy and Prophets in the Revelation of St. John," NTS 18 (1971/72) 406-11.

189 So also Strathmann, s.v. "μάρτυς," TWNT 4 (1942) 506; Brox, Zeuge und Märtyrer, 94; A. A. Trites, "Μάρτυς and Martyrdom in the Apocalypse: A Semantic Study," NovT 15 (1973) 74-75.

190 T. Holtz, Die Christologie der Apokalypse des Johannes (TU 85; Berlin: Akademie, 1962) 23-25. So also von Campenhausen, Die Idee des Martyriums, 42.

191 Holtz, Christologie, 55-57.

192   Brox, Zeuge und Märtyrer, 92-105.

193   Cf. E. Schussler-Fiorenza, Priester für Gott:
Studien zum Herrschafts- und Priestermotiv in der
Apokalypse (Neutestamentliche Handlungen, n.s. 7;
Münster: Aschendorff, 1973) 242-44. For a
detailed listing of scholars who do and of scholars
who do not believe the term μάρτυς contains the
notion of violent death, see Huss, Gemeinde, 230
n. 691;   see also Trites, "Μάρτυς and Martyrdom,"
72-80.

194   Schussler-Fiorenza, Priester für Gott, 244-46.
She correctly rejects any reference to the earthly
Jesus in the term μάρτυς.   Brox tends in the same
direction (Zeuge und Märtyrer, 98-99).   For him,
μάρτυς refers to the "Offenbarungstätigkeit" of
Jesus, especially that of the Revelation itself.

195   Holtz, Christologie, 156-59.

196   Those who prophesy and those who receive
prophecy are equally under the rule of Christ.
Hence, "to have the witness of Jesus" characterizes the entire community (cf. Rev 19:10; 22:9).
The Spirit of prophecy is no more a possession of
the prophet than of the believer receiving
prophecy, for it is finally a question of Christ's
rule, not of the special charism of an office.
The liturgical character of the introductory and
concluding sections shows that the Revelation is
a prophetic word from Christ to his congregation.

197   Schussler-Fiorenza, Priester für Gott, 246.

198   R. Schnackenburg, Gottes Herrschaft und
Reich: Eine biblisch-theologische Studie, 2nd ed.
(Freiburg: Herder, 1961) 235.

199   Cf. H. Schlier, "Jesus Christus und die
Geschichte nach der Offenbarung des Johannes,"
Besinnung auf das Neue Testament: Exegetische
Aufsätze und Vorträge II (Freiburg: Herder, 1964)
358-73.

200   This rule, once more, is exercised through
the Spirit of prophecy (cf. Rev 2:7,11,17,29;
3:6,13,22).   One cannot maintain that those who
suffer διὰ τὴν μαρτυρίαν ʾΙησοῦ did so because
they acted as μάρτυρες or spoke words of judgment
to the world.   ἡ μαρτυρία ʾΙησοῦ expresses the
rule of Jesus and does not itself assert anything
about the activity of the believers, but only that
they stand under the rule of Jesus.   Thus, when
those who were beheaded διὰ τὴν μαρτυρίαν ʾΙησοῦ
(Rev 20:4) are further described, they are said
to be those who did not worship the Beast and
receive his mark on their foreheads or hands.
ἔχειν τὴν μαρτυρίαν ʾΙησοῦ and to be μάρτυς are
nowhere identified in the Revelation, and one has
no cause to see every martyred saint after the
fashion of the two witnesses of chapter eleven.

Chapter 3

IGNATIUS OF ANTIOCH

The statements of Ignatius concerning his approaching martyrdom are fundamental to an understanding of his total thought. This does not mean that his thinking about martyrdom provided the matrix out of which he developed his views on other facets of Christian confession and life. Rather, to interpret his martyrdom, Ignatius employed those elements of Christian reality which were central to his thinking. It is essential, therefore, that the martyrological statements of Ignatius be understood in the light of his central concepts.

Some scholars have seen imitation as the guiding concept of Ignatius' understanding of his martyrdom. Von Campenhausen, Preiss, and Rathke represent this view.[1] According to these scholars, Ignatius understood his martyrdom to be a radical imitation of Jesus' own death. His death would possess its own independent value alongside that of Christ's; it would be parallel and analogous to the death of Christ. Thus, von Campenhausen summarizes his discussion of Ignatius in these words:

> Sie (Christ and the martyr) stehen nebeneinander und stehen einander in ihrem erlösendem Leiden um Gottes Willen tatsächlich gleich. . . . Ein grundsätzlicher Unterschied zwischen dem zur Vollkommenheit gelangten Lehrer und Schüler ist nicht mehr zu erkennen.[2]

In no way, however, does this view of imitation do justice to Ignatius. To be sure, Ignatius views the passion of Jesus and his martyrdom as two distinct, historical events. However, the relationship of one to the other is not merely that of external imitation. Rather, as our discussion below will indicate, the martyrdom of

111

Ignatius bears the imprint of the passion of Jesus because it is a form of the continuing eschatological, and salvific, presence of Jesus' passion in the Church. The minor role which the concept of imitation plays in Ignatius is reflected even in the incidence of terminology. Only once does Ignatius use μιμητής of himself (Rom. 6:3), while he uses it four times of his fellow Christians (Eph. 1:1; 10:3; Trall. 1:2; Phld. 7:2).[3]

Other scholars have attempted to interpret Ignatius in the light of his pagan environment. Schlier, for example, maintains that Ignatius was influenced by the gnostic myth of the Redeemed Redeemer.[4] On the other hand, Wetter and Bartsch maintain that Ignatius reflects conceptions of the mystery cults.[5] Yet, Ignatius can very well be interpreted without recourse to pagan religious phenomena. The structure of his thought is thoroughly biblical, being especially influenced by the theology of John. Wetter and Bartsch are correct when they assert a close connection between cult and martyrdom in Ignatius. Yet, there exists no substantial correspondence between Ignatius and the conceptions of the mysteries. Ignatius' insistence on the fleshly, historical character of both the passion of Jesus and his own martyrdom is inimical to the mystery cults.[6]

Scholars have also seen in the concepts of atonement and vicarious sacrifice the guiding principles by which Ignatius interpreted his martyrdom.[7] Four times Ignatius calls himself an ἀντίψυχον 'ransom' or 'substitute' (Eph. 21:1; Smyrn. 10:2; Pol. 2:3; 6:1), and twice he calls himself a περίψημα 'offscouring' or 'sacrifice' (Eph. 8:1; 18:1). Perler, pointing to the double occurrence of ἀντίψυχον in 4 Maccabees (6:29; 17:21), argues that the atonement ideas of that Jewish work were influential in the martyrological thinking of Ignatius as well.[8] Similarly, Stählin interprets Ignatius' use of ἀντίψυχον and περίψημα to mean that Ignatius vicariously goes into death for the Christian brethren, who thereby are spared in persecution. Indeed, Stählin concludes that the salvific death of Ignatius for the Church must--if systematically thought through--be understood as objectively parallel to and independent of the passion of Christ.[9]

It is, however, quite doubtful whether Ignatius conceived of his martyrdom as sacrificially vicarious for his fellow Christians. Certainly, as Bommes has amply demonstrated,[10] Ignatius did not think of his death as having atoning or sacrificial value alongside that of Christ's passion. Indeed, ideas of vicarious sacrifice are infrequent in the Ignatian letters even when attributed to Jesus' death. Concepts and terminology central to a sacrificial perspective--καθαρίζειν, ἁμαρτία, δικαιοσύνη, ἱλαστήριον-- either do not appear in Ignatius or they possess only peripheral significance in the total thought of Ignatius.[11] As we shall note throughout our discussion, for Ignatius man's predicament is not so much that he is a sinner (although certainly Ignatius knew of man as a sinner [Smyrn. 7:1]) but that man is separated from God. Salvation, therefore, lies not so much in the atonement for sin as in unification with God through the defeat of the powers of separation.[12]

Furthermore, the use of the terms ἀντίψυχον and περίψημα in the Ignatian letters does not support the view that Ignatius conceived his martyrdom as a vicarious, atoning sacrifice. First of all, the terms appear in letters to only two of the congregations addressed by Ignatius (Ephesus and Smyrna), a statistical datum which indicates that Ignatius may have had a special reason for addressing those churches in those terms. That reason is very likely the special relationship which Ignatius developed with the Ephesian and Smyrnaean congregations while on his way to Rome. Ignatius and his military escort made a stopover in Smyrna, and Ignatius was well befriended by the Smyrnaean Christians, especially their bishop Polycarp, while he was there. This probably explains the fact that twice (Smyrn. 10:2; Pol. 2:3) Ignatius calls himself ἀντίψυχον in contexts

which refer to the love shown to Ignatius by the
Smyrnaean Christians and their bishop. Similarly,
Ignatius mentions the special diligence which the
Ephesian community exhibited in its hospitality
toward him (Eph. 1:2-2:1). This hospitality was
shown especially in the special emissaries sent
by the Ephesian church to Ignatius. In Eph. 21:1,
Ignatius calls himself an ἀντίψυχον with an eye
toward those beloved visitors. In all these
passages we should attribute to ἀντίψυχον at most
a certain intercessory significance, as does
Bommes.[13]

Secondly, by the early second century the
term περίψημα had generally lost its strictly
sacrificial meaning and had become more and more
an expression of contempt or of self-humiliation.
Symmachus (Jer 22:28) uses the word as an
expression of disdain and odium, and Paul uses it
to express the lowly nature of his apostolic
ministry (1 Cor 4:13).[14] Other than in Ignatius,
περίψημα appears only twice in the Apostolic
Fathers, in Barn. 4:9; 6:5. Both times it
expresses the reserve of servanthood.[15] It is
along these lines that we should interpret Eph.
18:1: περίψημα τὸ ἐμὸν πνεῦμα τοῦ σταυροῦ. By
this Ignatius merely says that his Christian being
is completely defined by the cross; the passion
of Christ is the power, the form and the goal of
his Christian existence.[16]

In summary, Ignatius employs the terms
ἀντίψυχον and περίψημα in a more or less unreflective manner and without elaboration. They
certainly do not bear Ignatius' interpretation of
his coming martyrdom. Were that the case, it
would be strange indeed that Ignatius nowhere
designates himself ἀντίψυχον or περίψημα in
relation to the congregation at Antioch whose
bishop he was. It would be surprising as well
that the terms do not appear in the letter to the
Roman church in which Ignatius speaks almost
exclusively of his martyrdom.[17]

Finally, commentators sometimes enlist Rom.
2:2 (πλέον δέ μοι μὴ παράσχησθε τοῦ σπονδισθῆναι

114

θεῷ, ὡς ἔτι θυσιαστήριον ἕτοιμον ἐστιν) and Rom.
4:2 (λιτανεύσατε τὸν χριστὸν ὑπὲρ ἐμοῦ, ἵνα διὰ
τῶν ὀργάνων τούτων [the beasts] θεοῦ θυσία εὑρεθῶ)
to prove that Ignatius understood his martyrdom as
an atoning sacrifice. Obvious sacrificial terminology is used, but nowhere in these passages or
in their contexts is the idea expressed that
Ignatius dies for others. Rather, these passages,
along with other expressions in the same epistle
(ὑπὲρ θεοῦ ἀποθνήσκω [Rom. 4:1]; σῖτός εἰμι θεοῦ
[Rom. 4:1]), are to be interpreted in the light of
the fundamental Ignatian assertion that his
martyrdom shows God forth: God is the author of
martyrdom and the goal of martyrdom, for martyrdom is an expression of the passion of Christ
which supremely reveals God Himself.[18]

In turning now our attention to consideration
of Ignatius' understanding of martyrdom, one
obvious but absolutely essential fact must be kept
in mind: Ignatius reflects upon his own coming
martyrdom. This no doubt helps to explain the
passionate intensity of his martyrological statements, and in his intensity he is more like Paul
than any other early Christian figure. However,
important methodological consequences follow from
the fact that Ignatius speaks of his own death.
We should not expect, nor do we find, a systematic
reflection upon 'martyrdom' or 'the martyr'. In
the letters of Ignatius there is no 'community
view' of martyrdom; there is no 'theology' of
martyrdom. That is why all attempts to describe
Ignatius' understanding of his martyrdom in terms
of typical martyr motifs--whether they be
imitation, sacrifice, confession before the pagans,
or some other--are bound for disappointment.
Ignatius rather speaks directly out of his own
predicament. What he says, he says about himself
as one who is going into death because he is a
Christian. That is to say, what Ignatius says
about his martyrdom gives expression to what
Ignatius believes to be fundamentally true about
the Christian reality in which he exists. To put
it simply, Ignatius' understanding of his martyr-

115

dom reflects his Christian confession, the essential ingredients of his theology.

This close, inseparable connection between the creed of Ignatius and his martyrdom is made explicit twice. In the letter to the church at Tralles, Ignatius exhorts his readers to turn a deaf ear to anyone who does not speak of Jesus Christ, "who is from the family of David, who is from Mary, who was really born, ate and drank, who truly was persecuted under Pontius Pilate, who was truly crucified and died . . . who also truly was raised from the dead" (Trall. 9:1-2). Ignatius continues: "But if, as some atheists, that is, some unbelievers say, he seemed to have suffered, . . . why am I bound; why do I wish to fight the beasts? In that case, I die in vain. Indeed, in that case, I bear a false testimony against the Lord" (Trall. 10). Similarly, after speaking in a pseudo-creedal way about the real (ἀληθῶς) physical descent from David, the real birth and suffering of the Lord (Smyrn. 1:1-2), Ignatius writes of himself to the Christians at Smyrna: "For if these things seemingly (τὸ δοκεῖν) were done by our Lord, also I seemingly am bound. Why in that case have I given myself over to death, to fire, to the sword, to the beasts?" (Smyrn. 4:2).

Both of these creed-like passages (Trall. 9:1-2; Smyrn. 1:1-2; cf. also Eph. 7:2; 18:2; Mag. 11:1; Phld. 8:2) lead us to the center of Ignatian thinking: Jesus Christ was the incarnate God who truly suffered, died and rose in the flesh. And both of these passages lead to statements concerning the propriety of martyrdom. The reason for this is not hard to find. The creedal affirmations of Ignatius are not merely biographical of the man Jesus; they are affirmations concerning Jesus the Lord. Since Jesus--who lived, died and rose again in the flesh--is Lord, the Lordship, the active rule, of Jesus is fleshly. Therefore, Ignatius understands his martyrdom, which is in the flesh, to be an expression of the Lordship of Jesus. That is why Ignatius asserts that if, as the docetists said, Jesus had not

116

suffered and died in the flesh (τὸ δοκεῖν), his
death, which is fleshly, would be a "false witness
against the Lord" (Trall. 10). For Ignatius, his
martyrdom is a demonstration of Jesus--who really
suffered, died and rose again in the flesh--as
Lord. From this perspective, we can understand
Ignatius' praise of those Christians who received
him and gave him hospitality, and we can understand how his martyrdom can serve a polemical
function over against the docetists. Not to
confess the Lord is to dishonor the martyr; not
to honor the martyr is to dishonor the Lord. That
is precisely the argument in Smyrn. 5:2: "What
does anyone profit me, if he praises me but
blasphemes my Lord by not confessing him to be
the fleshbearer (μὴ ὁμολογῶν αὐτὸν σαρκοφόρον)?
He who does not say this denies him completely."[19]

Jesus, who truly suffered in the flesh, is
Lord, because in his passion Jesus destroyed the
"ancient kingdom" of the "ruler of this age" who
works division, separation and death (Eph. 17:1;
19:1-3; cf. 13). As the one who defeats Satan,
therefore, Jesus in his resurrection brings about
life and unity. To be united and to have life are
synonymous for Ignatius. However, unity and life
are only in the passion of Jesus, for only there
is Satan, the ruler of division and separation
and death, destroyed. For that reason, Ignatius
continually exhorts the churches to the unity of
the eucharist around the one bishop, for there
the flesh of the Savior who suffered is given,
there the powers of Satan are brought to naught
(Smyrn. 7:1; Eph. 13). Similarly, Ignatius knows
the goal and result of his martyrdom to be union
with God.

This connection between passion and unity is
fundamental to the thought of Ignatius. On the
one hand, the passion of Jesus establishes and
maintains unity, and on the other hand, the unity
of the Church so established expresses itself in
passion (i.e. eucharist and martyrdom). Essentially, of course, both the unity and the life are
of God, who gives both in Jesus Christ. Christ,

117

who is united to the Father (Eph. 5:1; Mag. 8:1;
Rom. 3:3; Phld. 7:2; 8:1), is in his passion the
revelation of the one God (Mag. 8:1). In his
passion, Christ destroyed the powers of division
thereby bringing about the Church, which is the
locus of the eschatological unity of God with His
people. The Church, therefore, participates in
the divine unity and partakes of the divine life
only when it lives out of and according to the
cross of Christ.

To illustrate this rather dynamic thinking of
Ignatius, we adduce two passages, Trall. 11:1-2
and Smyrn. 1:2.

> Trall. 11:1-2: Flee, therefore, the evil
> offshoots which bear death-carrying fruit, of
> which should anyone taste, he dies from it.
> For they are not a plant of the Father. For
> if they were, they would show themselves to
> be branches of the cross and their fruit
> would be incorruptible. Through it (the
> cross), in his passion he calls us, who are
> his members, to himself. A head is not able
> to come into existence without members,
> since God expresses unity, which He is.

> (φεύγετε οὖν τὰς κακὰς παραφυάδας τὰς γεννώσας
> καρπὸν θανατηφόρον, οὗ ἐὰν γεύσηται τις, παρ'
> αὐτὰ ἀποθνήσκει. οὗτοι γὰρ οὐκ εἰσιν φυτεια
> πατρός. εἰ γὰρ ἦσαν, ἐφαίνοντο ἂν κλάδοι τοῦ
> σταυροῦ, καὶ ἦν ἂν ὁ καρπὸς αὐτῶν ἄφθαρτος·
> δι' οὗ ἐν τῷ πάθει αὐτοῦ προσκαλεῖται ὑμᾶς
> ὄντας μέλη αὐτοῦ. οὐ δύναται οὖν κεφαλὴ
> χωρὶς γεννηθῆναι ἄνευ μελῶν, τοῦ θεοῦ ἔνωσιν
> ἐπαγγελλομένου, ὅ ἐστιν αὐτός.)

Ignatius exhorts his readers to flee from
"evil offshoots which bear death-carrying fruit".
Who these "evil offshoots" are is clear from
Trall. 7:1-2; 10. They are the "unbelievers" who
deny the reality of Christ's suffering and
separate themselves from the community which
gathers with its officers for the eucharist. The
"death-carrying fruit" is their division and
separation from the eucharistic communion (αἵρεσις

118

[Trall. 6:1]).[20] This division bestows death upon anyone who participates in it. This is because the schismatics do not belong to God; they are not the "plant of the Father" (φυτεία πατρός). The Father is conceived as a planter, and what He plants is characterized, unlike the schismatics, by unity and life. On the other hand, those who are the "plant of the Father" show themselves to be "branches of the cross" (κλάδοι τοῦ σταυροῦ), and their fruit is incorruptible. The imagery here becomes a little confused, for now the cross is conceived as a plant and the orthodox Christians as its branches, while in the image of the "plant of the Father" the Christians themselves were the plant. Yet, the thought is clear enough. That which the Father plants takes the form of the cross (that is, Christ in passion is the active revelation of God). The cross is the source of life and unity in which the Christians participate and which they themselves manifest (ἐφαίνοντο) because their behavior is characterized by the cross. From the context it is clear that the Christian community's manifesting of the cross consists in correct faith (Trall. 10) and in the eucharistic unity around the one bishop.[21]

In Trall. 11:2b there is a change from the plant-fruit metaphor to that of the head-members metaphor, and there is also a change in perspective. No longer does the text refer to the result of divine activity, the Christian community and its life, but to the divine activity itself. In his passion Jesus Christ "summons to himself" those who are his members. Christ in passion is the uniting center of the Church, and therefore the unity of the Church is organically bound to Christ in passion. That is, wherever Christ is in passion, there is the one Church.[22] The statement "a head is not able to exist without members" (οὐ δύναται οὖν κεφαλὴ χωρὶς γεννηθῆναι ἄνευ μελῶν) does no more than express by means of the head-members metaphor this organic relationship between Christ in passion and the creation of the united

119

believing and worshipping community. This organic necessity is grounded in the divine purpose which itself is expressive of the divine unity of God (τοῦ θεοῦ ἕνωσιν ἐπαγγελλομένου, ὅ ἐστιν αὐτός).[23] God, who is one, gives Himself expression, reveals Himself, by creating unity through the work of Jesus Christ in passion.

One further dimension, however, needs to be made explicit. The life of the Christian community, grounded in and given form by Christ in passion, is life in the power of the resurrection, as the various images--"branches of the cross", "incorruptible fruit", "head"--show. The present existence of the Church is resurrection existence in which the cross has received eschatological meaning, that is, an existence in which the cross brings about the final purposes of God, namely, life and unity. That Christ in his passion "calls us to himself" is the Ignatian equivalent of the Johannine thought that the dying grain bears much fruit (John 12:24) or that in being "lifted up from the earth" Jesus draws all men to himself (John 12:32; 11:51-52).

The second passage is Smyrn. 1:2.

Smyrn. 1:2: Under Pontius Pilate and Herod the tetrarch he was truly nailed in the flesh for us--from which fruit, that is, from his most divinely blessed suffering are we--in order that for the ages he might raise an ensign through his resurrection to his saints and believers, whether among the Jews or among the Gentiles, in the one body of his Church.

(ἀληθῶς ἐπὶ Ποντίου Πιλάτου καὶ Ἡρώδου τετράρχου καθηλωμένον ὑπὲρ ἡμῶν ἐν σαρκί, ἀφ' οὗ καρποῦ ἡμεῖς ἀπὸ τοῦ θεομακαρίστου αὐτοῦ πάθους, ἵνα ἄρῃ σύσσημον εἰς τοὺς αἰῶνας διὰ τῆς ἀναστάσεως εἰς τοὺς ἁγίους καὶ πιστοὺς αὐτοῦ, εἴτε ἐν Ἰουδαίοις εἴτε ἐν ἔθνεσιν, ἐν ἑνὶ σώματι τῆς ἐκκλησίας αὐτοῦ.)

The soteriological and eschatological significance of the cross is here clearly delineated.
Christ was nailed in the flesh "for us". The
participle "nailed" (καθηλωμένον) receives its
exposition in the following ἵνα clause, the clause
ἀφ᾽ οὗ καρποῦ . . . πάθους being parenthetical.
Yet, this parenthesis expounds the "for us". As
in Trall. 11:2, Christian existence is said to be
grounded solely in the passion of Christ. However,
as the ἵνα clause shows, this existence stands
under the event of the resurrection and takes
place within the one body of Christ's Church.
The words "that he might raise an ensign (ἄρῃ
σύσσημον) are a reference to the prophecies of
Isaiah that God will raise an ensign for His
scattered people to which they shall gather (Isa
5:26; 11:10,12; 49:22; 62:10). This would be the
great eschatological act of God which would
reverse the diaspora and unite His people in His
kingdom. For Ignatius this act of God occurred
in the resurrection of Christ through which the
cross was raised as an ensign.[24] Around this
ensign Christ's saints and believers gather into
the unity of his Church.

The passage climaxes in the phrase "in the
one body of his Church" (ἐν ἑνὶ σώματι τῆς
ἐκκλησίας αὐτοῦ). According to Bartsch, the
phrase "his saints and believers" (τοὺς ἁγίους καὶ
πιστοὺς αὐτοῦ) is developed by the phrase "whether
among the Jews or the Gentiles" and then is
summarized in the concept of the body.[25] However,
the body of the Church is more inclusive than the
mere collective of "the saints and believers".
The saints and believers gather around the cross
and thereby enter into the unity of God. As
Christ is not conceived without the Church,
neither is the Church conceived without Christ
(cf. Smyrn. 8:2). The life of the one Church is
the life which the cross gives through the
resurrection. Therefore, Ignatius can praise
the congregation at Smyrna for its life of faith
and love. The Christians there are complete in
steadfast faith "as though nailed to the cross of

the Lord Jesus Christ". They are established in love "by the blood of Christ" (Smyrn. 1:1).

Passion and unity, therefore, exist in closest relation. The God who is one revealed Himself in the passion of Christ. Through the resurrection the Church lives out of the passion as the one Church. That the unity of the Church is grounded in Christ's passion is an oft recurring theme in Ignatius.[26] Besides Trall. 11:2; Smyrn. 1:2, we may mention Eph. inscr. (ἡνωμένην καὶ ἐκλελεγμένην ἐν πάθει ἀληθινῷ); Trall. inscr. (εἰρηνευούσῃ ἐν σαρκὶ καὶ πνεύματι τῷ πάθει Ἰησοῦ χριστοῦ); Phld. inscr. (ἠλεημένῃ καὶ ἡδρασμένῃ ἐν ὁμονοίᾳ θεοῦ καὶ ἀγαλλιωμένῃ ἐν τῷ πάθει τοῦ κυρίου ἡμῶν ἀδιακρίτως); Phld. 4:1 (ἓν ποτήριον εἰς ἕνωσιν τοῦ αἵματος αὐτοῦ).[27]

Until now we have not made explicit mention of the Holy Spirit. This corresponds to the actual state of affairs in the letters of Ignatius. Only infrequently does he speak explicitly of the Holy Spirit.[28] This is not because he has no conception of the Spirit as a divine person (see the triadic formulation in Mag. 13:1-2), but rather because Ignatius, like early Christianity generally, conceived of the Spirit primarily in terms of its effectual working in the Church (note the phraseology of the third article of the various creeds). The Spirit is that divine person through whom the work of the Father and the Son takes on concrete shape in the present existence of the Church.[29] Therefore, it is through the Holy Spirit that the passion of Christ becomes the form of the Church's life.

Through the metaphor of building a temple, Ignatius gives pictorial expression to the life of the Christian community as a life in the passion of Christ by the power of the Spirit.

Eph. 9:1: Being stones of the Temple of the Father, having been prepared for the building of God the Father, (you) are carried into the heights by the machine of Jesus Christ, which

122

is the cross, being hoisted by a rope,
namely, the Holy Spirit.

(ὡς ὄντες λίθοι ναοῦ πατρός, ἡτοιμασμένοι
εἰς οἰκοδομὴν θεοῦ πατρός, ἀναφερόμενοι εἰς
τὰ ὕψη διὰ τῆς μηχανῆς Ἰησοῦ χριστοῦ, ὅς
ἐστιν σταυρός, σχοινίῳ χρώμενοι τῷ πνεύματι
τῷ ἁγίῳ.)

This figure, to be sure, expresses "the
powerful action of the Deity in redemption",[30] but
it expresses more than that. It is a picture of
the Church as the place of God's redemptive
activity which issues into unity with Him.[31]
Unity with God manifests itself in the unity of
the Church. In Eph. 9:1 the central position of
the cross again appears, but here there is also
explicit mention of the Holy Spirit. The Spirit
is pictured as a rope which, bound to the
"machine of Jesus Christ", the cross, draws the
Christians into the heights. The activity of the
Spirit is intimately connected with the cross.
The Spirit's activity is, so to speak, cross
activity which ends in the unity of the Temple of
the Father, that is, the Church. Therefore,
whenever Christians act in the power of the Spirit,
they act after the manner of the cross, and in so
acting, they foster unity. Therefore, Ignatius
calls the Ephesian Christians "Godbearers, Temple-
bearers, Christbearers, bearers of holy things"
(θεοφόροι καὶ ναοφόροι, χριστοφόροι, ἁγιοφόροι
[Eph. 9:2]), and as such he exhorts them under
the general rubric, "let us hasten to be imitators
of the Lord" (μιμηταὶ τοῦ κυρίου σπουδάζωμεν εἶναι
[Eph. 10:3]).[32] Such imitation consists in "being
mistreated", "being robbed", "being rejected", in
humility, prayers, firmness in faith, gentleness
(Eph. 10:2-3). The same relation between cross
and unity here again comes to view. The Church's
life in unity is expressed in a life of passion,
and the life of passion of the Church fosters
unity. Thus, Ignatius writes that the Ephesians
are to pray for other men and to allow them "to
learn from their works" (ἐκ τῶν ἔργων ὑμῖν
μαθητευθῆναι [Eph. 10:1]). Such language can

only mean that the Christians' life of passion
serves to bring others into the unity of the
Church. But is must be remembered that the
Church's unity is participation in the unity of
God,[33] and it is this precisely because the
passion of the Church is the eschatological
presence of the passion of Christ. Hence, just
as Christ's work destroyed the "ancient kingdom
of the ruler of this age", so now to be "imitators
of the Lord" means that "no plant of the Devil" is
allowed to exist (Eph. 10:3). The life of passion
banishes the Devil, which is to say that it
fosters unity.

The Church in unity is the resurrection
fruit of Christ's passion. Where Christ's passion
is, there is the Church in unity, there is
resurrection life. For Ignatius, nowhere is this
more evident than in the eucharistic fellowship
under the bishop. Here is clearly manifested
God's eschatological activity of gathering His
people around the cross (cf. Smyrn. 1:2). Here
is true life, the life of the resurrected Jesus,
and in that life communion with God. Here is the
passion of Jesus.

Indeed, on several occasions Ignatius uses
the term πάθος to designate the eucharist. In
Smyrn. 5:3, Ignatius writes that he does not even
wish to remember the names of the "unbelievers"
until "they repent unto the passion, which is our
resurrection" (μέχρις οὗ μετανοήσωσιν εἰς τὸ πάθος,
ὅ ἐστιν ἡμῶν ἀνάστασις). Ignatius here speaks of
the docetists who were staying away from the
eucharist because they did not confess that "the
eucharist is the flesh of our Savior Jesus Christ"
(Smyrn. 7:1). To reject this flesh, which the
Father raised by His goodness, is to die. Therefore, Ignatius says, it is to their benefit "to
love" (ἀγαπᾶν), that is, to participate in the
eucharist (cf. Rom. 7:3; Smyrn. 8:2),[34] in order
that "they might also rise again" (συνέφερεν δὲ
αὐτοῖς ἀγαπᾶν ἵνα καὶ ἀναστῶσιν [Smyrn. 7:1]).
At Phld. 3:3 Ignatius writes: "If anyone follows
a schismatic, he will not inherit the kingdom of

God. If anyone walks with another mind, he is not in agreement with the passion" (εἴ τις σχίζοντι ἀκολουθεῖ, βασιλείαν θεοῦ οὐ κληρονομεῖ· εἴ τις ἐν ἀλλοτρίᾳ γνώμῃ περιπατεῖ, οὗτος τῷ πάθει οὐ συγκατατίθεται). This passage and its context confirm the close relation between passion and unity and refer this relation to the eucharistic fellowship (σπουδάσατε οὖν μιᾷ εὐχαριστίᾳ χρῆσθαι [Phld. 4:1]). Apparently, in setting up their own eucharistic feasts, the heretics had split the unity of the Church. τῷ πάθει οὐ συγκατατίθεται expresses the consequence of the heretics' behavior: to separate oneself from the one eucharist is to separate oneself from the passion and its gifts, for the passion is present in the one eucharistic fellowship.

Likewise, πάθος in Trall. 11:2 and Mag. 5:2 probably refers to the eucharist. According to Trall. 11:2, in his passion Christ calls his people to himself (ἐν τῷ πάθει αὐτοῦ προσκαλεῖται ὑμᾶς).[35] Our assertion that πάθος refers to the eucharist is supported by the present tense, "Christ calls", which clearly has to do with a present reality in the Church, and by the fact that the Christians as the "branches of the cross" are contrasted with the schismatics who are refraining from the properly constituted eucharist under the bishop (Trall. 6:1-7:2).

In Mag. 5:2, Ignatius writes that men, like two types of coinage, bear a certain impress: "the unfaithful (bear the impress) of this world; the faithful in agape (bear) the impress of God the Father through Jesus Christ, through whom unless we willingly die into his passion, his life is not in us" (οἱ ἄπιστοι τοῦ κόσμου τούτου, οἱ δε πιστοι ἐν ἀγάπῃ χαρακτῆρα θεοῦ πατρὸς διὰ Ἰησοῦ χριστοῦ, δι' οὗ ἐὰν μὴ αὐθαιρέτως ἔχομεν τὸ ἀποθανεῖν εἰς τὸ αὐτοῦ πάθος, τὸ ζῆν αὐτοῦ οὐκ ἔστιν ἐν ἡμῖν). This passage is often interpreted as though it referred to the ethical activity of the Christian community, either to the daily dying of the 'old man' through the exercise of love[36] or to the martyrdom of Ignatius.[37]

However, the context (Mag. 4; 6:1) is clearly cultic, and, therefore, Mag. 5:2 probably refers to the eucharist.[38] Supporting this understanding of the text are the words, "the faithful in agape (have) the character of God the Father through Jesus Christ". If ἀγάπη is understood to mean the eucharist, as it must in Rom. 7:3 and Smyrn. 8:2 (cf. Smyrn. 7:1), then this phrase is an exact parallel to the last words of Trall. 11:2 (τοῦ θεοῦ ἔνωσιν ἐπαγγελλομένου, ὅ ἐστιν αὐτός). In Trall. 11:2, God is said to express His unity by uniting the Christians through Christ's passion. Here the Christians in the unity of the ἀγάπη (i.e. eucharistic fellowship) are said to bear the χαρακτῆρα of "God the Father through Jesus Christ". This χαρακτήρ is, of course, the unity itself. The Christians bear the "character" of God whenever they come together in eucharistic fellowship, which is here called "a dying into his (Christ's) death". πάθος, therefore, refers to the eucharist. The plurals, ἔχομεν and ἡμῖν, would tend to support this view.

Finally, it is likely that also in Eph. inscr. Trall. inscr. and Phld. inscr. πάθος refers to the eucharist.[39]

Ignatius' view of the eucharist is, therefore, thoroughly eschatological. The eucharist, for Ignatius, is the principal form the passion of Christ takes in the life of the Church. Through the resurrection the passion of Christ remains ever-present event, drawing the faithful into the one fellowship of the eucharistic unity. The Church in eucharistic fellowship, therefore, has all the characteristics of the resurrection life (cf. Smyrn. 5:3; 7:1). The Church is in unity, for through Christ's passion it lives in union with God (Eph. 4:2; 5:1; Mag. 5:2; 6:1; Trall. 11:2; Phld. 3:2). This union is essentially of the Spirit, for it is grounded in the union between Christ and the Father, which is Spiritual (Smyrn. 3:3).[40] When the Church is gathered into the eucharistic fellowship, the powers of evil are destroyed and the Church lives in peace (Eph. 13:2;

126

Trall. inscr.; Phld. 6:2) and joy (Phld. inscr.).
In the eucharist the community partakes of
ἀθανασία (Eph. 20:2; Trall. 2:1; Smyrn. 3:2),
ἀφθαρσία (Mag. 6:2; Trall. 11:2) and ζωή (Eph.
20:2; Mag. 5:2; cf. Eph. 18:1), for it is the
resurrected flesh of Christ of which the Church
partakes (Smyrn. 3:1-2; 7:1).

It is against the background of this relation
between passion and unity, made effective in the
Church through the Spirit and manifested most
clearly in the eucharist, that Ignatius understood
his martyrdom. For this reason, the statements of
Ignatius concerning his own martyrdom possess
the same dynamic as we have delineated concerning
the Church in the unity of its eucharistic
fellowship: martyrdom as a form of Christ's
passion reveals the union between Christ and the
Father; as the passion of Christ destroyed Satan,
the prince of separation, and thereby established
unity, so martyrdom as an eschatological manifestation of Christ's passion works to create and
foster unity; since through the resurrection
Christ in passion has become Lord of the Church,
martyrdom is endorsed and furthered by the Risen
Christ and the Church; and finally, martyrdom is
through the power of the Spirit.

As the passion of Christ revealed the one
God, so now the Church's life of passion reveals
the unity achieved by Christ's passion and
resurrection. This unity is essentially that
between Christ and the Father, but in Christ the
Church as well lives in this unity. Christ has
gone to the Father and in this exalted position
works through his Church.[41] This is the meaning
of Rom. 3:3: "Nothing visible is good. For our
God Jesus Christ, being with the Father, is all
the more visible. Not the work of persuasion,
but Christianity is great, whenever it is hated by
the world" (οὐδὲν φαινόμενον καλόν. ὁ γὰρ θεὸς
ἡμῶν Ἰησοῦς χριστὸς ἐν πατρὶ ὢν μᾶλλον φαίνεται.
οὐ πεισμονῆς τὸ ἔργον, ἀλλὰ μεγέθους ἐστὶν ὁ
χριστιανισμος, ὅταν μισῆται ὑπὸ κόσμου).

οὐδὲν φαινόμενον καλόν does not reflect a dichotomy between the material and the immaterial, nor does it deprecate things physical.[42] Rather, as the following sentence shows, it is a Christological statement. The union of Christ with the Father, invisible as it is, is paradoxically all the more visible, for as the one with the Father, Christ is active through what Ignatius calls "Christianity" (χριστιανισμός), whose greatness is shown whenever it is hated by the world. As an activity of χριστιανισμός, therefore, the martyrdom of Ignatius reveals "Jesus Christ who is with the Father" ('Ιησοῦς χριστὸς ἐν πατρὶ ὤν).[43] From this perspective we may also understand Rom. 4:2: "then I shall truly be a disciple of Jesus Christ, when the world will not see my body" (τότε ἔσομαι μαθητὴς ἀληθῶς 'Ιησοῦ χριστοῦ ὅτε οὐδὲ τὸ σῶμα μου ὁ κόσμος ὄψεται). Through his martyrdom Ignatius will cease to be visible to the world. Like Christ, he will be united with the Father and therefore truly a disciple.[44] Indeed, as a martyr Ignatius will become a "word of God" (λόγος θεοῦ [Rom. 2:1]), that is, he will be a revelation of God as was Christ, who as λόγος revealed God in all that he did (Mag. 8:2).

Two related passages, Smyrn. 4:2 and Trall. 10, further develop the theme that martyrdom is a form of the Lordship of Christ in passion.

Smyrn. 4:2: For if these things were done by our Lord only in appearance, I am bound also in appearance. Why have I given myself completely to death, to fire, to the sword, to the beasts? But, close to the sword is close to God. Close to the beasts is close to God. Only (may this happen) in the Name of Jesus Christ! To suffer with him I endure all things, since he who is become the perfect man empowers me.

(εἰ γὰρ τὸ δοκεῖν ταῦτα ἐπράχθη ὑπὸ τοῦ κυρίου ἡμῶν, κἀγὼ τὸ δοκεῖν δέδεμαι. τί δὲ καὶ ἑαυτὸν ἔκδοτον δέδωκα τῷ θανάτῳ, πρὸς πῦρ, πρὸς μάχαιραν, πρὸς θηρία; ἀλλ' ἐγγὺς

128

μαχαίρας, ἐγγὺς θεοῦ, μεταξὺ θηρίων μεταξὺ
θεοῦ· μόνον ἐν τῷ ὀνόματι Ἰησοῦ χριστοῦ.
εἰς τὸ συμπαθεῖν αὐτῷ πάντα ὑπομένω, αὐτοῦ
με ἐνδυναμοῦντος τοῦ τελείου ἀνθρώπου
γενομένου).

After a short parenthesis (Smyrn. 4:1),
Ignatius resumes from Smyrn. 3:3. Characteristic
of the entire context (Smyrn. 1-7) is the anti-
docetic assertion that salvation, resurrection
life, is sarkic. Indeed, one could label the
entire section as sarko-centric: Jesus was nailed
for us ἐν σαρκί (Smyrn. 1:2); even after the
resurrection Jesus was ἐν σαρκί (Smyrn. 3:1);
after the resurrection Jesus ate and drank ὡς
σαρκικός (Smyrn. 3:3); the resurrected Jesus is
σαρκοφόρος (Smyrn. 5:2); the eucharist is the
σάρξ of the Savior, which flesh suffered for us
and which the Father raised (Smyrn. 7:1). Similarly, Jesus was truly (ἀληθῶς) from David's line,
truly born, truly crucified and truly raised
(Smyrn. 1-2). The salvific events were done in
flesh and are done in flesh. This is Ignatius'
great concern about his martyrdom. If the
salvific events were accomplished by Christ in
appearance only (τὸ δοκεῖν), then his own
suffering, which is in flesh, would be a sham,
that is, his own suffering and death would not be
the present salvific working of Christ. However,
if Christ did suffer in the flesh and did rise in
the flesh--and this is Ignatius' confession--,
then the martyrdom of Ignatius is an activity of
the Risen Lord, who, while united Spiritually
with the Father (Smyrn. 3:3),[45] continues to act
as the σαρκοφόρος (Smyrn. 5:2) in a sarkic manner.
No more is being asserted when Ignatius says that
"he who is become the perfect man empowers me"
(αὐτοῦ με ἐνδυναμοῦντος τοῦ τελείου ἀνθρώπου
γενομένου). Jesus is the "perfect man" because
he has reached God through death and resurrection,[46] but as the "perfect man", he is σαρκοφόρος
who is with the Father and who through the martyr
continues to act in flesh. Therefore, Ignatius'
goal is likewise to become a "man". That will

129

happen when he arrives at the "pure light" (<u>Rom.</u>
6:2), that is, when he is martyred and reaches
God (ἐκεῖ παραγενόμενος ἄνθρωπος ἔσομαι).[47]

> <u>Trall</u>. 10: But if, as some who are atheists
> --that is, unfaithful--say, he suffered in
> appearance (they themselves exist in appear-
> ance), then why am I bound? Why do I ask to
> fight the beasts? Therefore, I die in vain.
> Indeed, I am bearing false witness concerning
> the Lord.
>
> (εἰ δέ, ὥσπερ τινὲς ἄθεοι ὄντες τουτέστιν
> ἄπιστοι, λέγουσι, τὸ δοκεῖν πεπονθέναι αὐτόν,
> αὐτοὶ ὄντες τὸ δοκεῖν, ἐγὼ τί δέδεμαι τί δὲ
> καὶ εὔχομαι θηριομαχῆσαι; δωρεὰν οὖν
> ἀποθνήσκω. ἄρα οὖν καταψεύδομαι τοῦ κυρίου).

This passage says essentially the same as
does <u>Smyrn</u>. 4:2. As in <u>Smyrn</u>. 4:2, Ignatius
inserts a statement concerning his martyrdom
which is sharply anti-docetic and stands after a
listing of the salvific events, which were all
"truly" done. Again the reality of the resurrection receives special attention (ὃς καὶ ἀληθῶς
ἠγέρθη ἀπὸ νεκρῶν), as does also the life given
by the Resurrected One (<u>Trall</u>. 9:2; cf. <u>Smyrn</u>.
3:1-2). If the docetists are correct, Ignatius
argues, then his martyrdom speaks falsely concerning the κύριος, that is, the resurrected
Christ. Unless it is true that the life of Christ
is grounded in real passion and resurrection, then
the real martyrdom which Ignatius will suffer can
not be an expression of that life. If Jesus
Christ is not κύριος through real death and
resurrection, the κύριος is not at work in his
martyrdom, which is in flesh. It would indeed in
that case be "in vain", of none effect.[48]

That the Holy Spirit is the formative power
bringing about the passion of Christ in the
worship and ethical life of the Church is clear
from <u>Eph</u>. 9-10.[49] That the Holy Spirit is the
formative power bringing about the passion of
Christ in the martyrdom of Ignatius is clear from
<u>Rom</u>. 7:2.

Rom. 7:2: For living, I write to you, desiring to die. My desire is crucified and in me there is no fire of attachment to material things. Rather, living water speaks in me, saying in me, "Come to the Father".

(ζῶν γὰρ γράφω ὑμῖν, ἐρῶν τοῦ ἀποθανεῖν. ὁ ἐμὸς ἔρως ἐσταύρωται, καὶ οὐκ ἔστιν ἐν ἐμοὶ πῦρ φιλόϋλον· ὕδωρ δὲ ζῶν καὶ λαλοῦν ἐν ἐμοί, ἔσωθέν μοι λέγον· Δεῦρο πρὸς τὸν πατέρα).

In the preceding context, Ignatius had exhorted the Romans not to hinder his martyrdom. They are not to be such as talk of Jesus Christ but desire the world (Rom. 7:1). Rather, they are to join forces with him and aid him on his way. This will occur if they, being governed by the same power of life as is Ignatius, will obey his wish for martyrdom.[50] His desire for martyrdom comes from the divine life that is in him. He writes as one who is "living", that is, as one in whom the "living water" is speaking, "Come to the Father". ζῶν and ἐρῶν τοῦ ἀποθανεῖν are synonymous and are contrasted with ὁ ἔρως and πῦρ φιλόϋλον.[51] The contrast is not between "life" and an imprisonment in matter (ὕλη), but between "life" and "desire" (ἔρως=also πῦρ φιλόϋλον). It is a contrast between the "flesh" (σάρξ) as the power of Satan and the "mind of God" (γνώμη θεοῦ) (cf. Rom. 7:1; 8:3).

The "living water" (ὕδωρ ζῶν) extinguishes the "fire of attachment to material things" (πῦρ φιλόϋλον), and the "desire" (ἔρως) is "crucified" (ἐσταύρωται), thereby bringing about "living" (ζῶν) or "desiring to die" (ἐρῶν τοῦ ἀποθανεῖν). ἐσταύρωται is metaphorically used, to be sure, but the choice of image remains significant. Elsewhere Ignatius uses σταυροῦν and, with one exception (Rom. 5:3), σταυρός only of Christ's crucifixion (σταυροῦν: Eph. 16:2; Trall. 9:1; σταυρός: Eph. 9:1; 18:1; Trall. 11:2; Phld. 8:2; Smyrn. 1:1). The use of this metaphor allows Ignatius to bring the cross of Christ into relation with the "living

131

water". The "living water" brings the power of the cross into the life of Ignatius and leads Ignatius to give expression to the cross in his martyrdom.

The allusion to the "living and speaking water" has aroused considerable comment but little agreement as to its meaning. Much of the difficulty has been doubt concerning the background of Ignatius' reference. Lightfoot asserts that John 4:10-11 inspired the entire passage, and he is therefore prepared to accept the long recension's emendation of ἀλλόμενον for καὶ λαλοῦν (cf. John 4:14). He rejects as "more than doubtful" the suggestion that Ignatius may have borrowed the expression ὕδωρ λαλοῦν from the "speaking" fountain at Daphne, the famous suburb of Antioch.[52] According to ancient belief, those who drank from the waters of Daphne were inspired to poetry and prophecy.[53] Such an influence on Ignatius was certainly possible, but Ignatius' statement is of a different nature. The idea of ecstatic utterance is completely absent. It is not Ignatius who speaks, but the water which speaks in him.

A close parallel to Rom. 7:2 (certainly closer than John 4:10-11) is Ode of Solomon 11:6-9.[54] Here there is the association of both "living" and "speaking" water and movement toward the Father. Kraeling suggested that the "living water" of Ode 11:6 may be a draught of water at baptism which confers the Spirit.[55] A sacrament of drinking water did later occur among the Mandaeans. Schlier also thinks of Taufsekten, pointing out that the contrast between ὕδωρ and πῦρ is often encountered in baptist circles.[56] However, it is unlikely that Rom. 7:2 refers to baptism. Ignatius does connect baptism and passion in one rather esoteric passage (Eph. 18:2), but otherwise baptism plays no special role in his letters (cf. Pol. 6:2). The language of Ode 11:6, nevertheless, makes it difficult to believe that a conceptual relationship of some kind does not exist between Ode 11 and Rom. 7:2

Be that as it may, another possible background deserves attention. While Rom. 7:2 itself contains no eucharistic allusions,[57] Rom. 7:3 shows that the eucharist was not far from Ignatius' mind. We have seen that for Ignatius the eucharist was the experienced eschatological act of God whereby He gathered His people into one through the passion of Christ. The call, "Come to the Father", implies that the same ingathering occurs through martyrdom as well. Within Jewish eschatology the great celebration of God's ingathering of His people into the renewed sanctuary at Jerusalem was the Feast of Booths, during which one of the most solemn and popular ceremonies was the libation of water upon the altar. This was symbolic of "that day" when streams of water would flow from the Temple (Ezek 47:1-12; Joel 3:18) or Jerusalem (Zech 14:8) and the nations would gather at Jerusalem (Joel 3:11-12; Zech 14:16; cf. 10:6-12). Early Christian eschatology made use of the symbolism of the Feast of Booths, although it was reinterpreted. So, in John 7:37-39 Jesus interprets the water ceremony in such a way that he himself becomes the Temple, while John tells us that the "rivers of living water" (ποταμοὶ ὕδατος ζῶντος) refer to the Spirit. Similarly, Rev 21:6b; 22:1-2,17b partake of the water symbolism. Here the Temple has been replace by "the Lord God the Almighty and the Lamb" (Rev 21:22; 22:1) and the stream is the "water of life" (ὕδωρ τῆς ζωῆς). Rev 21:24-26 refers to the gathering of the nations (cf. John 12:20ff.; Rev 7:9-17).[58]

The ὕδωρ ζῶν of Rom. 7:2 is certainly the Holy Spirit, as the words for "speak" show (cf. Phld. 7:1-2). It is possible that Ignatius had the imagery of "living water" flowing from the throne of God in mind when he wrote this passage. The Spirit, coming from the source of life, speaks within Ignatius, Δεῦρο πρὸς τὸν πατέρα. This may be Ignatius' application of the invitation that he who is "thirsty" should "come" (ἐρχέσθω) to the source of life and "drink" (John 7:37; Rev 22:17).

The Spirit is the eschatological power of God
which flows from the Father and through the
suffering of martyrdom leads Ignatius to unity
with the Father.

The resurrected Christ, who is with the
Father, or the Spirit from the Father urges
Ignatius on his way. But the one Church also
helps the martyr on his way. This is so because
the Christ who "empowers" Ignatius is also the
Christ who is at work in and through the Church.

> <u>Rom</u>. 2:1: For I do not wish that you please
> <u>men</u>. Rather, please God, as indeed you are.
> For I shall never again have such an oppor-
> tunity to attain to God. Nor will you, if
> you remain silent, be accredited with a
> better work. For if you remain silent about
> me, I shall be a word of God, but if you love
> my flesh, I shall again be a noise.

> (οὐ γὰρ θέλω ὑμᾶς ἀνθρωπαρεσκῆσαι, ἀλλὰ θεῷ
> ἀρέσαι, ὥσπερ καὶ ἀρέσκετε. οὔτε γὰρ ἐγὼ
> ἔξω ποτὲ καιρὸν τοιοῦτον θεοῦ ἐπιτυχεῖν, οὔτε
> ὑμεῖς, ἐὰν σιωπήσητε, κρείττονι ἔργῳ ἔχετε
> ἐπιγραφῆναι. ἐὰν γὰρ σιωπήσητε ἀπ᾽ ἐμοῦ,
> ἐγὼ λόγος θεοῦ· ἐὰν δὲ ἐρασθῆτε τῆς σαρκός
> μου, πάλιν ἔσομαι φωνή).

That Ignatius does not conceive his martyrdom
as an individualistic ethical imitation but as an
expression of community love is apparent in this
passage. Martyrdom is Ignatius' opportunity
(καιρός) to reach God, but the Roman community as
well is an active participant, either working for
the fulfillment of the martyrdom or its hindrance.
The Romans are to keep silent, but that is not
understood passively. It is a "work" (ἔργον) in
which the Romans are engaged and for which they
are credited (ἔργῳ ἐπιγραφῆναι). Their keeping
silent is contrasted to an ἔρως, which no less
than that of Ignatius (<u>Rom</u>. 7:2) directs one's
loyalties away from God. If they keep silent, if
they please God, the martyred Ignatius will be a
λόγος θεοῦ, that is, he shall reveal God who sent
His λόγος to die.[59]

Rom. 6:3-7:1: Allow me to be an imitator of
the passion of my God. If anyone has him
(Christ) in him, let him understand what I
desire; let him suffer with me, knowing
those things which compel me. The leader of
this age wishes to seize me and to corrupt
my disposition toward God. Therefore, let
no one of you who are present assist him.
Rather, be on my side, that is, on God's. Do
not speak Jesus Christ but desire the world.

(ἐπιτρέψατέ μοι μιμητὴν εἶναι τοῦ πάθους τοῦ
θεοῦ μου. εἴ τις αὐτὸν ἐν ἑαυτῷ ἔχει,
νοησάτω ὃ θέλω, καὶ συμπαθείτω μοι, εἰδὼς τὰ
συνέχοντά με. ὁ ἄρχων τοῦ αἰῶνος τούτου
διαρπάσαι με βούλεται καὶ τὴν εἰς θεόν μου
γνώμην διαφθεῖραι. μηδεὶς οὖν τῶν παρόντων
ὑμῶν βοηθείτω αὐτῷ· μᾶλλον ἐμοῦ γίνεσθε,
τουτέστιν τοῦ θεοῦ. μὴ λαλεῖτε Ἰησοῦν
χριστόν, κόσμον δὲ ἐπιθυμεῖτε.)

Within a context of urgent exhortation to the
Romans not to prevent his martyrdom, Ignatius
introduces the idea of motivation. However,
unlike Rom. 7:2, which speaks of the martyr's
motivation alone, here Ignatius speaks generally
of the motivation which impels both martyr and
Christian community. The Roman congregation is
not a mere bystander which is supposed to allow
something to happen. It is an active participant
in the same struggle and quest as is Ignatius.
Both Ignatius and the Romans must choose either to
act out of Christ's passion or to desire the
world (Rom. 3:2; 7:1,2). Both may either "be of
God" or give way to Satan (Rom. 6:2; 7:1).

Both martyr and congregation are impelled by
the God who suffered.[60] For Ignatius that means
to be "an imitator of the passion of my God" in
martyrdom; for the Romans it means "to suffer
with" Ignatius. When Ignatius exhorts the Romans
"to suffer with" him (συμπαθείτω μοι), he means
no more than when he exhorts them to "be of like
mind" with him (συγγνώμην μοι ἔχετε [Rom. 5:3];
σύγγνωτε μοι [Rom. 6:2]). Ignatius "knows"

135

(γινώσκειν) what is beneficial to him (Rom. 5:3),
namely, martyrdom. He "seeks" and "desires" him
who died and rose (Rom. 6:1). For the Romans to
"be of like mind" with Ignatius means for them to
direct their minds and behavior toward the
successful completion of Ignatius' martyrdom, for
them to seek and desire for Ignatius what he seeks
and desires for himself. Thus, Ignatius, writing
"according to the mind of God" (κατὰ γνώμην θεοῦ
[Rom. 8:3]), urges them not to aid "the ruler of
this age" who wishes "to destroy my disposition
toward God" (τὴν εἰς θεόν μου γνώμην διαφθεῖραι
[Rom. 7:1]). For the Romans, to send Ignatius
on his way is to suffer with him. One may say
that by so doing the Romans themselves become
imitators of Christ. Virtually the same thought
occurs in Eph. 1:1-2. There the Ephesians, "being
imitators of God (in that they are) inflamed into
life by the blood of God", are said to have
enthusiastically endorsed Ignatius and sent him on
his way (cf. Eph. 12:2).

It is not just the Roman community which
helps Ignatius. He is aided by every Christian
community which worships in unity. He, like all
Christians, is under the constant attack of Satan
(Rom. 5:3; 7:1), but unlike them he cannot participate in the unity of the Church's eucharistic
fellowship where "the powers of Satan are destroyed
and the ruin which he brings brought to naught by
the concord of faith" (Eph. 13:1). Christians in
the eucharistic fellowship have "peace" (Eph. 13:2)
and the "bread of God" (Eph. 5:2) which Ignatius
still seeks (Rom. 7:3). Therefore, he urges them
to assemble more often for the eucharist (Eph.
13:1), and he repeatedly reminds them to give him
their prayers and their love (Eph. 11:2; 21:1;
Mag. 14; Trall. 12:3; Rom. 8:3; Phld. 5:1; 8:2;
Smyrn. 11:1).[61] The prayers and love of the
assembled Church are efficacious and will help
Ignatius to reach God.[62] In a similar way,
Ignatius urges the churches to pray for the congregation at Antioch (Eph. 21:1; Mag. 14; Trall.
13:1; Rom. 9:1), and when he learns that the

Church there has been returned to peace, he attributes this to the efficacy of their prayers (Smyrn. 11:1,3; Pol. 7:1).[63] Ignatius' fate as a martyr and the division within the Antiochene community appear to be related. It is Ignatius' exhortation that both martyr and divided Church be aided by the united prayers of the churches in eucharist by which the divisive powers of Satan are destroyed and the unifying power of Christ's passion exerted.

Ignatius' martyrdom, therefore, is an expression of life which comes from union with the Father. He is empowered to martyrdom by the Risen Christ, who is with the Father (Rom. 3:3; 6:3; Trall. 10; Smyrn. 4:2); he is called to martyrdom by the Spirit, who comes from the Father (Rom. 7:2); he is furthered on his way to martyrdom by Christians united with God in the eucharist. As one who "lives", he writes to the Romans not to prevent his martyrdom.

However, Ignatius' martyrdom itself effects and fosters unity. This is most clearly seen in Ignatius' own fate. He calls his martyrdom and "attaining to God" (θεοῦ ἐπιτυχεῖν [Eph. 12:2; Mag. 14; Trall. 12:2; 13:3; Rom. 1:2; 2:1; 4:1; 9:2; Smyrn. 11:1; Pol. 7:1]), an "attaining to Jesus Christ" ('Ιησοῦ χριστοῦ ἐπιτυχεῖν [Rom. 5:3]), or simply an "attaining" (ἐπιτυχεῖν [Eph. 1:2; Trall. 12:3; Rom. 8:3; Phld. 5:1]), where θεοῦ or 'Ιησοῦ χριστοῦ is the implied object. In these passages ἐπιτυχεῖν, with God or Christ as its object, refers indeed to the moment of martyrdom, but it does not have the suffering of martyrdom so much in view as that which is reached in martyrdom, namely, unity with God.[64] To suffer martyrdom and to attain to God, to be united with Him, is one and the same thing.

Interesting in this regard is Rom. 7:3.

Rom. 7:3: I do not desire corruptible food nor the pleasures of this life. I wish the bread of God, which is the flesh of Jesus Christ, who is from the seed of David. I

137

desire a drink, his blood, which is incorruptible love.

(οὐχ ἥδομαι τροφῇ φθορᾶς οὐδὲ ἡδοναῖς τοῦ
βίου τούτου. ἄρτον θεοῦ θέλω, ὅ ἐστιν σὰρξ
Ἰησοῦ χριστοῦ, τοῦ ἐκ σπέρματος Δαυίδ, καὶ
πόμα θέλω τὸ αἷμα αὐτοῦ, ὅ ἐστιν ἀγάπη
ἄφθαρτος.)

While possessing a certain grammatical
parallelism, the construction of this passage is
not logically parallel: the exact parallel to
ὅ ἐστιν σάρξ Ἰησοῦ χριστοῦ would be ὅ ἐστιν αἷμα
αὐτοῦ, not the ὅ ἐστιν ἀγάπη ἄφθαρτος of the text.
The fact that mention of the blood is made already
in the clause πόμα θέλω τὸ αἷμα αὐτοῦ raises the
question whether the final relative clause (ὅ
ἐστιν ἀγάπη ἄφθαρτος) refers to the whole preceding
sentence, that is, to both the flesh and the
blood,[65] or only to the blood (τὸ αἷμα αὐτοῦ).[66]
However, the obvious eucharistic terminology in
the context (ἄρτος-σάρξ; πόμα-αἷμα) and the
obvious contrast of ἀγάπη ἄφθαρτος to τροφή φθορᾶς
demand that we--in analogy to Smyrn. 7:1; 8:2;
Mag. 5:2--interpret ἀγάπη ἄφθαρτος to mean "incorruptible love feast" (i.e. the eucharist).[67]

The context of Rom. 7, and indeed the context
of the entire letter of Ignatius to the Romans,
makes clear, however, that Rom. 7:3 speaks not of
the eucharist as such but of Ignatius' martyrdom.[68]
Through the use of eucharistic terminology,
Ignatius gives expression to that which he will
receive in his martyrdom, namely, union with
Christ, and since union with Christ, then union
with the Father.[69] However, Ignatius does not
radically distinguish between his suffering of
martyrdom itself and the goal or benefit he will
attain through his martyrdom. His very martyrdom
itself contains the goal to which it leads, and
this is so because martyrdom is a form in which
the Lordship of Christ, who remains Christ in
passion, receives expression in the life of the
Church. As we argued above,[70] through the
resurrection the passion of Christ has become the

138

instrument of God's eschatological power by which and in which God effects His will in the Church and brings into actuality His final purposes. For this reason, Ignatius throughout his letters directly relates to the passion of Jesus Christ the benefits and power of life (Eph. 1:1; 18:1; Mag. 9:1; Trall. inscr.; 2:1; 11:2; Phld. inscr.; Smyrn. 1:1-2; 5:3; 12:2).

The principal form which the passion of Christ takes in the Church is the eucharist, participation in which effects unity with God, since in the passion of Christ Satan, the prince of division, is destroyed.[71] When, therefore, Ignatius speaks of his martyrdom in eucharistic terms, he is not merely borrowing terminology from one reality in order to express symbolically another, different reality. Rather, he speaks of his martyrdom in the language of the eucharist because both, eucharist and martyrdom, are essentially the same thing: both are participation in the passion of Christ. Martyrdom is eucharistic; one might even say that Ignatius conceived of his martyrdom as a participation in the eucharist.[72] What the Church receives within its eucharistic fellowship, Ignatius will receive in his martyrdom. Both partake of the same reality: the resurrected σάρξ of Christ (Rom. 7:3; Smyrn. 3:1-2; 7:1), the ἄρτος τοῦ θεοῦ (Rom. 7:3; Eph. 5:2), ἀφθαρσία (Rom. 7:3; Trall. 11:2; Eph. 20:2 [ἀθανασία]). As the Church is united with God in the eucharist (Eph. 5:1; Mag. 5:2; 6:1; Trall. 11:2; Phld. 3:2), so Ignatius will be united with God in his martyrdom (Eph. 12:2; Mag. 14; Trall. 12:2; 13:3; Rom. 1:2; 2:1; 4:1; 9:2; Smyrn. 11:1).[72] Moreover, since it is in martyrdom that Ignatius shall partake of the same reality as the Church in the eucharistic fellowship, it is in martyrdom that Ignatius shall rejoin the unity of the Church. This is the proper perspective from which to assess Ignatius' wellknown and much discussed statements of his unworthiness.[74]

139

If we are correct that Ignatius viewed his martyrdom as participation in the eucharist, as a rejoining in the Church's unity with God, we ought not be surprised if we find reason to believe that Ignatius saw a broader significance in his martyrdom than that of his own personal salvation. Ignatius writes in Trall. 12:2: "My chains which I bear for the sake of Christ--in my quest to attain to God--beseech you, 'Remain in your harmony and in your united prayer'."[75] Similarly, he writes in Mag. 1:2:

> Being found worthy of this most honored name, in these chains which I bear I sing the churches, in which I pray that there be unity of the flesh and spirit of Jesus Christ, our eternal life, unity of faith and of love, which nothing surpasses, and above all unity of Jesus and the Father.[76]

As one who "carries about chains", Ignatius' great concern is the unity of the churches under the bishop (Trall. 12:2). It does not appear to be a case of Ignatius' exhorting out of a special authority which he had acquired as martyr. Rather, the fact of Ignatius' suffering itself exhorts the community to unity. Ignatius' chains beseech the Trallians: "Remain in unity!" Like elsewhere, this unity is primarily the unity which exists in the eucharist. In the suffering status of the martyr the eschatological power of Christ's cross is working for the uniting of God's people, which union occurs already in the gathering for the eucharist. This is also why Ignatius is so con-cerned about the temptations presented by those who "puff" him up (Trall. 4:1-2). Only the cross has the power to promote unity, and only in humility will the cross take shape in the martyr. Therefore, Ignatius has need for "humility"; therefore, he fears the "zeal" warring in him.

More significant, however, is the relation-ship between Ignatius' martyrdom and the unity of the Church in Syria. As noted above,[77] in his request for the prayers of the Asian churches,

Ignatius often connects his fate with that of the Syrian congregation. Nowhere is this more clear than in Mag. 14: "I need your prayer, which is united in God, and your love, in order that the Church in Syria may be worthy to be refreshed through your Church."[78] Here a statement concerning Ignatius' need for prayers that he reach martyrdom gives way to a purpose clause that the Church in Syria be refreshed. Prayers for the faithful completion of Ignatius' martyrdom are to be made in view of the troubled situation in Syria.

Exactly what that situation was remains a mystery. However, the possibility that internal strife was at least part of the problem may not be dismissed. A century ago, Zahn observed that the anti-heretical remarks of Ignatius were too exact for them to have been formed only by the fleeting encounters in Asia Minor, and he wondered if Ignatius already had not encountered the same teaching in Antioch.[79] Harrison held that the use of εἰρηνεύειν in Phld. 10:1; Smyrn. 11:2; and Pol. 7:1 suggested the achievement of internal harmony and presupposed that there had been internal dissension.[80] More recently, Corwin has postulated that there were two opposing factions in Antioch, with Ignatius representing a third, centrist party.[81] Whatever the situation might have been, it is clear that the congregation in Antioch was in a state of disunity and very likely one which was affecting the unity of its eucharist.[82] This appears to have governed Ignatius' attitude toward his martyrdom.

In a recent article, Swartley has examined Ignatius' terminology dealing with ethics (μιμητής, μαθητης, ἄξιος, etc.), Christology (πάθος, ἀληθής, etc.), unity (ἔνωσις, ὁμόνοια, etc.) and obedience (ὑποτάσσω, γνώμη, etc.).[83] Swartley observes that when Ignatius learned that the Church in Syria had attained unity, "then his own concern about being worthy, being a true disciple, attaining God, etc. appears to be relieved and virtually non-existent!"[84] The relationship between Ignatius'

141

desire for martyrdom and the unity of the Church in Syria, not imitation, is then an important consideration in understanding Ignatius: "Only when the church over which he is bishop is united (and less decisively, the whole church), and only when the church in Syria unitedly celebrates the Eucharist, will his death be a true martyrdom, certifying his attaining God, his true discipleship, and his actual participation in the sufferings of God (the cross) which the Eucharist when unitedly shared celebrates."[85] In this conclusion, Swartley is in substantial agreement with Snyder, who proposed that Ignatius understood his calling to be that of a bishop-unto-martyrdom. Since the Church as Christ's body is called to suffering, and the Church focuses in the bishop's office, "if the church is not united, then his death will have no meaning because the bishop of Syria would not be 'the church'".[86]

Swartley and Snyder correctly perceive the problematic which lies behind Ignatius' thinking about his martyrdom, the relationship between passion and unity. However, while they would make the success and significance of Ignatius' martyrdom dependent upon events in Syria, our study leads us in the opposite direction. It is passion, and especially that of the eucharist, which creates and fosters unity. In that Ignatius suffers martyrdom and thereby partakes in the eucharist, he enters the battle against the powers of division and asserts the power of God's peace and concord on behalf of the divided Church in Syria. Ignatius' martyrdom effects not only his own unity with God but works for the union of the Syrian Church with God.[87] In this way as well, his martyrdom is an instrument of God's eschatological ingathering and is therefore understood to be of the Spirit.

From this perspective Ignatius' desire to attain martyrdom becomes understandable. It is not evidence that he has reduced soteriology to the quest for personal immortality. Rather, he desires martyrdom and is anxious that he not be

hindered from martyrdom because his martyrdom
stands, as it were, under the eschatological
necessity of uniting God's people, specifically
those in Syria, into one with Him. For this
reason, Ignatius' feels relief upon learning of
the return of peace in Syria; he is relieved of
the burden he bears for the Syrian community. He
may now more cheerfully enter into his death, for
therein he will rejoin his own Christian community
in the peace and concord of unity with God.

Finally, we must briefly discuss the question
of whether Ignatius believed that he possessed
special pneumatic gifts because he was condemned
to martyrdom. Michel and Schlier answer in the
affirmative.[88] It is clear that Ignatius
possessed pneumatic gifts: he receives revelations (Eph. 20:2); he foresees the plots of the
Devil (Trall. 8:1); he knows of heavenly things
and angelic orders (Trall. 5:1-2); he speaks
words of the Spirit (Phld. 7:1-2). Obviously,
these gifts are special, that is, they are not the
common possession of all Christians. However,
nowhere in his letters does Ignatius even imply
that these special Spiritual gifts were given to
him because of his position as one condemned to
martyrdom. They appear to be expressions of a
continual Spirit possession, perhaps to be associated with Ignatius' office as bishop (see Pol.
2:2).[89]

Yet, on two occasions Ignatius mentions his
chains alongside the exercise of his pneumatic
charismata (Trall. 5:1-2; Phld. 7:1-2).[90] These
two passages have led Bommes to suggest that while
one cannot say that the chains of Ignatius were
the cause of his Spiritual gifts, yet his situation as martyr exercised an influence on the
actualization of those gifts.[91] However, it is
doubtful that there is, even in this attenuated
sense, an internal, organic connection between
Ignatius' position as martyr and his possession of
pneumatic gifts. When Ignatius writes οὐ καθότι
δέδεμαι καὶ δύναμαι νοεῖν τὰ ἐπουράνια (Trall. 5:2),
his being in chains and his knowing of heavenly

things are not placed in any kind of dependent relationship but are listed as independent, coordinate situations.[92]   Indeed, the special pneumatic powers of Ignatius may actually prove to be a hindrance to the humble completion of his martyrdom (Trall. 4).

Phld. 7:1-2 reflects an actual occurrence in which Ignatius exhorted the congregation at Philadelphia, which was threatened by schism, to maintain its unity around its bishop. Ignatius asserts that he did not know beforehand of the schismatic intentions of some but that the Spirit, who is not deceived, spoke through him. Here also there is no compelling reason to assume that this prophetic activity in Philadelphia happened only because Ignatius was in chains and for that reason given special Spiritual insight. The content of Ignatius' exhortation--to do nothing without the bishop, to love unity, to flee divisions, to be imitators of Christ--is common to all of Ignatius' letters to the churches (Mag. 4; Trall. 7:2; Smyrn. 8:2; Smyrn. 7:2; Eph. 10:3). One has the impression that despite the special relevance of these exhortations to the community at Philadelphia, they were not conceived specifically with the church at Philadelphia in view.[93] These exhortations probably reflect the common exhortations Ignatius was wont to make even prior to his condemnation.

SUMMARY

Attempts to interpret Ignatius of Antioch's understanding of his martyrdom in terms of ethical imitation, vicarious sacrifice, or his pagan religious environment are inadequate. They are unable to incorporate Ignatius' martyrology into the whole of Ignatius' theological outlook.

Central to the thinking of Ignatius is the relationship between unity and passion. God revealed Himself as one through the sending of Christ whose passion is the instrument by which

God through the power of the Holy Spirit accomplishes His final eschatological act of uniting His people to Himself. By participating in Christ's passion, which takes present form principally in the celebration of the eucharist, the Christian participates in God's ingathering of His people into one with Him.

The eucharist, understood as God's ingathering of His people, provided the pattern by which Ignatius interpreted his martyrdom. In the passion of his martyrdom Ignatius will participate in the same eschatological movement as does the Church in its celebration of the eucharist. As the Church is united to God through the power of the Spirit in the eucharist, so will Ignatius be united to God through the power of the Spirit in his martyrdom. In his martyrdom, Ignatius will partake of the same "incorruptible agape" as does the Church in the eucharist.

In the eucharist, the resurrected Christ continues the work of his passion. He continues to act sarkically, for in the eucharist that flesh is given which suffered for our sins and which the Father raised from the dead. In the same way the martyrdom of Ignatius is the activity of the resurrected Christ who works in passion, who works sarkically. Therefore, Ignatius writes urgently against the docetists, who deny the reality of the flesh of Christ. If Christ was not born in the flesh, did not die in the flesh, and did not rise in the flesh, then Ignatius' martyrdom, which will be in the flesh, would not be of Christ. It would be vain, meaningless. Indeed, it would bear false witness against the Lord.

In his martyrdom, Ignatius will rejoin the unity of the eucharistic fellowship of the Church. Since his martyrdom is a participation in the passion of Christ, it is a participation in that eschatological movement of God by which the divisions caused by Satan are overcome and union with God is achieved.

145

NOTES TO CHAPTER THREE

1 H. von Campenhausen, Die Idee des Martyriums
in der alten Kirche, 2nd ed. (Göttingen:
Vandenhoeck & Ruprecht, 1964) 74-78; Theodor
Preiss, "La mystique de l'imitaion du Christ et
de l'unité chez Ignace d'Antioche," RHPR 18 (1938)
199-210; Heinrich Rathke, Ignatius von Antiochien
und die Paulusbriefe (TU 99; Berlin: Akademie,
1967).

2 Von Campenhausen, Die Idee des Martyriums, 78.
Cf. Preiss, "La mystique de l'imitation," 210:
"c'est qu'il choisit librement et souffre une
passion semblable et en quelque sort parallèle à
celle de son modèle"; Rathke, Ignatius von
Antiochien, 72-73: "Christus ist für Ignatius
nicht so sehr der Erlöser von der Sünde, sondern
der Vorbild für den Weg zu Gott. Das Martyrium
des Ignatius geschieht in Analogie zum Leiden
Christi. Wie Christi Weg durch den Tod zur
Auferstehung, zum Leben, zu Gott führt, so auch
der Weg des Ignatius." See also Norbert Brox,
Zeuge und Märtyrer: Untersuchungen zur frühchristlichen Zeugnis-Terminologie (SANT 5:
München: Kösel, 1961) 219; G. Stählin, s.v.
"περίψημα," TWNT 6 (1959) 92.

3 See the good criticism of the views of von
Campenhausen, Preiss, and Rathke by Karin Bommes
(Weizen Gottes: Untersuchungen zur Theologie des
Martyriums bei Ignatius von Antiochien
[Theophaneia 27; Köln/Bonn: Peter Hanstein, 1976]
95-107). Cf. also W. M. Swartley, "The Imitatio
Christi in the Ignatian Letters," VigChr 27 (1973)
81-103.

4 H. Schlier, Religionsgeschichtliche Untersuchungen zu den Ignatiusbriefen (BZNW 8;
Giessen: Alfred Töpelmann, 1929) 125-74.

5 G. P. Wetter, Altchristliche Liturgien: Das
christliche Mysterium. Studie zur Geschichte des

Abendmahles (FRLANT 30; Göttingen: Vandenhoeck &
Ruprecht, 1921) 116-23; H.-W. Bartsch,
Gnostisches Gut und Gemeindetradition bei Ignatius
von Antiochien (BFCT 44; Gütersloh: C. Bertelsmann,
1940) 80-98.

6   Bartsch defines the fundamental conception of
the mysteries as "die Wiederholung eines
mythologischen Geschehens mit dem Ziel der
Vergottung des Gläubigen" (Gnostisches Gut, 79).

7   So von Campenhausen, Die Idee des Martyriums,
71-73; O. Michel, Prophet und Märtyrer (BFCT 37/2;
Gütersloh: C. Bertelsmann, 1932) 55; W. Bauer,
Die Briefe des Ignatius von Antiochia, in Die
Apostolischen Väter (HNT, Ergänzungsband;
Tübingen: J. C. B. Mohr, 1923) 207-8, 219;
Stählin, s.v. "περίψημα," TWNT 6 (1959) 91-92;
O. Perler, "Das vierte Makkabaeerbuch, Ignatius
von Antiochien und die Aeltesten Martyrerberichte,"
RArchCr 25 (1949) 51-52, 63.

8   Perler, "Ignatius von Antiochien," 48-65.

9   Stählin, s.v. "περίψημα," TWNT 6 (1959) 92:
"Sein Tod ist eine Opferleistung für Gott und ein
heilsbedeutendes Sterben für die Gemeinden, das,
wenn die Gedanken systematisch durchdacht werden,
als in Konkurrenz mit Christi Leiden stehend
erkannt werden müsste."

10   Bommes, Weizen Gottes, 86-107.

11   Note, on the other hand, the terminology of
atonement and sacrifice in the passages of 4
Maccabees mentioned by Perler (n. 8): 4 Macc
6:29: καθάρσιον αὐτῶν ποιῆσον τὸ ἐμὸν αἷμα καὶ
ἀντίψυχον αὐτῶν λαβὲ τὴν ἐμὴν ψυχήν; 4 Macc
17:21-22: καὶ τὸν τύραννον τιμωρηθῆναι καὶ τὴν
πατρίδα καθαρισθῆναι, ὥσπερ ἀντίψυχον γεγονοτας
τῆς τοῦ ἔθνους ἀμαρτίας καὶ διὰ αἵματος τῶν
εὐσεβῶν ἐκείνων καὶ τοῦ ἱλαστηρίου τοῦ θανατου
αὐτῶν ἡ θεία πρόνοια τὸν Ἰσραηλ προκακωθεντα
διέσωσεν (cf. 4 Macc 1:11; 7:8-9; 9:24; 12:17;

16:16; 18:4). In the letters of Ignatius, the verb ἁμαρτάνειν occurs only once, as a parallel to μισεῖν (Eph. 14:2). The noun ἁμαρτία occurs in a traditional formula (Smyrn. 7:1), but it plays no role in Ignatius' argument (cf. Rom. 6:1; Smyrn. 1:2).

12 So also Bartsch, Gnostisches Gut, 82: "Für Ignatius ist Gott nicht in erster Linie der Gerechte, dem gegenüber der Mensch Sünder ist, sondern Gott ist der Eine, von dem der Mensch getrennt ist." See also Virginia Corwin, St. Ignatius and Christianity in Antioch (Yale Publications in Religion 1; New Haven: Yale University, 1960) 162, 247; Georg Wustmann, Die Heilsbedeutung Christi bei den apostolischen Vätern (BFCT 9/2-3; Gütersloh: C. Bertelsmann, 1905) 97.

13 Bommes, Weizen Gottes, 222: "sein Martyrium ist in einer umfassenderen Weise ein fürbittendes Opfer um jegliche Hilfe für die Kirche, deren sie auf ihrem Weg zu Gott bedarf. 'Stellvertretung' ist es dabei in dem Sinn, in dem schon jedes wirklich engagierte Fürbittgebet ein Sich-selbst-einsetzen für den anderen ist." J. B. Lightfoot generalizes the meaning even more: "the idea of devotion to and affection for another stands out prominently" (The Apostolic Fathers, Part 2: S. Ignatius. S. Polycarp, 3 vols. [London: Macmillan, 1889], 2/1:88).

14 ΣJer 22:28: μὴ περίψημα φαῦλον καὶ ἀπόβλητον ὁ ἄνθρωπος; 1 Cor 4:13: ὡς περικαθάρματα τοῦ κόσμου ἐγενήθημεν, πάντων περίψημα ἕως ἄρτι.

15 Barnabas wishes to write many things, "not as a teacher, but as befits one who loves" (οὐχ ὡς διδάσκαλος, ἀλλ' ὡς πρέπει ἀγαπῶντι); therefore, he hastens to write, being an "offscouring" (περίψημα ὑμῶν). περίψημα is antithetical to διδάσκαλος. In similar fashion, Barnabas writes in Barn. 6:5 that as an "offscouring of your love" (περίψημα τῆς ἀγάπης ὑμῶν) he writes simply so

that his readers can comprehend his teaching.

16 So also Bommes, Weizen Gottes, 84.

17 See the balanced discussion of Bommes (Weizen
Gottes, 221-27). Our argument is not that
Ignatius saw no benefit in his martyrdom for the
Church, but that he did not see this benefit in
sacrificial terms.

18 Cf. Bommes, Weizen Gottes, 153-59.

19 σαρκοφόρος refers to the sarkic nature of the
resurrected Jesus, who is Lord, not to the incar-
nation as such (against Wustmann, Die Heilsbedeutung Christi, 86; Bauer, Briefe des
Ignatius, 268-69). Since the Lord is "fleshbearer",
his active rule has fleshly character.

20 Bartsch opines that the "death-carrying fruit"
refers to the eucharist of the schismatics
(Gnostisches Gut, 29). The words οὗ ἐὰν γεύσηται
makes such an interpretation possible. However,
it seems more likely that the image of tasting
simply continues the metaphor of fruit and rather
than signifying an actual tasting is the metaphor
for participation in αἵρεσις, the separation from
the properly constituted eucharist.

21 See also Phld. 3:1-2. Here also the
Christians are called φυτεία πατρός and are
contrasted with the schismatics who divide the
Church. Those who are of God and of Jesus Christ
live within the unity of the Church under the
bishop (ὅσοι γὰρ θεοῦ καὶ ᾿Ιησοῦ χριστοῦ, οὗτοι
μετὰ τοῦ ἐπισκόπου εἰσίν). This is "to live
according to Jesus Christ" (κατὰ ᾿Ιησοῦν χριστὸν
ζῆν).

22 For a good discussion of Trall. 11:2, see
Bommes, Weizen Gottes, 75-76.

23 ἐπαγγελλομένος, while often translated
"promising", is better rendered here by

"asserting", "expressing", or the like. Ignatius
uses the word two other times (Eph. 14:2), both
times with the meaning "to proclaim of onesself"
or "to show forth". God gives His unity
expression in that Christ in passion calls to
himself his members.

24 σύσσημος surely refers to the cross (so also
Lightfoot, S. Ignatius, 2/1:292; Corwin, St.
Ignatius, 99,170,178). Lightfoot refers to some
remarks of Jerome on Isa 5:26: Legi in cuiusdam
commentariis, hoc quod dicitur Levabit signum in
nationibus procul et sibilabit ad eum de finibus
terrae de vocatione gentium debere intelligi,
quod elevato signo crucis et depositis oneribus
peccatorum velociter venerint atque crediderint.

25 Bartsch, Gnostisches Gut, 26 n. 1.

26 For a good discussion of the passion of
Christ as the ground of the Church and the very
form of the Church's life, see Bommes, Weizen
Gottes, 69-79.

27 The phrase εἰς ἔνωσιν τοῦ αἵματος αὐτοῦ
(Phld. 4:1) is ambiguous and probably inten-
tionally so. It may mean either the unity of
those celebrating the eucharist brought about by
the blood (so Bauer, Briefe des Ignatius, 257) or
the unity with the blood through the common
partaking of the cup (so Schlier, Religionsgeschichtliche Untersuchungen, 168). Both
meanings are no doubt equally in view: "die
Einheit der Gemeinde gründet in der Einheit des
einzelnen Gläubigen mit dem Herrn in seinem Blut
und umgekehrt: Die wahre Einheit der Glaubenden
mit dem Herrn manifestiert sich in der Einigkeit
der Gemeinde, die sich auch in ihrer einmütigen
Teilhabe am einen Kelch und am einen Altar
verwirklichen muss" (Bommes, Weizen Gottes, 60).

28 For discussion of the pneumatology of
Ignatius, see Karl Hörmann, "Das Geistreden des
Heiligen Ignatius von Antiochia," Mystische

Theologie, Jahrbuch 2 (1956) 39-53; Theodor
Rüsch, _Die_ Entstehung _der_ Lehre _vom_ Heiligen
Geist _bei_ Ignatius _von_ Antiochia, Theophilus _von_
Antiochia _und_ Irenäus _von_ Lyon (Studien zur
Dogmengeschichte und systematischen Theologie 2;
Zürich: Zwingli, 1952) 46-76; J. P. Martín, _El_
Espiritu Santo _en_ los Origenes _del_ Cristianismo:
Estudio _sobre_ I Clemente, Ignacio, II Clemente
_y_ Justino Martir (BibScRel 2; Zürich: Pas, 1971)
67-142.

29   Therefore, Ignatius can say that according to
Christ's will the bishop, presbyters, and
deacons of the Church were established by the
Holy Spirit (οὓς κατὰ τὸ ἴδιον θέλημα ἐστήριξεν
ἐν βεβαιωσύνῃ τῷ ἁγίῳ αὐτοῦ πνεύματι [Phld.
inscr.]).

30   Corwin, St. Ignatius, 142-43.

31   Martín, El Espiritu Santo, 99-100: "se trata
de la realización de la Iglesia por la obra del
Padre, de Cristo y del Espíritu Santo. . . . La
Iglesia es el lugar del Espíritu. Es la
comunidad de los 'pneumáticos', donde los
carnales no tiene cabida." According to Martín,
there may be a skeletal formula underlying this
passage: ἐκκλησία (=ναός, οἰκοδομή) θεοῦ πατρὸς
διὰ ᾽Ιησοῦ χριστοῦ τῷ πνεύματι ἁγίῳ.

32   For a discussion of the ethics of Ignatius,
see P. Meinhold, "Die Ethik des Ignatius von
Antiochien," HJ 77 (1958) 50-62.

33   Martín, El Espiritu Santo, 123: "El
cristiano que vive en la comunidad participa de
la unidad divina."

34   That ἀγαπᾶν refers to the eucharist is held
by Theodor Zahn, Ignatius von Antiochien (Gotha:
1873) 347-48; Schlier, Religionsgeschichtliche
Untersuchungen, 168; Wetter, Altchristliche
Liturgien, 119; Bartsch, Gnostisches Gut, 117;
C. Maurer, Ignatius von Antiochien und das

Johannesevangelium (ATANT 18; Zürich: Zwingli,
1949) 38-39.

35 See our discussion of Trall. 11:2 above,
pp. 118-20.

36 So E. von der Goltz, Ignatius von Antiochien
als Christ und Theologe: eine dogmengeschichtliche
Untersuchung (TU 12/3; Leipzig: J. C. Hinrichs,
1894) 35: "ein sittliches bedingtes Absterben
des alten Menschen"; also Wustmann, Die Heilsbedeutung Christi, 101; Bauer, Briefe des
Ignatius, 222-23; Lightfoot, S. Ignatius, 2/1:117.
Corwin believes Mag. 5:2 is an expression of the
Two Ways (St. Ignatius, 223).

37 So J. Schneider, Die Passionsmystik des
Paulus: ihr Wesen, ihr Hintergrund und ihre
Nachwirkungen (UNT 15; Leipzig: J. C. Hinrichs,
1929) 127; M. Viller, "Martyre et Perfection,"
RAsMys 6 (1925) 8-9; Brox, Zeuge und Märtyrer,
206; D. Aune, The Cultic Setting of Realized
Eschatology in Early Christianity (NovTSup 28;
Leiden: E. J. Brill, 1972) 157-61.

38 So also Wetter, Altchristliche Liturgien,
118; Bartsch, Gnostisches Gut, 59,122-23; F. A.
Schilling, The Mysticism of Ignatius of Antioch
(Philadelphia: 1932) 47. Schlier perceives the
cultic setting but believes Ignatius speaks of
the reading of the gospel rather than the
eucharist (Religionsgeschichtliche Untersuchungen,
166 n. 1). The plural ἔχομεν excludes an
reference to martyrdom.

39 According to Eph. inscr., the Ephesian
community is "united and chosen out in the passion"
(ἡνωμένην καὶ ἐκλελεγμένην ἐν πάθει ἀληθινῷ).
The appearance of εἰρηνεύειν in Trall. inscr.
reminds one of Eph. 13:2: peace is a result of
the eucharist in which every fight is overcome.
According to Phld. inscr., the community is "made
to rejoice" (ἀγαλλιωμένη) by the passion,
probably a reference to the joy at the eucharist.

Also the phrase ἐν τῷ πάθει stands in a certain
relation to ἐν ὁμονοίᾳ θεοῦ, which according to
Mag. 6:1 exists whenever the Church gathers
under its three-fold ministry. Also in Eph. 4:2
Ignatius refers to Christians within the
eucharistic fellowship as being ἐν ὁμονοίᾳ (cf.
1 Clem. 34:7: καὶ ἡμεῖς οὖν ἐν ὁμονοίᾳ ἐπὶ τὸ
αὐτὸ συναχθέντες τῇ συνειδήσει, ὡς ἐξ ἑνὸς
στόματος βοήσωμεν πρὸς αὐτόν. Here the
eucharistic context is obvious).

40 πνευματικῶς (Smyrn. 3:3) does not refer to
the divine nature of Christ (Hörmann, "Das
Geistreden," 45) or to Christ's belonging to the
divine plane after the resurrection (Martín, El
Espiritu Santo, 78). πνευματικῶς predicates
nothing of Christ. Rather, as its adverbial
form shows, it modifies ἡνωμένος, describing the
manner or quality of Christ's union with the
Father. The significance of Smyrn. 3:3 is
twofold: 1) even after the resurrection, Christ
acts among his disciples in a sarkic manner,
2) this activity flows from Christ's union with
the Father, which union is of the Spirit.

41 Cf. Schlier, who correctly refers to the
affinity of Ignatius to John at this point
(Religionsgeschichtliche Untersuchungen, 76-77).
John 14:28: εἰ ἀγαπᾶτέ με, ἐχάρητε ἂν ὅτι
πορεύομαι πρὸς τὸν πατέρα, ὅτι ὁ πατὴρ μείζων μού
ἐστιν.

42 Against von der Goltz, who see in Rom. 3:3
an ascetic tendency which easily leads to a
depreciation of the flesh (Ignatius von Antiochien,
53-54) and Schlier, who identifies φαινόμενον
with ὕλη (Religionsgeschichtliche Untersuchungen,
148).

43 Cf. Eph. 14:2: φανερὸν τὸ δένδρον ἀπὸ τοῦ
καρποῦ αὐτοῦ· οὕτως οἱ ἐπαγγελλόμενοι χριστοῦ
εἶναι δι' ὧν πράσσουσιν ὀφθήσομαι. οὐ γὰρ νῦν
ἐπαγγελίας τὸ ἔργον, ἀλλ' ἐν δυνάμει πίστεως ἐάν
τις εὑρεθῇ εἰς τέλος.

44 On several occasions Ignatius uses the term
μαθητής 'disciple' to designate that position
reached in and through martyrdom (Eph. 1:2; 3:1;
Trall. 5:2; Rom. 4:2; 5:3; Pol. 7:1). As such
it receives the meaning of one who is united
with God (see Brox, Zeuge und Märtyrer, 207-9:
μαθητής is "ein Ersatzwort für den Märtyrertitel";
also the good discussion of μαθητής by Bommes
[Weizen Gottes, 41-47]).

45 See n. 40 above. Smyrn. 3:1-3 is not simply
anti-docetic proof for the reality of the body
of the resurrected Jesus (against Maurer,
Ignatius von Antiochien, 93). Ignatius' interest
lies in the reality of resurrection life within
the Christian community which exists and acts in
time and space, that is, sarkically. Therefore,
Christians are contrasted to the heretics who
exist only in appearance (αὐτοὶ τὸ δοκεῖν ὄντες).

46 Schlier, Religionsgeschichtliche Untersuchungen,
173; Martin, El Espiritu Santo, 118; Aune,
Realized Eschatology, 150. However, against
Schlier, no similarity is to be discerned between
Ignatius' use of "perfect man" and that of the
Naassene Hymn. Cf. Corwin, St. Ignatius, 111-13.

47 There is no thought of Ignatius becoming
identical or equal with Christ. Nor is there any
idea of a freed heavenly Man becoming what he
once was (against Schlier, Religionsgeschichtliche
Untersuchungen, 72-74).

48 Following Bauer (Briefe des Ignatius, 268),
Brox calls Ignatius' martyrdom a "Beweisstück"
for the reality of Jesus' suffering (Zeuge und
Märtyrer, 214). According to this view, Ignatius
reason backwards from his own martyrdom to
Christ's passion. Aune argues in a similar way
(Realized Eschatology, 149): "Ignatius regarded
his own suffering as a demonstration of the
reality of the Passion of Jesus . . . ; the
sufferings of Jesus Christ had to be real because
the sufferings of Ignatius were real." This is

not, however, how Ignatius argues. In <u>Trall</u>. 10; <u>Smyrn</u>. 4:2, Ignatius argues not from the reality of his own suffering to the reality of Jesus' suffering, but from the reality of Christ's suffering to the significance and efficacy of his own.

49   See above, pp. 122-24.

50   See below, pp. 134-36.

51   Origen interpreted Ignatius' ὁ ἐμὸς ἔρως to mean Christ: denique memini aliquem sanctorum dixisse Ignatium nomine de Christo: Meus autem amor crucifixus est, nec reprehendi eum pro hoc dignum judico (<u>Prol</u>. <u>in</u> <u>Cant</u>. 3 [PG 13:70]). Ps.-Dionysius (<u>De div</u>. <u>nom</u>. 4.12 [PG 3:709]) and Theodore the Studite (<u>Serm</u>. <u>Cat</u>. 3 [PG 99:512]) follow Origen in this interpretation. However, ἔρως is clearly synonymous with πῦρ and refers to his attachment to the world (so also Lightfoot, <u>S</u>. <u>Ignatius</u>, 2/1:222-24; Bauer, <u>Briefe des Ignatius</u>, 251-52).

52   Lightfoot, <u>S</u>. <u>Ignatius</u>, 2/1:224-25. The suggestion that the fountain at Daphne was behind <u>Rom</u>. 7:2 was first made by J. Jortin (<u>Remarks</u> <u>on Ecclesiastical History</u> [London: 1751], 1:356). See the discussion by J. R. Harris, who responds positively to Jortin's suggestion (<u>The</u> <u>Odes</u> <u>and Psalms</u> <u>of</u> <u>Solomon</u> [Manchester: 1920], 2:270-71).

53   The fountain at Daphne is mentioned by Sozomen (<u>Hist</u>. <u>eccl</u>. 5.19 [GCS 50:223ff.]).

54   "And speaking waters drew near my lips/ From the fountain of the Lord plenteously/ And I drank and was inebriated/ With the living water that doth not die;/ And my inebriation was not one without knowledge/ But I forsook vanity/ And I turned to the Most High my God/ And I was enriched by His bounty" (trans. by Harris, <u>Odes</u> <u>of</u> <u>Solomon</u>, 2:266). Cf. Harris, <u>Odes</u> <u>of</u> <u>Solomon</u>, 2:265-71; Corwin, <u>St</u>. <u>Ignatius</u>, 74-75.

55 C. H. Kraeling, "The Apocalypse of Paul and
the 'Iranische Erlosungsmysterium'," HTR 24 (1931)
223-24.

56 Schlier, Religionsgeschichtliche Untersuchungen,
146-48. Cf. Aune, who also sees a connection
between baptism and passion in Rom. 7:2 (Realized
Eschatology, 146).

57 Bartsch suggests that ὕδωρ ζῶν may refer to
the second element of the eucharist (Gnostisches
Gut, 110-11). This steps beyond the evidence.
The simple proximity of eucharistic language in
Rom. 7:3 is not enough to assume that Rom. 7:2
contains eucharistic language as well.

58 See J. Comblin, "La Liturgie de la Nouvelle
Jerusalem (Apoc. XXI.1-XXII.5)," ETL 29 (1953)
29-35.

59 It is most likely that Ignatius' idea that
Jesus Christ, the λόγος ἀπὸ σιγῆς, "pleased" God
in all that he did (Mag. 8:2) stands behind the
contrast which Ignatius makes between "pleasing
men" and "pleasing God" in Rom. 2:1.

60 The neuter plural τὰ συνέχοντά με is difficult
to interpret. It must mean essentially the same
as the αὐτος ἐν ἑαυτῷ. Perhaps the eucharistic
elements are meant (cf. Eph. 1:1).

61 Ignatius' concern for the Church in the unity
of the eucharist makes it probable that προσευχή
and ἀγάπη are to be eucharistically understood.
προσευχή would refer to prayer offered within the
eucharistic fellowship and ἀγάπη to the love
operative among the assembled Christians.
Passages such as Mag. 7:1; 14; Trall. 12:2-3;
Phld. 6:2; Smyrn. 7:1 argue in favor of such as
interpretation. Certainly ἀγάπη in Mag. 14; Trall.
12:3; Smyrn. 9:2 (cf. Rom. 9:1) cannot mean a
direct ethical activity, for Ignatius writes when
he no longer has any direct contact with his
readers. Note also the greeting ἀσπάζεται ὑμᾶς

157

ἡ ἀγάπη Σμυρναίων καὶ Ἐφεσίων (Trall. 13:1; also
Rom. 9:3; Phld. 11:2; Smyrn. 12:1).

62 Eph. 11:2: γένοιτό μοι ἀναστῆναι τῇ προσευχῇ
ὑμῶν; Mag. 14: ἵνα θεοῦ ἐπιτύχω; Rom. 8:3: ἵνα
ἐπιτύχω; Trall. 12:3: εἰς τὸ καταξιωθῆναι με τοῦ
κλήρου, οὗ περίκειμαι ἐπιτυχεῖν; Phld. 5:1: ἡ
προσευχὴ ὑμῶν εἰς θεόν με ἀπαρτίσει; Smyrn. 11:1:
ἵνα ἐν τῇ προσευχῇ ὑμῶν θεοῦ ἐπιτύχω. Also Phld.
8:2 (θέλω ἐν τῇ προσευχῇ ὑμῶν δικαιωθῆναι) which
refers to Ignatius' martyrdom (von der Goltz,
Ignatius von Antiochien, 31-32; Bartsch,
Gnostisches Gut, 42). M. Pellegrino, "Le sens
ecclésial du martyre," RevSR 35 (1961) 171: "Pour
Ignace, la prière est le lien de charité qui unit
les chrétiens, elle est la source mystérieuse de
grâce qui supplée aux insuffisances de l'homme.
Cette prière est authentiquement catholique, en
ce qu'elle s'appuie sur la foi inébranlable dans
la communion des saints et sur la solidarité des
disciples du Christ, tenus de s'aider mutuellement
par un échange de dons spirituels."

63 Smyrn. 11:1: ἡ προσευχὴ ὑμῶν ἀπῆλθεν ἐπὶ τὴν
ἐκκλησίαν τὴν ἐν Ἀντιοχείᾳ τῆς Συρίας; Smyrn.
11:3: ὅτι λιμένος ἤδη ἔτυχον ἐν τῇ προσευχῇ ὑμῶν;
Pol. 7:1: ἐπειδὴ ἡ ἐκκλησία ἡ ἐν Ἀντιοχείᾳ τῆς
Συρίας εἰρηνεύει . . . διὰ τὴν προσευχὴν ὑμῶν.
According to Rom. 9:1, the ἀγάπη of the Romans
"watches over" the Church in Syria.

64 R. A. Bower, "The Meaning of ΕΠΙΤΥΓΑΝΩ in the
Epistles of St. Ignatius of Antioch," VigChr 28
(1974) 9: "Ἐπιτυχεῖν, when used with God as its
object, can be described as union: i.e. as the
highest form of identification with or participation in the reality of that to which one is
united." See also Brox, Zeuge und Märtyrer,
209-11; Bommes, Weizen Gottes, 161-64.

65 So Zahn, Ignatius von Antiochien, 348-50;
Schlier, Religionsgeschichtliche Untersuchungen,
149 n. 1; Bauer, Briefe des Ignatius, 252;
Maurer, Ignatius von Antiochien, 91.

66 Lightfoot, S. Ignatius, 2/1:227; Schneider, Passionsmystik, 129; J. Colson, "Agape chez Saint-Ignace d'Antioche," TU 78 (Berlin: Akademie, 1961) 341. See also Bommes, who, while recognizing the possibility of the other interpretation, appears to favor "blood" alone as the antecedent of the final clause (Weizen Gottes, 63-64).

67 Opponents of this view (such as Lightfoot and Bommes [n. 66]) often appeal to Trall. 8:1 which identifies ἀγάπη with αἷμα (ἀνακτίσασθε ἑαυτοὺς ἐν πίστει, ὅ ἐστιν σὰρξ τοῦ κυρίου, καὶ ἐν ἀγάπῃ, ὅ ἐστιν αἷμα Ἰησοῦ χριστοῦ). However, this is not a true parallel: it does not have clear eucharistic terminology, as does Rom. 7:3. Moreover, in Trall. 8:1 "love" is said to be the "blood" of Christ, not the "blood" to be "love", as in Rom. 7:3.

68 Ignatius is not expressing a desire to partake of the eucharist before he is martyred, as Corwin suggests (St. Ignatius, 208: "To sustain himself as he goes on toward martyrdom, it is the eucharist that he craves."); cf. also Schlier, Religionsgeschichtliche Untersuchungen, 151-52.

69 Lightfoot, S. Ignatius, 2/1:226: "The reference here is not to the eucharist itself but to the union with Christ which is symbolized and pledged in the eucharist. . . . Ignatius is contemplating the consummation of his union with Christ through martyrdom"; Bauer, Briefe des Ignatius, 252: "Wir dürfen also wohl annehmen, dass der Genuss der Gemeinschaft mit Christus, die das Martyrium ermöglicht, mit Bildern, die aus dem Abendmahlsgebrauch entlehnt sind, geschildert wird."

70 See above, pp. 120-21.

71 See above, pp. 124-27.

72 Bartsch, Gnostisches Gut, 78: "dass Ignatius sein Martyrium, um das sein ganzes Denken kreist,

nicht nur bildhaft mit der Eucharistie und ihren
Begriffen umschreibt, sondern tatsächlich als
Eucharistie versteht" (against Maurer, Ignatius
von Antiochien, 90). While agreeing with Bartsch
that martyrdom is conceived by Ignatius as participation in the eucharist, we differ with him in
his assertion that martyrdom formed the center of
Ignatius' thinking so that one could even assume
"dass das Martyrium und sein Verständnis auf das
Verständnis des Sakraments eingewirkt hat"
(Gnostisches Gut, 79). The opposite is true.
The eucharist, as the locus of God's eschatological action of gathering His dispersed people,
formed the center of Ignatius' thinking and
provided him with the conceptual and termino-
logical equipment with which to interpret his
martyrdom.

73   P. Meinhold, "Episkope-Pneumatiker-Märtyrer:
Zur Deutung der Selbstaussagen des Ignatius von
Antiochien," Saeculum 14 (1963) 321: "Die durch
das Martyrium erlangte Gottes- oder Christus-
gemeinschaft . . . wird der in der Eucharistie
gewonnenen gleichgestellt."

74   So long as Ignatius is a prisoner and cannot
participate in the eucharist of the Church he is
unworthy and in danger. But once he is martyred
and thus participates in the eucharist with the
Church he will be τις (Rom. 9:2), πιστός (Rom.
3:2), χριστιανός (Rom. 3:2), μαθητής (Rom. 4:2).
See the good discussion by Bommes (Weizen Gottes,
200-8); cf. also Bartsch, Gnostisches Gut, 96-98;
von Campenhausen, Die Idee des Martyriums, 75;
Rathke, Ignatius von Antiochien, 70: "Seine
Unwürdigkeit liegt nicht zuerst an seiner Person,
sondern an seinem Zustand. Er ist aus der Einheit
der Gemeinde herausgerissen, für die Heil und
Erlösung ja schon in dem geeinten Leben unter dem
Bischof und in dem Teilhaben an der Eucharistie
gegenwärtig ist."

75   Trall. 12:2: παρακαλεῖ ὑμᾶς τὰ δεσμά μου, ἃ
ἕνεκεν 'Ιησοῦ χριστοῦ περιφέρω αἰτούμενος θεοῦ

ἐπιτυχεῖν· διαμένετε ἐν τῇ ὁμονοίᾳ ὑμῶν καὶ τῇ μετ' ἀλλήλων προσευχῇ.

76 Mag. 1:2: καταξιωθεὶς γὰρ ὀνόματος θεοπρεπεστάτου, ἐν οἷς περιφέρω δεσμοῖς ᾄδω τὰς ἐκκλησίας, ἐν αἷς ἕνωσιν εὔχομαι σαρκὸς καὶ πνεύματος Ἰησοῦ χριστοῦ, τοῦ διὰ παντὸς ἡμῶν ζῆν, πίστεώς τε καὶ ἀγάπης, ἧς οὐδὲν προκέριται, το δε κυριώτερον Ἰησοῦ καὶ πατρός.

77 See above, pp. 136-37.

78 Mag. 14: ἐπιδέομαι γὰρ τῆς ἡνωμένης ὑμῶν ἐν θεῷ προσευχῆς καὶ ἀγάπης, εἰς τὸ ἀξιωθῆναι τὴν ἐν Συρίᾳ ἐκκλησίαν διὰ τῆς ἐκκλησίας ὑμῶν δροσισθῆναι.

79 Zahn, Ignatius von Antiochien, 365-66.

80 P. N. Harrison, Polycarp's Two Epistles to the Philippians (Cambridge: 1936) 83,94-95.

81 Corwin, St. Ignatius, 52-65. See also Bartsch, Gnostisches Gut, 12.

82 This may account for Ignatius' use of εἰρηνεύειν. Through a reunited eucharist the Syrian community again experiences the peace of God (cf. Eph. 13:2).

83 Swartley, "Imitatio Christi," 81-103.

84 Swartley, "Imitatio Christi," 93. Swartley refers especially to Pol. 7:1.

85 Swartley, "Imitatio Christi," 102.

86 Graydon F. Snyder, "The Continuity of Early Christianity: A Study of Ignatius in Relation to Paul" (Diss.: Princeton University, 1961) 234.

87 Snyder and Swartley may well be correct in maintaining a close relationship between Ignatius'

fate as martyr and his office as bishop of a
troubled Antioch congregation.

88 Michel, Prophet und Märtyrer, 58: "Der
Märtyrer hat den Heiligen Geist"; p. 59:
"Ignatius war Prophet, Märtyrer, Bischof; nicht
als Bischof Prophet, sondern als Märtyrer Prophet.
Sein Martyrium macht ihn zum Prophet"; Schlier,
Religionsgeschichtliche Untersuchungen, 140: "Den
Weg geht Ignatius als Pneumatiker. Seine Fesseln
machen ihn dazu."

89 So also Bommes, Weizen Gottes, 174-75.

90 Trall. 5:1-2: μὴ οὐ δύναμαι ὑμῖν τὰ ἐπουράνια
γράψαι; ἀλλὰ φοβοῦμαι, μὴ νηπίοις οὖσιν ὑμῖν
βλάβην παραθῶ· καὶ συγγνωμονεῖτέ μοι, μήποτε οὐ
δυνηθέντες χωρῆσαι στραγγαλωθῆτε. καὶ γὰρ ἐγώ, οὐ
καθότι δέδεμαι καὶ δύναμαι νοεῖν τὰ ἐπουράνια καὶ
τὰς τοποθεσίας τὰς ἀγγελικὰς καὶ τὰς συστάσεις τὰς
ἀρχοντικάς, ὁρατά τε καὶ ἀόρατα, παρὰ τοῦτο ἤδη
καὶ μαθητής εἰμι. πολλὰ γὰρ ἡμῖν λείπει, ἵνα θεοῦ
μὴ λειπώμεθα. Phld. 7:1-2: εἰ γὰρ καὶ κατὰ
σάρκα μέ τινες ἠθέλησαν πλανῆσαι, ἀλλὰ τὸ πνεῦμα
οὐ πλανᾶται ἀπὸ θεοῦ ὄν. οἶδεν γάρ, πόθεν ἔρχεται
καὶ ποῦ ὑπάγει, καὶ τὰ κρυπτὰ ἐλέγχει. ἐκραύγασα
μεταξὺ ὤν, ἐλάλουν μεγάλῃ φωνῇ, θεοῦ φωνῇ· τῷ
ἐπισκόπῳ προσέχετε καὶ τῷ πρεσβυτερίῳ καὶ
διακόνοις. οἱ δὲ ὑποπτεύσαντές με ὡς προειδότα
τὸν μερισμόν τινων λέγειν ταῦτα· μάρτυς δέ μοι, ἐν
ᾧ δέδεμαι, ὅτι ἀπὸ σαρκὸς ἀνθρωπίνης οὐκ ἔγνων.
τὸ δὲ πνεῦμα ἐκήρυσσεν λέγον τάδε· χωρὶς τοῦ
ἐπισκόπου μηδὲν ποιεῖτε, τὴν σάρκα ὑμῶν ὡς ναὸν
θεοῦ τηρεῖτε, τὴν ἕνωσιν ἀγαπᾶτε, τοὺς μερισμοὺς
φεύγετε, μιμηταὶ γίνεσθε Ἰησοῦ χριστοῦ, ὡς καὶ
αὐτὸς τοῦ πατρὸς αὐτοῦ.

91 Bommes, Weizen Gottes, 175: "Sind seine
Fesseln auch nicht grundsätzlich und schlechthin
die Ursache seines Pneumatikerseins, so haben sie
doch offensichtlich einen so wesentlichen Einfluss
auf die Aktualisierung seiner pneumatischen
Begabung gegenüber den ihn auf seinem Wege
begegnenden Gemeinden."

92 Bommes recognizes this (<u>Weizen</u> <u>Gottes</u>, 174)

93 Cf. Bommes, <u>Weizen</u> <u>Gottes</u>, 168-70. In his
study on the Greek imperatives in the New Testament and related literature, James Voelz asserts
that the present imperative was predominantly used
to express "policy" commands, that is, commands
not situationally oriented nor confined to one
occasion or to a very limited number of occasions.
He asserts that Ignatius adheres to this usage in
92% of his policy imperatives or prohibitions
("The Use of the Present & Aorist Imperatives &
Prohibitions in the New Testament" [Diss.:
Cambridge University, 1978] esp. 24-25). If Voelz
is correct, the present imperatives in the exhortations in <u>Phld</u>. 7:2 (ποιεῖτε, τηρεῖτε, ἀγαπᾶτε,
φεύγετε, γίνεσθε) aid to corroborate our view
that these exhortations were common to Ignatius
and not very specially formulated with Philadelphia
in mind.

Chapter 4

THE MARTYRDOM OF POLYCARP

The authenticity of the Martyrdom of Polycarp
has generally been assumed since Lightfoot's
discussion of the problems.[1] The uneven textual
transmission, however, has given rise to important
theories of interpolations. Müller argued that
the text suffered much interpolation from the
desire to pattern Polycarp's suffering and death
after that of Jesus.[2] On the other hand, Baden,
Reuning, and Delehaye argued against Müller that
the idea of imitation was early and widespread
and, therefore, imitation passages in the
Martyrdom of Polycarp need not be interpolations.[3]
Recently von Campenhausen in a well-argued article
took up and expanded Müller's arguments.[4] Basing
his comparison on the Eusebian text (Hist. eccl.
4.15.3-45), von Campenhausen argues that the
original text underwent at least two redactions,
an anti-Montanist redaction in the late second or
early third century[5] and a fourth-century gospel
redaction which sought to paint Polycarp's passion
as a close imitation of Christ's passion.[6] To
these interpolations have been added also others
intended to increase the wonderful character of
Polycarp's passion.[7]

If von Campenhausen's arguments be true, the
original text of the Martyrdom of Polycarp would
have been virtually devoid of interpretative
commentary. It is, however, highly improbable
that the Smyrnaean church would have written of
its bishop's martyrdom without any attempt to
express its significance and meaning. As for the
alleged redactions themselves, even if Mart. Pol. 4
is an anti-Montanist polemic--which is by no means
certain[8]--that would not require the hypothesis of
a redactor. Secondly, the thesis of an
"Euangelion-Redaktor" rests on an over-estimation
of the role which the imitatio motif plays in the
Martyrdom of Polycarp.[9] Finally, von Campenhausen

165

finds many of his textual deviations within Eusebius, Hist. eccl. 4.15.4-14 (Mart. Pol. 1:1b-7:3) where Eusebius is obviously paraphrasing and, therefore, this passage may not be used for textual comparison and criticism.[10] There is, therefore, no solid ground for rejecting the text of pseudo-Pionius as the basis of study.[11]

It seems clear that the Martyrdom of Polycarp was written within a reasonably short time after the martyrdom (Mart. Pol. 18:3; 20:1), yet the date of martyrdom remains an open and much-debated question.[12] For our purposes, this question is not of great importance. However, the arguments favoring 155/156 or 156/157 seem most cogent.

The Martyrdom of Polycarp exhibits several incidents in which the "supernatural" plays a role. While Holl may exaggerate in calling the Martyrdom "eine ununterbrochene Kette von Geisteswundern",[13] von Campenhausen errs in the opposite direction by denying any role to the Holy Spirit within the narrative.[14] As we shall see, the Spirit is clearly implied as present at the climax of the narrative, the martyrdom itself (Mart. Pol. 15).

The "supernatural" elements, however, are not haphazardly recounted but serve to confirm that Polycarp's death was a "martyrdom according to the gospel" (τὸ κατὰ τὸ εὐαγγέλιον μαρτύριον [Mart. Pol. 1:1; 19:1; 22:1]). Indeed, according to Mart. Pol. 1:1 the very purpose of the events which transpired in Smyrna was so that "the Lord might show us from above a martyrdom according to the gospel" (ἵνα ἡμῖν ὁ κύριος ἄνωθεν ἐπιδείξῃ τὸ κατὰ τὸ εὐαγγέλιον μαρτύριον).

What is a martyrdom "according to the gospel"? Mart. Pol. 1:2 explains what is involved:

> For he tarried (περιέμενεν) in order that he might be handed over (παραδοθῇ), as was also the Lord, in order that also we might become his imitators, caring not only for our own welfare but also for that of the neighbor. For it is characteristic of a true and valid love that one desire not

166

only his own salvation but the salvation of all the brethren.[15]

First of all, then, a martyrdom "according to the gospel" is not voluntary. A true martyr must be "handed over", as was Christ himself (Mark 9:31; 10:33). For Lightfoot, the clause περιέμενεν ἵνα παραδοθῇ provides "an incentive to rather than a discouragement of martyrdom", and he explains περιέμενεν to mean "he lingered about so as to be in the way of his captors".[16] However, the point is certainly in the παραδοθῇ and not in the περιέμενεν, as the comparison with Christ implies, and the Quintus episode confirms this (Mart. Pol. 4). Quintus, a Phrygian only recently come from Phrygia, had given himself up and had forced others as well voluntarily to give themselves over to persecution and martyrdom.[17] However, in the arena Quintus is brought to apostasy, which leads the Martyrdom to make the programmatic statement: "for this reason we do not approve of those who come forward on their own, since the gospel does not teach that to be the way" (ἐπειδὴ οὐχ οὕτως διδάσκει τὸ εὐαγγέλιον [Mart. Pol. 4]).[18] The martyrdom of Quintus, being voluntary, was not an expression of the divine will, and for that reason Quintus was unable to endure steadfastly. Polycarp's martyrdom, on the other hand, was an expression of the divine will (cf. the δεῖ in Mart. Pol. 5:2); he is "handed over" (God is the unexpressed subject of παραδοθῇ), and therefore Polycarp is enabled to endure without wavering.

However, as Mart. Pol. 1:2 also makes clear, a martyrdom "according to the gospel" is a martyrdom which engenders in the Christian community behavior which, in imitation of the martyr, looks to the welfare and salvation of the brethren. Here likewise the Quintus episode provides a direct contrast. While the rash conduct of Quintus involves others in the same folly, the death of Polycarp serves to strengthen the Christian community as it prepares and trains others for steadfast martyrdom (Mart. Pol. 18:3).

A martyrdom "according to the gospel", therefore, has three essential elements: 1) it is in
obedience to a divine call and not a voluntary
quest for suffering; 2) it serves to promote
faithful endurance on the part of the brethren
and thus their salvation; and 3) the martyr
himself endures steadfastly his own suffering and
death (note also here the contrast between the
timidity of Quintus in the face of the beasts
[Mart. Pol. 4] and the express lack of fear of
Polycarp [Mart. Pol. 11:1-2]).

The story of Polycarp's death in fact may be
divided along these lines. The story commences
with Polycarp's hearing the call for his arrest
(Mart. Pol. 5:1), and it concludes with the
mention of the Church's intention to meet yearly
at Polycarp's grave (Mart. Pol. 18:3).[19] Mart.
Pol. 5-8 reports the vision which Polycarp
receives informing him of the divine necessity of
his martyrdom (δεῖ [Mart. Pol. 5:2]) and of
Polycarp's subsequent obedience to the divine
will when he allows himself to be arrested with
the prayer "the will of God be done" (Mart. Pol.
7:1).[20] Mart. Pol. 9-16 concerns Polycarp's
steadfastness under interrogation, his death and
the accompanying wonders. Mart. Pol. 17-18
reports the gathering of Polycarp's bones and the
intended cultic gatherings at Polycarp's grave,
the purpose of which was "for remembrance of those
who have fought the fight before and for the
training and preparation of those who will yet
fight it" (εἰς τε τὴν τῶν προηθληκότων μνήμην καὶ
τῶν μελλόντων ἄσκησιν τε καὶ ἑτοιμασίαν [Mart. Pol.
18:3]). The martyrdom of Polycarp led to an
intensified community life and served to prepare
others faithfully to endure future persecution.[21]

The "supernatural" elements pervading
Polycarp's martyrdom are to be understood within
the above context. They serve to confirm what the
will of God is and that that will is being
effected. A vision informs Polycarp what the will
of God is. It is the will of God that Polycarp
suffer martyrdom (Mart. Pol. 5:2; 12:3); his

martyrdom is the working out of the divine δεῖ.[22] Since Polycarp's martyrdom is willed by God, Polycarp may expect divine aid in order to endure steadfastly the hostile threats and subsequent suffering. This connection between God's willing martyrdom and God's assisting in martyrdom is explicitly made in Mart. Pol. 13:3. Polycarp refuses to be nailed to the stake at which he is to be burned: "Leave me thus, for He who deemed that I should undergo fire shall grant that I remain unmoved in the fire even without the assurance you offer by the use of nails" (ὁ γὰρ δοὺς ὑπομεῖναι τὸ πῦρ δώσει καὶ χωρὶς τῆς ὑμετέρας ἐκ τῶν ἥλων ἀσφαλείας ἄσκυλτον ἐπιμεῖναι τῇ πυρᾷ). ὁ δοὺς clearly refers to God. The aorist shows that God's "giving to endure" alludes to a prior execution of God's will, perhaps the arrest but more probably the condemnation to the fire. The expression ἡ ὑμέτερα ἐκ τῶν ἥλων ἀσφάλεια implies a corresponding ἡ ἡμέτερα ἀσφάλεια or ἡ θεῖα ἀσφάλεια which does not require nails for steadfastness. God shall guarantee that which He wills.[23] Hippolytus would later make this point with admirable clarity: "whenever anyone of the saints should be called to martyrdom, certain great deeds will be done by God to him" (ἡνίκα γὰρ ἄν τις τῶν ἁγίων ἐπὶ μαρτύριον κληθῇ καὶ μεγαλεῖα τινα ὑπὸ θεοῦ εἰς αὐτὸν γενηθῇ [Comm. Dan. 2:38]).

Assurance that God will indeed enable him to endure faithfully is given to Polycarp through a heavenly voice. As Polycarp enters the stadium, a "voice from heaven" (φωνὴ ἐξ οὐρανοῦ) comes to Polycarp: ἴσχυε Πολύκαρπε καὶ ἀνδρίζου (Mart. Pol. 9:1).[24] The exhortation ἴσχυε καὶ ἀνδρίζου is common in the Septuagint, often occurring with the corresponding exhortation μὴ φοβοῦ, μὴ δειλιάσῃς, or μὴ πτοθῇς (Deut 31:6,7,23; Josh 1:6,7,9,18; 10:25; 1 Chr 22:13; 28:20; 2 Chr 32:7; Dan 10:19; cf. Ps 26:14; 30:25; 1 Macc 2:64). Two Greek manuscripts, c (Chalcensis) and v (Vindobonensis), add μετὰ σοῦ γὰρ εἰμι after ἀνδρίζου: "be strong and take courage, for I am with you". This is surely a later interpolation. Yet, the addition accurately expresses the sense of the passage. In

several passages of the Septuagint the words
ἴσχυε καὶ ἀνδρίζου are combined with the promise
of the faithful presence of God which guarantees
the faithful execution of God's will. Deut 31:6
is typical: "For it is the Lord your God who goes
before you, who will not fail or desert you"
(cf. also Deut 31:8,23; Josh 1:9; 1 Chr 28:20;
2 Chr 32:7). Twice a promise that God shall
conquer the enemies of His people accompanies the
exhortation (Josh 10:25; 2 Chr 32:7). According
to Dan 10:19, God's very speaking of the exhortation was the instrument of encouragement and
strength: καὶ ἐν τῷ λαλῆσαι αὐτὸν μετ᾽ ἐμοῦ
ἴσχυσα. Similar ideas were no doubt meant when
the author of the Martyrdom of Polycarp wrote of
the heavenly voice. It is the heavenly sign that
God through His presence will assist and
strengthen Polycarp in his ordeal to its appointed
end.[25]

The wonder reported in Mart. Pol. 15:2 at
once confirms that Polycarp is a chosen and
faithful instrument of God and gives the reason
why Polycarp has continuing significance for the
life of the Church. When Polycarp finished his
prayer, the fire was lit around him, and those
"to whom it was given to see" saw a "wonder"
(θαῦμα): "For the fire formed the shape of a
vault, as a sail which is filled by the wind (ὑπὸ
πνεύματος), and surrounded the body of the martyr
as with a wall."[26]

Schlatter and Surkau regard this as a
"Schutzwunder".[27] Von Campenhausen correctly
rejects this view; the martyr is in fact not
protected.[28] The wonder is rather a graphic
actualization of Polycarp's prayer recorded in
Mart. Pol. 14. Polycarp blessed God for finding
him worthy to receive a share in the number of the
martyrs "in the cup of Christ for the resurrection
to eternal life of both soul and body in the
incorruptibility of the Holy Spirit" (ἐν τῷ
ποτηρίῳ τοῦ χριστοῦ σου εἰς ἀνάστασιν ζωῆς αἰωνίου
ψυχῆς τε καὶ σώματος ἐν ἀφθαρσίᾳ πνεύματος ἁγίου
[Mart. Pol. 14:2]). When the fire is blown as a

sail filled "by the wind" (ὑπὸ πνεύματος) leaving
Polycarp's body untouched, we are to understand
that the "incorruptibility of the Holy Spirit" for
which Polycarp prayed has been granted. ὑπὸ
πνεύματος is a play on words allowing the author
vividly to express this salvific occurrence.
Polycarp's body cannot be burned (<u>Mart</u>. <u>Pol</u>. 16:1a)
for it has become the recipient of the incorruptibility of the Holy Spirit.[29] Polycarp has
received "the crown of incorruptibility" (<u>Mart</u>.
<u>Pol</u>. 17:1; 19:2). This reception of the incor-
ruptibility of the Spirit by the body of Polycarp
explains the desire of the Smyrnaean community to
collect his remains (<u>Mart</u>. <u>Pol</u>. 17:1; 18:2). The
Smyrnaean Christians regard the victorious martyr,
crowned with "the crown of incorruptibility", as
participating in the heavenly liturgy with the
apostles and all the righteous (<u>Mart</u>. <u>Pol</u>. 19:2).
Gathered at his grave, they participate with
Polycarp, the victorious martyr, in the liturgy
of praise and blessing, and in so doing others are
prepared for persecution and martyrdom.[30]

Possibly the "fragrance as of smoking incense
or some other precious perfume" (<u>Mart</u>. <u>Pol</u>. 15:2)
belongs to the same complex of ideas as does the
flame blown by the wind. The words λιβανωτοῦ
πνέοντος perhaps imply the presence of the Spirit.
A sweet odor was often symbolic of the divine
presence (cf. 2 Cor 2:15-16). The letter of the
Lyons martyrs speaks of Christ's presence as
ἡ εὐωδία ἡ χριστοῦ (Eusebius, <u>Hist</u>. <u>eccl</u>. 5.1.35),
and according to Hippolytus, Basilides spoke of
the odor brought down from above by the Holy
Spirit (ἡ ἀπὸ τοῦ πνεύματος τοῦ ἁγίου φερομένη
ὀσμὴ ἄνωθεν κάτω [<u>Philosophumena</u> 7:22]). In
some sources the Spirit's presence at Pentecost
was indicated by a sweet odor.[31] Not only the
Spirit but also his gifts, such as life and
incorruptibility, could be indicated by a sweet
smell (cf. 2 Cor 2:14-16; Ign. <u>Eph</u>. 17:1).[32] The
εὐωδία of <u>Mart</u>. <u>Pol</u>. 15:2 may just as well,
however, allude to the notion of the acceptable
sacrifice of a just man (cf. Sir 35:5-6; Eph 5:2;
Phil 4:18; <u>Barn</u>. 2:10).[33]

171

The vision (Mart. Pol. 5:2), the heavenly voice (Mart. Pol. 9:1), and the flame blown by the wind (Mart. Pol. 15:2) may be considered Spirit-effected wonders, for they are divine actions rooted in God's will which are accomplished on the martyr. To this list one should perhaps add Mart. Pol. 7:3: Polycarp, "full of the grace of God", was unable to stop praying for two hours. However, the relation this Spirit-driven prayer has with Polycarp as martyr must remain problematic. It may simply testify to the Spirit-filled character of Polycarp as bishop. Clearly, Polycarp was held to be a Spirit-filled man even before his arrest: he was an "apostolic and prophetic teacher" (διδάσκαλος ἀποστολικὸς καὶ προφητικός [Mart. Pol. 16:2]). On the other hand, it is not a Spirit-effected wonder when the blood from Polycarp's pierced side extinguishes the flame (Mart. Pol. 16:1).[34] The account merely asserts that in his death Polycarp escaped the eternal fire. It is a parallel to Mart. Pol. 2:3.[35]

We must now turn to the brief account the letter gives of the other martyrs (Mart. Pol. 2-3).[36] All the martyrdoms occurred according to the will of God who is the real source of the martyrs' glory, "for it is necessary that we be devout and ascribe to God the power in all things" (Mart. Pol. 2:1). Both von Campenhausen and Surkau have remarked that despite these words the martyrs immediately appear as objects of wonder, praise, and honor. The martyrs' endurance (ὑπομονή) has become a virtue; the martyr has become a hero.[37] One can hardly deny that the language of Mart. Pol. 2-3 gives cause for this view. The words τὸ γενναῖον αὐτῶν καὶ ὑπομονητικὸν καὶ φιλοδέσποτον (Mart. Pol. 2:2) lend themselves much better to the idea of heroic virtue as a possessed quality than to the idea of God's active working in the martyr. The word ὑπέμειναν (Mart. Pol. 2:2) takes on unmistakeable heroic dimensions from its immediate context: although torn by whips so that the structure of their bodies was visible as far as the inner veins and arteries, the martyrs endured, so that even the

172

bystanders wept for mercy. The courage of Germanicus is shown supremely when he pulls the beast upon himself to leave this evil life more quickly (Mart. Pol. 3:1). These passages do seem devoid of any eschatological perspective in their treatment of martyrdom.

A good example of this heroic view of martyrdom is Mart. Pol. 2:2b: some of the martyrs reached such courage "that they neither cried nor uttered a sound thereby showing to all of us that while being tormented in that hour, these most courageous martyrs of Christ were not present in the flesh (τῆς σαρκὸς ἀπεδήμουν), or rather that the Lord was present speaking to them (παρεστὼς ὁ κύριος ὡμίλει αὐτοῖς [cf. Mart. Isa. 5:14; Eusebius, Hist. eccl. 5.1.51,56]). The words τῆς σαρκὸς ἀπεδήμουν seem to point toward the idea of ecstasy, but the silence of the martyrs is explained by the letter itself. The Lord is talking to them. The presence of Christ is the cause of the martyrs' heroic courage. Here Christ brings about, not an eschatological event, but heroes.[38]

However, an eschatological perspective is not entirely missing from Mart. Pol. 2. Mart. Pol. 2:3 contains the famous comparison of the martyrs with angels:

> But the fire of their inhuman tormentors was cool to them. For they kept in mind their flight from the eternal fire, which is never quenched, and with the eyes of the heart looked at those good things held for those who have persevered, which neither ear has heard nor eye seen nor has entered into the heart of man. But to them these things were revealed by the Lord, since they were no longer men but already angels.[39]

The source of this idea remains somewhat of an enigma. However, the words "what ear has not heard, nor eye seen, nor has come into the heart of man" present the motif of the hidden and the revealed and appear in various formulations in a

173

wide variety of literature.[40]   The underlying
thought seems to be that ordinary men do not have
the capacity to perceive and appropriate as their
own the things of the heavenly world (cf. 1 Cor
15:50).   Since such things cannot be received by
men, those who receive them can no longer be men
but must be heavenly beings, angels.[41]   Related to
this is the view that the future life will be like
that of the angels (cf. Matt 22:30; Mark 12:25;
Luke 20:35-36).[42]

However, the interest of Mart. Pol. 2:3 is
not to describe the martyrs but to explain why
they withstood their torments.   The fire of their
tormentors was cool to the martyrs.   Negatively
this is explained by reference to the martyrs'
cognizance that they were escaping the eternal
fire.   Positively, their steadfastness is attributed to the revelation of "the good things held
for those who have endured" (τοῖς ὑπομείνασιν).
The aorist (τοῖς ὑπομείνασιν) implies that "the
good things" are held for those who have completed
their trials, that is, the Christian dead.   But to
"those who have endured" the martyrs stand in
strongest contrast (ἐκείνοις δέ).   The martyrs are
not yet dead, but they nevertheless receive from
the Lord a revelation of "the good things" usually
held only for those who already have completed
successfully their Christian sojourn.   For this
reason the martyrs held steadfast, and for this
reason their steadfastness is itself a revelation
of the eschatological "good things".

In this argument we may very well see the
redactorial hand of the author.   Very likely the
tradition the author knew had a present participle
(τοῖς ὑπομένουσιν) instead of the aorist
participle.   Both Isa 64:3 (LXX), which forms the
basis of the passage, and 1 Clem 34:8 have the
present participle of μένειν.   At 1 Cor 2:9,
although the verb is different, a present participle also occurs (τοῖς ἀγαπῶσιν).   Changing the
participle from the present to the aorist tense
enabled the author to demark the suffering,
persecuted Christian as the object of a special

174

grace, the perception of the eschatological glory in anticipation. Of course, by doing this the author drew a distinction between the martyr and the ordinary Christian. The martyr has become the recipient of special spiritual gifts. Yet, this was not the point of the author. He was not interested in making the martyr extraordinary but in proclaiming the gracious aid of the Lord even within the worst of times (cf. 1 Cor 10:13).

SUMMARY

The Martyrdom of Polycarp was written for the edification of the Church, although it possesses overtones of a didactic, polemical nature. The martyrdom of Polycarp is presented as a "martyrdom according to the gospel". Such a martyrdom consists of three features: 1) the will of God calls the martyr to martyrdom; 2) the martyr obeys God's will through steadfast faithfulness in the midst of suffering; 3) the martyrdom is an ecclesial event, for through the remembrance of the martyr the Christian community faithfully trains itself for future struggles.

The wonders of the Spirit which occur to the martyr are to be understood in this context. A vision informs Polycarp what the will of God is. As Polycarp enters the arena, a voice from heaven confirms that God will grant that which He has willed. A wind blows the flames away from the body of Polycarp signifying that it has received the incorruptibility of the Holy Spirit. For that reason, the martyr has continuing significance for the Church, which prepares itself for future martyrdoms through its remembrance of the martyr. Although the Martyrdom of Polycarp belies the tendency to view the martyr as a hero, and therefore individualistically, this ecclesial dimension still predominates.

NOTES TO CHAPTER FOUR

1 J. B. Lightfoot, The Apostolic Fathers, Part 2:
S. Ignatius. S. Polycarp, 3 vols. (London:
Macmillan, 1889), 1:604-45.

2 H. Müller, "Das Martyrium Polycarpi: Ein
Beitrag zur altchristlichen Heiligengeschichte,"
RQ 22 (1908) 1-16.

3 H. Baden, "Der Nachahmungsgedanke im
Polykarpmartyrium," TGl 3 (1911) 115-22; W.
Reuning, Zur Erklärung des Polykarp-Martyriums
(Darmstadt: 1917) 10-20; H. Delehaye, Les
passions des martyrs et les genres littéraires
(Bruxelles: Société des Bollandistes, 1921) 14-20.

4 H. von Campenhausen, "Bearbeitungen und
Interpolationen des Polykarpmartyriums," Aus der
Frühzeit des Christentums: Studien zur Kirchen-
geschichte des ersten und zweiten Jahrhunderts
(Tübingen: J. C. B. Mohr, 1963) 253-301. For
criticism of von Campenhausen's argument, see
L. W. Barnard, "In Defense of Pseudo-Pionius'
Account of Polycarp's Martyrdom," Kyriakon:
Festschrift Johannes Quasten, 2 vols. (Münster:
Aschendorff, 1970), 1:192-204.

5 Von Campenhausen, "Bearbeitungen," 268-71. To
this redaction belongs primarily the Quintus
episode (Mart. Pol. 4).

6 Von Campenhausen, "Bearbeitungen," 256-66. To
the "Euangelion-Redaktor" von Campenhausen assigns
Mart. Pol. 1:1b-2:2a; 2:2c-2:3; 4 (last sentence);
6:2-7:1a; 19:1b-19:2; 22:1. Cf. Müller, "Das
Martyrium Polycarpi," 6-13.

7 Von Campenhausen, "Bearbeitungen," 271-74.

8 Cf. Lightfoot, S. Polycarp, 1:619-20,622;
T. D. Barnes, "Pre-Decian Acta Martyrum," JTS n.s.
19 (1968) 511-12; Barnard, "In Defense of Pseudo-
Pionius," 197-99.

9　See especially Reuning, Erklärung des Polykarp-
Martyriums, 10-20.　To be sure, parallels between
the death of Jesus and the death of Polycarp exist
and at times are expressly accentuated (e.g. Mart.
Pol. 1:2; 6:2).　But what parallels exist are not
of the kind one would expect of a redactor who
had a free hand to create parallels at his discre-
tion.　The refusal of Polycarp to be nailed (Mart.
Pol. 13:3) hardly argues in favor of a conscious
imitatio redaction.

10　See Barnard, "In Defense of Pseudo-Pionius,"
194;　Barnes, "Pre-Decian Acta," 511.

11　We shall use the text of K. Bihlmeyer-W.
Schneemelcher, Die Apostolischen Väter:　Neubearbeitung der Funkschen Ausgabe, Part 1,
3rd ed. (Tübingen: J. C. B. Mohr, 1970) 120-32.

12　Lightfoot (S. Polycarp, 1:646-724) and E.
Schwartz ("Christliche und jüdische Ostertafeln,"
AGG n.s. 8 [1905] 125ff.) argued for the date
155/156, and that date was largely accepted until
H. Grégoire suggested the date 177 A.D. ("La
véritable date du martyre de S. Polycarpe (23
février 177) et le 'Corpus Polycarpianum'," AnBoll
69 [1951] 1-38).　P. Meinhold argued cogently
against Grégoire and upheld the old dating
("Polykarpos," PW 21/2 [1952] 1676-80).　H. I.
Marrou ("La date du martyre de S. Polycarpe,"
AnBoll 71 [1953] 5-20) suggested a date between
161 and 168/169 and has been followed by M.
Simonetti ("Alcune osservazioni sul martirio di
S. Policarpo," Giornale Italiano di Filologia
9 [1956] 328-32) and von Campenhausen
("Bearbeitungen," 253-54).　Recently, T. D. Barnes
reviewed the evidence and concluded that 156/157
was the most probable date ("A Note on Polycarp,"
JTS n.s. 18 [1967] 433-37;　"Pre-Decian Acta,"
510-14).

13　K. Holl, "Die Vorstellung vom Märtyrer und die
Märtyrerakte in ihrer geschichtlichen Entwicklung,"
Gesammelte Aufsätze zur Kirchengeschichte, vol. 2:

Der Osten (Tubingen: J. C. B. Mohr, 1928) 77.
Holl lists Mart. Pol. 5:2; 7:3; 9:1; 12:1; 15:1,2;
16:1; 20:1.

14 H. von Campenhausen, Die Idee des Martyriums
in der alten Kirche, 2nd ed. (Göttingen:
Vandenhoeck & Ruprecht, 1964) 90 n. 3. Von
Campenhausen distinguishes sharply between the
special presence of Christ during martyrdom and
the sending of the Spirit, which is "urchristlich".

15 Mart. Pol. 1:2: περιέμενεν γάρ, ἵνα παραδοθῇ,
ὡς καὶ ὁ κύριος, ἵνα μιμηταὶ καὶ ἡμεῖς αὐτοῦ
γενώμεθα, μὴ μόνον σκοποῦντες τὸ καθ' ἑαυτούς,
ἀλλὰ καὶ τὸ κατὰ τοὺς πέλας. ἀγάπης γὰρ ἀληθοῦς
καὶ βεβαίας ἐστίν, μὴ μόνον ἑαυτὸν θέλειν σῴζεσθαι,
ἀλλὰ καὶ πάντας τοὺς ἀδελφούς.

16 Lightfoot, S. Polycarp, 1:619,619 n. 1.

17 In Eusebius, Hist. eccl. 4.15.8, Quintus'
behavior is called "irreverent" (ἀνευλαβῶς) and
"foolhardy" (ῥιψοκινδύνως). Eusebius, Hist. eccl.
4.15.8 implies that the others were willing
accomplices with Quintus, while Mart. Pol. 4
states that Quintus forced them to give themselves
over voluntarily: οὗτος δε ἦν ὁ παραβιασάμενος
ἑαυτόν τε καὶ τινας προελθεῖν ἑκόντας. Whether
Quintus was a Montanist is a question impossible
to answer with certainty. Certainly Φρύξ need not
designate a Montanist; it might just relate the
fact that Quintus was by nationality a Phrygian.
Yet, the behavior of Quintus (so characteristic of
some Montanist enthusiasts), the significant
position the Quintus episode takes within the
narrative, and the fact that the Phrygian city of
Philomelium was the prime destination of the
letter tend to support the suspicion that Quintus
was a Montanist.

18 R. Reitzenstein calls the Martyrdom of
Polycarp a "Lehrschrift" against the ἑκουσίως
προσιέναι ("Bemerkungen zur Martyrienliteratur. I.
Die Bezeichnung Märtyrer," NGG [Berlin: Weidmann,

179

1916] 451-52,459). Reitzenstein compares
ἐκουσίως προσιέναι to the Hellenistic concepts of
execution and performance which presuppose
voluntary action as a way to fame and glory (cf.
Epictetus, Diss. 3.24.11).

19 Mart. Pol. 19:1 begins: "such are the events
which pertain to the blessed Polycarp" (τοιαῦτα
τὰ κατὰ τὸν μακάριον Πολύκαρπον). The story of
Polycarp's martyrdom does not end with his death
but includes, or perhaps better, is itself
incorporated into the continuing life of the
Christian community.

20 The account is not without some inconsist-
encies. Although the vision is reported in Mart.
Pol. 5:2, Polycarp is said in Mart. Pol. 6:1 to
have moved yet another time to escape capture.
While Mart. Pol. 7:1 reports that Polycarp
refused further safety in order to follow God's
will, Mart. Pol. 6:2 appears to attribute
Polycarp's arrest to the infidelity of servants
whose collaboration made it impossible for
Polycarp to continue in hiding.

21 For a discussion of Mart. Pol. 18:3, see W.
Rordorf, "Aux origines du culte des martyrs,"
Irénikon 46 (1972) 315-25. Most likely an account
of Polycarp's martyrdom was read at these
gatherings.

22 The psychologizing of H. Weinel is devoid of
any basis in the text and amounts to vain specula-
tion (Die Wirkungen des Geistes und der Geister
im nachapostolischen Zeitalter bis auf Irenäus
[Freiburg: J. C. B. Mohr, 1899] 174-75).

23 This motif may be present in the middle portion of the prayer which interprets Polycarp's
martyrdom in eucharistic terms (Mart. Pol. 14:2).
Polycarp prays that he might be accepted as an
acceptable sacrifice καθὼς προητοίμασας καὶ
προεφανέρωσας καὶ ἐπλήρωσας, ὁ ἀψευδὴς καὶ ἀληθινὸς
θεός. The three participles perhaps refer to the

divine will, the revealing of that will in the
vision, and the fulfillment of that will. However,
the typology of the bound ram as sacrifice may
rather be the background (cf. G. Kretschmar,
"Christliches Passa im 2. Jahrhundert und die
Ausbildung der christlichen Theologie," Judeo-
Christianisme. Recherches historiques et
théologiques offertes en hommage au Cardinal Jean
Daniélou [Paris: Recherches de science religieuse,
1972] 294-95).

24 The text of Mart. Pol. 8:3-9:1 may have
suffered some interpolation and tendencious
growth, but there is insufficient cause to regard
the incident of the heavenly voice itself as a
later interpolation. See Reuning, Erklärung des
Polykarp-Martyriums, 27-29; against Müller, "Das
Martyrium Polycarpi," 13-14; von Campenhausen,
"Bearbeitungen," 272.

25 It is significant that the voice speaks as
Polycarp enters the arena. Polycarp is from the
beginning under the assisting hand of God. H.-W.
Surkau believes Mart. Pol. 9:1 is parallel to the
report of a heavenly voice during the martyrdom of
Chananja ben Teradjon (Martyrien in jüdischer und
frühchristlicher Zeit [FRLANT 54; Göttingen:
Vandenhoeck & Ruprecht, 1938] 131 n. 123).
According to Weinel, the account of the heavenly
voice is "die symbolische Ausdeutung oder
Weiterbildung eines Gegenstandes oder Vorganges
aus der Sinnenwelt". A voice from the crowd was
heard and unconsciously interpreted according to
the strong desire of the Christians that Polycarp
remain steadfast (Wirkungen des Geistes, 166-67).
Such idle psychologizing does not aid in understanding the text.

26 Mart. Pol. 15:2: τὸ γὰρ πῦρ καμάρας εἶδος
ποιῆσαν, ὥσπερ ὀθόνη πλοίου ὑπὸ πνεύματος
πληρουμένη κύκλῳ περιετείχισεν τὸ σῶμα τοῦ
μάρτυρος.

27 A. Schlatter, Der Märtyrer in den Anfängen der
Kirche (BFCT 19/3; Gütersloh: C. Bertelsmann, 1915)
35ff.; Surkau, Martyrien, 131 n. 124.

28 Von Campenhausen, Die Idee des Martyriums,
84 n. 1. Lightfoot writes that "this may be
explained as a strictly natural occurrence". He
refers to the martyrdoms of Savonarola (1498) and
of John Hooper (1555) during which the wind's
blowing the flames was perceived as a miracle
(S. Polycarp, 1:614-15).

29 Mart. Pol. 18:1 does not contradict this. The
wonder expresses what was happening to, but
nevertheless supernaturally beyond, the physical
body of Polycarp. It is expressly a statement of
Christian faith (cf. Mart. Pol. 15:1b). Cf.
Rordorf, "Aux origines du culte des martyrs," 318:
"aux yeux des Smyrniotes chrétiens, le corps même
du martyr est devenu le 'temoin' de la puissance
de l'Esprit qui communique l'incorruptibilité à
la matière corruptible".

30 Von Campenhausen argues that the martyr cult
did not evolve organically from a concept of
martyrdom or from a belief in a special communion
with the Spirit in martyrdom. Rather, the martyr
cult arose from general notions of holiness and
sainthood (Die Idee des Martyriums, 80 n. 9). He
refers to Mart. Pol. 13:2 (ὅστις τάχιον τοῦ
χρωτὸς αὐτοῦ ἅψηται) and to Mart. Pol. 17:1
(κοινωνῆσαι τῷ ἁγίῳ σαρκίῳ). The Martyrdom of
Polycarp does not support this view: 1) "To touch
his flesh" and "to have communion with the holy
flesh" are not synonymous. κοινωνῆσαι τῷ ἁγίῳ
σαρκίῳ does not refer to a physical touching but
to the gatherings at the martyr's tomb. τῷ ἁγίῳ
σαρκίῳ is dativus comitativus. The Christians
wish to share with the holy flesh in something
else. This something else is not expressed, but
the "incorruptibility of the Holy Spirit" is a
likely possibility. 2) When the Christians in
fact do come into contact with the martyr's
remains (Mart. Pol. 18:2), nothing is made of

this. Of sole importance is that Polycarp's body be laid in a "suitable place", that is, in a place where the community can gather (see Rordorf, "Aux origines du culte des martyrs," 318). 3) The purpose of the gatherings at the grave is to prepare for future martyrdoms. This would be meaningful only if the holiness were that of the martyr and not just a "general holiness".

31 See E. Nestle, "Der süsse Geruch als Erweis des Geistes," ZNW 4 (1903) 272.

32 See A. von Harnack, "Zu Eusebius IV.15.37," ZKG 2 (1878) 291-96; E. Lohmeyer, Vom göttlichen Wohlgeruch (Heidelberg: 1919) 48. Lucian reports that Peregrinus artificially produced a sweet odor when he was on the bier (Pereg. 3). Apparently Lucian was satirizing the Christians' belief that martyrs give off a sweet odor.

33 See Reuning, Erklärung des Polykarp-Martyriums, 43-45; Kretschmar, "Christliches Passa," 293; A. Stumpff, s.v. "εὐωδία," TWNT 2 (1935) 808-10.

34 Against Holl, "Die Vorstellung vom Märtyrer," 77. The Greek manuscripts (G) add περιστερὰ καὶ after ἐξῆλθεν. These words are missing in Eusebius and are surely a later interpolation (cf. Lightfoot, S. Polycarp, 2/2:974-77; Reuning, Erklärung des Polykarp-Martyriums, 9-10). Reuning is correct in refusing to see a passion parallel in Mart. Pol. 16:1 (Erklärung des Polykarp-Martyriums, 20; against Müller, "Das Martyrium Polycarpi," 11; Barnard, "In Defense of Pseudo-Pionius," 195).

35 Cf. Cyprian, Ep. 10:2: fluebat sanguis qui incendium persecutionis extingueret, qui flammes et ignes gehennae glorioso cruore sopiret. 4 Macc 9:20 is no true parallel.

36 Reitzenstein ("Bemerkungen zur Martyrien-literatur," 460-61) and von Campenhausen ("Bearbeitungen," 284-89) argue that the original

letter contained some account of the other martyrdoms and did not report so exclusively of Polycarp.
For criticism of this view, see Reuning, Erklärung
des Polykarp-Martyriums, 1.

37 Von Campenhausen, Die Idee des Martyriums, 80;
Reuning, Erklärung des Polykarp-Martyriums, 127.

38 On the other hand, the Letter of the martyrs
of Lyons and Vienne understands the converse of
Christ from the eschatological perspective of
Rom 8:18 (Eusebius, Hist. eccl. 5.1.51,56 [see
below, p. 197]).

39 Mart. Pol. 2:3: καὶ τὸ πῦρ ἦν αὐτοῖς ψυχρὸν
τὸ τῶν ἀπανθρώπων βασανιστῶν· πρὸ ὀφθαλμῶν γὰρ
εἶχον φυγεῖν τὸ αἰώνιον καὶ μηδέποτε σβεννύμενον,
καὶ τοῖς τῆς καρδίας ὀφθαλμοῖς ἐνέβλεπον τὰ
τηρούμενα τοῖς ὑπομείνασιν ἀγαθά, ἃ οὔτε οὖς
ἤκουσεν οὔτε ὀφθαλμος εἶδεν οὔτε ἐπι καρδίαν
ἀνθρώπου ἀνέβη, ἐκείνοις δὲ ὑπεδείκνυτο ὑπὸ τοῦ
κυρίου, οἵπερ μηκέτι ἄνθρωποι, ἀλλ' ἤδη ἄγγελοι
ἦσαν.

40 See H. Conzelmann, Der erste Brief an die
Korinther (MeyerK; Göttingen: Vandenhoeck &
Ruprecht, 1969) 81-82. Cf. Isa 64:3; 45:3; Ps
30:20; Prov 2:3-5; Asc. Isa. 11:34; 1QS 11:5ff.;
Gos. Thom. 17; 1 Clem. 34:8; 2 Clem. 11:7; Apost.
Const. 7.32.5. For rabbinic parallels, see
Str-B, 3:327-29.

41 Cf. Origen, in Lev. 9:11: addit post haec
Scriptura: 'et non erit' inquit 'homo, cum
ingredietur pontifex intra velamen interius in
tabernaculo testimonii'. Quomodo 'non erit homo'?
Ego sic accipio quod, qui potuerit sequi Christum
et penetrare cum eo interius tabernaculum et
caelorum excelsa conscendere, iam 'non erit homo,'
sed secundum verbum ipsius erit 'tamquam angelus
Dei' (GCS 29:438-39).

42 For a discussion of the life of the ascetic
as a vita angelica, see P. Nagel, Die Motivierung

der Askese in der alten Kirche und der Ursprung
des Mönchtums (TU 95; Berlin: Akademie, 1966)
34-48. Concerning the martyrs, Tertullian writes
that as victors they receive a brabium angelicae
substantiae (Ad mart. 3:3). Cyprian speaks of
the martyr becoming equal to the angels (angelis
adaequari [Ad Fort. 13]). Cf. also Didaskalia
apost. 19: qui enim ob nomen domini dei
condemnatur, hic martyr sanctus, angelus dei vel
deus in terra a vobis reputetur, spiritualiter
indutus spiritu sancto dei. Concerning Luke 20:36
Tertullian writes: similes enim erunt angelis,
qua non nupturi, quia nec morituri, sed qua
transituri in statum angelicum per indumentum
illud incorruptibilitatis, per substantiae
resuscitatae tamen, demutationem (De resurr. mort.
36:5 [CChr 2:969])'.

Chapter 5

THE LETTER OF THE MARTYRS
OF LYONS AND VIENNE

A large portion of the letter from the
Christians of Lyons and Vienne to their brethren
in Asia and Phrygia has been preserved by Eusebius
in his Historia Ecclesiastica (Hist. eccl. 5.1-2).
Eusebius dates the persecution in Gaul in "the
seventeenth year of the Emperor Antoninus Verus",
that is, in the year 177 A.D. (Hist. eccl. 5.pref.).
There is no reason to doubt this dating or the
authenticity of the letter.[1] While authorship
cannot be proven, the eminent position which
Irenaeus possessed in the Gallic community makes
it a priori probable that he played at least a
participatory role in the writing of the document.
Indeed, Nautin has shown certain verbal similarities between the letter and the writings of
Irenaeus.[2] A degree of scepticism that such
similarities prove authorship may be allowed, but
that there was in fact a close relationship
between the martyrs and Irenaeus is shown by
Eusebius' mention of a letter to the Bishop of
Rome, Eleutherus, in which the martyrs warmly
recommend Irenaeus (Hist. eccl. 5.4.1-2).[3] Close
affinities do exist between our letter and
Irenaeus, and we shall proceed regarding Irenaeus
as a broader context for understanding this
letter.

The programmatic motif for the entire letter
occurs in Eusebius, Hist. eccl. 5.1.5-6. The
events of persecution and martyrdom which occurred
in Lyons were a breaking in of the final eschatological battle between God and Satan.[4] The
tortures, the fury and hate of the mob were fore-
tastes of the Adversary's final assault (Hist.
eccl. 5.1.5).[5] They were the fulfillment of the
prophecy concerning the last days: "Let the
wicked be wicked still and let the righteous
continue to do righteousness" (Hist. eccl. 5.1.58;

187

cf. Rev 22:11). As those under the power and
leadership of Satan, the pagans take on his
characteristics. Since Satan is the "wild Beast"
(Hist. eccl. 5.1.57), the pagans act like beasts
and no longer behave as human beings.[6]

Against Satan stands "the grace of God" which
is represented as an opposing general directing
the operation of his army. This operation is two-
fold: 1) the grace of God saves the weak,[7] and
2) the grace of God arranges in opposition to
Satan "sturdy pillars" who through their endurance
are able to absorb every attack of the Evil One
(Hist. eccl. 5.1.6).[8] The image given is that of
a general sending a military unit to engage the
enemy. By defeating the enemy, victory is
achieved, not only for the conquering army itself,
but also for the populace, including the cowardly,
which did not directly participate in the battle.
The result is that in victory both the soldiers
and those for whom they fought have peace and,
since the enemy has no power to interfere, they
are able to live that life which is proper to
them. This idea is given expression in the concluding lines of the letter:

> In every respect they went to God victorious,
> having always loved peace and always
> commending peace. With peace they went to
> God, leaving behind no pain for the Mother
> nor any strife or conflict for the brethren,
> but rather joy, peace, harmony and love
> (Hist. eccl. 5.2.7).

The martyrs, therefore, despite the special role
they play in time of persecution are not regarded
apart from the good of the Christian community.
This theme is especially clear in those passages
which speak of the martyrs' attitude toward those
who had fallen (Hist. eccl. 5.1.45; 5.2.5-6).[9]

That which takes place in and through the
martyrs is a breaking in of the eschatological
victory of God over Satan. The letter expresses
this in Hist. eccl. 5.1.6b:

> (The martyrs) charged into battle enduring
> every form of abuse and torment. Indeed,
> they hastened to Christ regarding their
> great burden as of no account, showing with-
> out question that the sufferings of the
> present time are not to be compared to the
> glory which shall be revealed to us
> (cf. Rom 8:18).[10]

Brekelmans maintains that in this passage
"glory" has lost its eschatological meaning and
refers simply to the immediate reward given to the
martyrs who as imitators of Christ rush to their
heavenly Lord.[11] However, quite the opposite is
true. This entire letter is, so to speak, a
commentary on Rom 8:18, which is quoted here, and
"glory" must be understood in terms of that
passage. "Glory" is not a reward for a work well
done, but is the final, heavenly state of peace,
joy, and newness won by Christ in his victory over
Satan. It is this "glory" which is the proper and
present inheritance of those who have received the
"Spirit of sonship" and in its power "suffer with
Christ in order that they might also be glorified
with him" (Rom 8:15-17). Through their sufferings
and deaths the martyrs show forth (ἐπιδεικνύμενοι)
the coming glory. For by remaining unbroken in
the midst of persecution, the martyrs show that
there is something greater, more powerful at work
in them, namely, the glory to be revealed, than
the sufferings of this age.[12] As those who resist
and disregard Satan's attacks, the martyrs hasten
to Christ; that is, by not giving in they reach
the goal. Not to be defeated is to gain victory.
This is why martyrdom is a victory.

As a breaking in of the future glory, the
story of the martyr is the work of the victorious
Christ. The martyr gains victory because Christ
is victorious. Because it is Christ's victory
which appears in the martyr, the martyr's victory
is also Christ's victory. This thought is clearly
expressed in <u>Hist</u>. <u>eccl</u>. 5.1.36:

> From this time on the witnesses of their
> deaths were of every variation. For having

woven one crown from many different colors
and all kinds of flowers, they offered it
to the Father. Certainly it was right that
these noble athletes, having sustained
(ὑπομείναντας) a many-faceted struggle and
having conquered (νικήσαντας) in a magnifi-
cent manner, received the great crown of
incorruptibility.

The different deaths of the martyrs are a varied
witness which, as a victory crown woven from
different flowers, is presented to the Father.[13]
Yet, the "noble athletes" themselves, being
victors, receive "the great crown of incorruptibility". In the one act of the martyr's death,
both the Father and the martyr are victors.[14]
This theme recurs in Hist. eccl. 5.1.42 where the
small, weak Blandina, having "put on the great,
invincible athlete Christ", defeats the Adversary
and is "crowned with the crown of incorruptibility".
There are two athletes fighting, Blandina and
Christ, and therefore two victors.

Since the martyr's victory is the victory of
Another, the letter in a variety of ways speaks of
the divine subject whose active presence is
manifested in the steadfastness of the martyr in
suffering and death. This divine subject is
sometimes the Father, sometimes Christ, sometimes
the Spirit. While distinguished as subjects, all
three--Father, Christ, Spirit--partake of the same
work, and therefore they appear as parallel
subjects in all possible combinations.[15] However,
generally it is Christ whom the letter mentions as
the divine agent of victory. It is Christ, "the
faithful and true witness and the first-born of
the dead and the leader of the life of God", who
took up the martyrs in their confession thereby
sealing their witness through death (Hist. eccl.
5.2.5).[16] The death of the martyr is the work
of the victorious Christ. Similarly, according to
Hist. eccl. 5.1.27, many Christians died in prison,
the Lord thereby "showing his glory" (ἐπιδεικνύων
τὴν αὑτοῦ δόξαν).[17] The endurance (ὑπομονή) of
the blessed is the tool of Christ for overcoming

190

the Tyrant (Hist. eccl. 5.1.27). It is Christ who
through the weak Blandina shows that that which is
contemptuous before men is made worthy of great
glory before God (Hist. eccl. 5.1.17). Through
the "grace of Christ" the tortures become healing
for Sanctus (Hist. eccl. 5.1.24). ἡ τέχνη χριστοῦ
accomplishes wonders through those imprisoned
(Hist. eccl. 5.1.32). The confessors exude a
"sweet odor" which shows the presence of Christ
(Hist. eccl. 5.1.35). Christ suffers in the
martyr, performing great works of glory (Hist.
eccl. 5.1.23).

The subject of "glory", therefore, is always
the victorious Christ (or the Father or Spirit).
This will remain clear as long as it is remembered
that it is the future glory which is manifested in
the martyrs. The glory won by the martyr is not
conceived as reward but as the final state of
victory over Satan and death in which the martyr
shall participate but which is present already in
the martyr who endures and conquers the sufferings
of the present age.[18]

The letter speaks of five ways in which the
future glory appeared in the martyrs: 1) confession of the Name of Christ, 2) endurance,
3) triumph over bodily weakness, 4) experiences of
glory, 5) love for the brother. These five are in
no way sharply distinguished but as expressions of
the one glory are mutually related and may even be
strikingly equated.[19] However, if there is one
which serves to provide focus for the other four,
it is confession of the Name Christian.[20] In our
discussion, therefore, we will not directly
discuss this theme, for it will appear in each of
the remaining four.

5.1. Endurance.

The letter repeatedly mentions the martyrs'
"endurance" (ὑπομονή [Hist. eccl. 5.1.6,27,39,45;
5.2.4]; ὑπομένειν [Hist. eccl. 5.1.4,7,16,20,36,
51]). The verb ὑπομένειν invariably means "to
endure" tortures, abuses, struggles. Three times
it is adverbially modified by γενναίως (Hist.

eccl. 5.1.7,20,54). The verb, therefore, appears
to denote the ethical activity of the hero who
endures unjust punishment without bending. In one
instance the noun (ὑπομονή) takes on a similar
nuance. The confessors showed their "nobility"
(εὐγένεια) through their "endurance" (ὑπομονή),
"fearlessness" (ἀφοβία), and "courage" (ἀτρομία)
(Hist. eccl. 5.2.4).

However, ὑπομονή usually appears as a
positive force. The martyrs are able through
their "endurance" to absorb all the attacks of the
Evil One (Hist. eccl. 5.1.6); through the
"endurance" of the saints Christ renders the
tyrant's instruments of torture useless (Hist.
eccl. 5.1.27); the immeasurable mercy of Christ
is shown through the "endurance" of the martyrs
(Hist. eccl. 5.1.45); the "endurance" of the
martyrs must be defeated (Hist. eccl. 5.1.39). In
these instances ὑπομονή is not simply an ethical
virtue which does not bend in suffering (see Hist.
eccl. 5.1.27 where Christ is the subject of the
martyrs' "endurance"). Rather, ὑπομονή is understood as steadfastness in the confession of the
Name of Christian. Of course, in reality this
also means steadfastness under torment but only
because that is, so to speak, the physical form
which steadfastness in confession takes in time of
persecution. Sanctus provides the best example.
The pagans hope that severe and persistent torture
will induce Sanctus to say a blasphemous word.
But Sanctus answers directly none of their questions, responding to each question with the
refrain, "I am a Christian" (Hist. eccl. 5.1.20).[21]
Repeated confession is the real content of Sanctus'
endurance. That this is so is clear from Hist.
eccl. 5.1.39. The maddened pagans torture the
martyrs, "wishing to conquer their endurance, but
from Sanctus they heard nothing other than what he
had said from the beginning, the confession"
(βουλόμενοι νικῆσαι τὴν ἐκείνων ὑπομονήν. καὶ οὐδ'
ὡς παρὰ Σάγκτου ἕτερον τι εἰσήκουσιν παρ' ἣν ἀπ'
ἀρχῆς εἴθιστο λέγειν τῆς ὁμολογίας φωνήν). Likewise, the holy martyrs endure indescribable torments because Satan wishes a blasphemous word to

192

escape their lips (Hist. eccl. 5.1.16). According
to Hist. eccl. 5.1.19 the confession itself was
Blandina's refreshment and rest from, and insensibility to, her tortures (καὶ ἦν αὐτῆς ἀνάληψις καὶ
ἀνάπαυσις καὶ ἀναλγησία τῶν συμβαινόντων τὸ λέγειν
ὅτι χριστιανή εἰμι καὶ παρ᾽ ἡμῖν οὐδὲν φαῦλον
γίνεται). The confession is the very stuff of the
confessor's "endurance". In Hist. eccl. 5.1.45
the "endurance" of the martyrs is the instrument
of Christ's mercy to lead the apostates to renewed
confession. Not the unyielding endurance of
suffering as courageous act but the steadfastness
in confession is the meaning of ὑπομονή in this
passage.[22] Thus, the martyrs have doubts about
the clarity of their confession, not fearing the
torments but fearing that in the presence of an
unclear confession others might fall away (Hist.
eccl. 5.1.12). Confession not only is the content
of the martyrs' "endurance" but serves to
strengthen others to continual confession, that is,
to "endurance".

5.2. Triumph over bodily weakness.

Characteristic of this letter is its repeated
contrast between the power at work in the martyrs
and their physical weakness. The bishop of Lyons,
Pothinus, appears as the epitome of physical
infirmity: he is over ninety years of age; he is
very weak in body; he hardly breathes on account
of his bodily weakness; his body is decimated by
age and illness; hardly breathing, he is returned
to prison where he expires (Hist. eccl. 5.1.29-31).
Yet, against this weakness stands the "eagerness
of the Spirit" (προθυμία πνεύματος) by which
Pothinus is "strengthened" (ἀναρρωννύμενος) and
which appears in the martyr as an intense desire
to give witness (Hist. eccl. 5.1.29).[23] Indeed,
the strengthening which the Spirit gives is the
very maintaining of Pothinus' life so that Christ
might triumph through it.[24] The triumph of Christ
is the confession which Pothinus makes before the
tribunal. Therefore, the activity of the Spirit
reaches its goal in Pothinus' giving "the good

confession" (Hist. eccl. 5.1.30).[25] The desire
of the Spirit is the confession of the martyr.

It is clear that the narrative concerning
Pothinus is modelled on the synoptic passage,
"the Spirit is willing, but the flesh is weak"
(Matt 26:41; Mark 14:38). Irenaeus presents an
interpretation of this passage which precisely
corresponds to the use of Mark 14:38 in our letter.
In fact, the prime examples whom Irenaeus selects
to demonstrate the passage are the martyrs. In a
passage concerning the "life-giving Spirit",
Irenaeus speaks of the "willing Spirit" as a
"prodder" or "stimulus" which makes the weak flesh
do what it desires. The weakness of the flesh is
absorbed by the power of the Spirit, man thereby
becoming no longer sarkic but Spiritual, having
communion with the Spirit. He is then a "living
man". Such are the martyrs who witness and
despise death "not according to the weakness of
the flesh but according to the willingness of the
Spirit" (Adv. haer. 5.9.2).[26]

The holy Blandina is an example for her
earthly mistress that the weakness of the body is
not an insuperable obstacle to boldness in confession (Hist. eccl. 5.1.18). For through
Blandina Christ showed that "those things which
seem cheap, ugly, and contemptuous to men are made
worthy of great glory before God because of love
to Him, which love is shown in power and not
merely vaunted as a show" (Hist. eccl. 5.1.17).[27]
When filled with divine power, the weak physical
constitution of Blandina in no way presents itself
as an obstacle to confession but rather becomes
the very vehicle of defeat for the pagan
torturers: "Blandina was filled with such power
that even those who took turns to torture her in
every way from morning to evening became faint and
exhausted, admitting that they were defeated and
that there was nothing more they could do to her"
(Hist. eccl. 5.1.18).[28] Similarly, the "small,
weak, and insignificant" Blandina, having put on
the "great athlete" Christ, defeats the Adversary
(Hist. eccl. 5.1.42).

<u>Hist. eccl.</u> 5.1.17-19 has a parallel in
Irenaeus, <u>Adv. haer.</u> 5.3.1. Against the Gnostics
Irenaeus adduces Paul's words, "Strength is made
perfect in weakness" (2 Cor 12:9). Irenaeus
argues that man's infirmity allows him to discern
the power of God. For man could not learn that he
is weak and mortal and that God is powerful and
immortal unless man experienced both his own
weakness and God's strength. Irenaeus concludes:
"But the experience of both confers upon man true
knowledge as to God and man and increases his love
towards God. For where an increase of love exists,
there greater glory is wrought by the power of God
for those who love Him."[29]

A third example of the contrast between the
divine power at work in the martyr and the
martyr's physical weakness is the passage concerning Sanctus (<u>Hist. eccl.</u> 5.1.20-24). The body
of Sanctus is witness to the tortures he has
suffered, for it is all one wound and welt and
distorted out of any human shape. Yet, it is in
this body that Christ suffers and thereby accomplishes great deeds of glory (<u>Hist. eccl.</u> 5.1.23).[30]
That Sanctus did not break was a manifestation of
Christ's glory.[31] The presence of this glory was
shown in a most striking fashion. Although so
swollen and inflamed that it could not endure the
touch of a hand, "beyond any glory of man" (παρὰ
πᾶσαν δόξαν ἀνθρώπων)[32] the body of Sanctus is
straightened under further tortures and it again
receives its former appearance. Through the grace
of Christ the second application of tortures had
become healing for Sanctus (<u>Hist. eccl.</u> 5.1.24:
ἀλλ᾽ ἴασιν διὰ τῆς χάριτος τοῦ χριστοῦ τὴν
δευτέραν στρέβλωσιν αὐτῷ γενέσθαι). The healing
of Sanctus showed the presence of the resurrection
glory.[33]

A final example of this motif occurs in
<u>Hist. eccl.</u> 5.1.28. The Christians in prison had
been mishandled so severely that it seemed they
could not survive even if given every medical aid.
Yet, "devoid of all human care", they were
strengthened by the Lord in both body and soul.

195

5.3. Experiences of glory.

The future glory was manifest in the martyrs also in what we may call experiences of glory. The martyrs are insensitive to pain, are healed, have shining countenances, exude a sweet odor, have conversation with Christ. Such elements occur to a greater or lesser degree throughout the literature of martyrdom. They are sometimes understood as special charisms given to the martyr to show the martyr to be a man of the Spirit.[34] But with each occurrence the question must be asked, "What function do these elements play within the total context of the presentation of martyrdom?" This is not always easy, and sometimes impossible, to determine. The letter of the Christians at Lyons and Vienne, however, understands them in the light of Rom 8:18 (Hist. eccl. 5.1.6). The "supernatural" elements are appearances of the future glory. They show the sufferings of this age in defeat.

The future glory is the resurrection glory. Through the mouths of the pagans the letter states that the hope of the resurrection was the reason why the martyrs "despised the torments" and "went with joy to their deaths" (Hist. eccl. 5.1.63).[35] "The hope in those things promised" strengthened the martyrs in prison (Hist. eccl. 5.1.34). "The hope and concentration on those things believed" kept Blandina insensible to pain (Hist. eccl. 5.1.56). Similarly, Blandina's confession was her insensibility to suffering (Hist. eccl. 5.1.19). For Sanctus there is no pain, for Christ's glory is present (μηδὲ ἀλγεινὸν ὅπου χριστοῦ δόξα [Hist. eccl. 5.1.23]). This view that in the coming kingdom there would be no pain or misery was widespread in Jewish literature[36] and exists also within Christian literature. According to Rev 21:4, God will be with His people in the last days, and He "will wipe away every tear from their eyes, death shall be no more, nor shall there be grief, nor mourning, nor pain".[37]

196

The confessors in prison are cheerful. Their countenances reflect glory and great beauty (Hist. eccl. 5.1.35).[38] This glory is the future glory.[39] The chains of the confessors are worn like a "beautiful ornament as though for a bride adorned with golden embroidered tassels" (Hist. eccl. 5.1.35; cf. Ign. Eph. 11:2; Pass. Mont. et Luc. 6:2). The words "as for a bride adorned" (ὡς νύμφῃ κεκοσμημένῃ) remind one of Rev 21:2 where the new, holy city of Jerusalem is adorned as a bride. The imagery is that of the eschatological presence of God. The odor which the martyrs exude is interpreted by the letter itself as the presence of Christ (Hist. eccl. 5.1.35).

Twice the martyrs are said to be speaking to God, or to Christ, during martyrdom (Hist. eccl. 5.1.51,56).[40] Certainly for this letter there is no interest in the ecstatic nature of the speech, and there is no interest in psychologizing this speech.[41] The silence of the martyr is proof of the presence of the future glory. Thus, Irenaeus writes that when man has been renewed and lives in an incorruptible state, never becoming old, there shall be a new heaven and a new earth in which the new man shall remain "ever anew holding converse with God" (Adv. haer. 5.36.1).[42]

Similarly, the healing which Sanctus experiences is a clear instance of the future glory overcoming the sufferings of the present age (Hist. eccl. 5.1.24). The last age of God was conceived by the Jews as a time of healing (cf. Isa 35:5-6).[43] The acts of healing done by Jesus were also understood as acts of the new age (cf. Luke 4:18; Irenaeus, Adv. haer. 5.12.5-6; 5.13.1).

5.4. Love for the brethren.

Finally, the future glory is shown in the martyrs because of the communal dimension of their suffering and death. When Blandina is hung upon a post, she appears in the form of a cross, and through her those suffering with her saw "with their physical eyes him who was crucified for

197

them, so that he might convince those who believe on him that whoever suffers for the glory of Christ has eternal fellowship with the living God" (Hist. eccl. 5.1.41). In the martyr, he who was crucified "for them" (ὁ ὑπὲρ αὐτῶν ἐσταυρωμένος) is present. Christian martyrdom has community-building power, for he who suffered on behalf of others suffers now in the martyr (cf. Hist. eccl. 5.1.23).

The confession and suffering of the martyr has as its aim the defeat and destruction of Satan. Since Satan is the enemy, his defeat means victory not only for the martyr but also for the non-combatant brethren. Either the brethren remain steadfast in their confession because Satan no longer has the power of attack, or the brethren who have fallen confess anew because Satan no longer has the power to hold them prisoner. A good example of the former is the passage Hist. eccl. 5.1.32-35. Here is talk of "a great action of God" (μεγάλη τις οἰκονομία τοῦ θεοῦ), of the appearance of the "immeasurable mercy of Jesus" Hist. eccl. 5.1.32). There follows a long description of the continued deprivation of those who had apostatized. Their denial had gained them nothing. There is also the description of the striking difference between the confessors, who are joyous and beautiful, and the apostates, who are dejected and ugly (Hist. eccl. 5.1.35). However, a careful reading of this passage shows that these things are not the "great act of God" or the mercy of Christ. Rather, the passage finds its zenith in the last sentence: "When the others saw these things, they were strengthened and those who were arrested confessed without hesitation, giving no thought to the Devil's prompting" (Hist. eccl. 5.1.35). The "great act" was the "strengthening" on the one hand and the ready confession of those arrested on the other. What occurred to the confessors in prison was the tool by which Christ effected a faithful steadfastness in the brethren which manifested itself in faithful confession.

Similarly, the victory of the weak Blandina over her tormentors becomes, as it were, Christ's answer to the fear of Blandina's earthly mistress that her weak flesh will prevent her from making a bold confession (Hist. eccl. 5.1.18). Here also the victory of the martyr extends itself to others in the Christian community, enabling them also to overcome their persecutors.

Here we may mention as well the episode concerning Alcibiades (Hist. eccl. 5.3.2-3). Alcibiades, one of the Christians in prison, practiced a strict asceticism, eating only bread and water. After his first round of tortures, another confessor, one Attalus, received a revelation that Alcibiades was not doing good in rejecting God's creation and was giving a bad example to the others. Alcibiades was convinced, changed his ways, and gave thanks to God: "For they were not unvisited by the grace of God, but the Holy Spirit was their advisor" (οὐ γὰρ ἀνεπίσκεπτος χάριτος θεοῦ ἦσαν, ἀλλὰ τὸ πνεῦμα τὸ ἅγιον ἦν σύμβουλον αὐτοῖς [Hist. eccl. 5.3.3]).[44]

However, the communal dimension of the Christian martyr most strikingly appears when the letter speaks of the restoration of fallen brethren through the martyrs.[45] An interval in the proceedings is said to have been not idle and fruitless for the martyrs. Through their perseverance the mercy of Christ was manifested, for through the living that which was dead was brought to life; the martyrs brought grace to those who were not martyrs, and there was great joy to the Virgin Mother when she recovered alive those whom she had aborted as dead. Through the martyrs those who had formerly denied were again conceived and quickened in the womb, and having learned again to confess, they went living and strengthened to their interrogation, since the God who wishes not the death of a sinner but his repentance made it easy (Hist. eccl. 5.1.45-46). Toward the end of the letter we read that the martyrs "humbled themselves under the mighty hand by which they have now been exalted. Then they

gave defense to all but accused no one. They
loosed all but bound none. Indeed, they prayed
for those who had tortured them" (Hist. eccl.
5.2.5). Finally, through the love of the martyrs
the Beast was forced to disgorge alive those whom
he had formerly swallowed: "For they (the martyrs)
did not boast in view of the fallen, but having
motherly love and shedding many tears to the
Father on their behalf, they gave of that which
they had in abundance to those in need. They
besought life and He gave it to them and this they
shared with their neighbor when they went off
completely victorious to God" (Hist. eccl. 5.2.6).

These are the three major passages which
speak of the martyrs' having a role in the
strengthening or the restoration of the brethren.
How are we to understand this role of the martyr?
There is no proof that the martyrs engaged in an
act of penance and forgiveness which in any way
could be compared to later practice.[46] There is
some interest to exhibit the exemplary attitude
of the martyrs toward the fallen--the martyrs
pray for the fallen and their attitude is one of
motherly love (Hist. eccl. 5.2.5-6)--and in this
there may very well be a polemical thrust.[47]

Yet, in view of this "mild" attitude toward
the fallen, to speak of a "mild" penitential
system would be to force a problem on the letter
which is foreign to it. The question of penance
involves the elements of contrition by the sinner,
satisfaction for the sin, forgiveness of the sin,
and the resumption of full Church membership.
There is no hint of any such practice in the
letter. Rather, our letter speaks of denial and
renewed confession. In other words, the letter
speaks not of the Church's office of the keys,
whether mildly or harshly administered, but of
the power which brings the apostate to renewed
confession and therefore to renewed membership in
the Church.[48] In this process the martyr plays
his role.

The martyr prays for the fallen. Yet, the
letter gives no basis for speaking of a special

prerogative of the martyr before God or of a special power of intercession.[49] The martyr's prayer may have been considered efficacious, but, if so, this theme receives no development in this letter. The role of the martyr in the restoration of the fallen lies elsewhere.

The role of the martyr lies in the victory motif of which we have previously spoken. It is as those who go as victors to God that the martyrs share that life with their neighbors which they have received from God (Hist. eccl. 5.2.7). The martyrs waged war on the Beast in order that he might be choked and thus disgorge his prey alive (Hist. eccl. 5.2.6). By defeating Satan, the prince of death, the martyrs receive life and give it to others.[50] But the martyrs defeat Satan through their constant perseverance in suffering (Hist. eccl. 5.1.27,42), that is, through their constant confession of the Name Christian (Hist. eccl. 5.1.19,20,25-26,35,39). Such confession is, however, a sign of the presence of the future glory and therefore a work of the victorious Christ who now works victory in and through the martyrs. Thus, "through their perseverance" and "through the living"--that is, through those who confess the "life-giving Name" (Hist. eccl. 5.1.35) and suffer, showing their communion with the living God (Hist. eccl. 5.1.41)--the apostates come to renewed confession (Hist. eccl. 5.1.45-46). For he who gives the power for the martyr himself to confess is he who suffers in the martyr (Hist. eccl. 5.1.23), is seen in the martyr (Hist. eccl. 5.1.41), and works glories through the martyr (Hist. eccl. 5.1.23). Through the confessing martyr the victorious Christ works confession in the apostate.

The image the letter uses to describe this activity is that of a Mother and the giving of birth. To deny is to be "cast off stillborn" (ἐξετρῶσαι [Hist. eccl. 5.1.11,45]). Those who renew their confession go through the process of birth (ἀνεμετροῦντο καὶ ἀνεκυΐσκοντο καὶ ἀνεζωπυροῦντο [Hist. eccl. 5.1.46]). Alexander

in exhorting to confession is said to be "in birth
pangs" (ὠδίνειν [Hist. eccl. 5.1.49]). Twice the
image of Mother is given to the Church: there is
great joy to "the Virgin Mother" (ἡ πάρθενος
μήτηρ) when she receives back alive those whom she
had cast off as dead (Hist. eccl. 5.1.45); the
martyrs went in peace to God leaving no pain for
the Mother (Hist. eccl. 5.2.7). However, the
image of Mother is also applied to the martyrs
themselves. They are said to have a "motherly
love" (μητρικὰ σπλάγχνα) for the fallen (Hist.
eccl. 5.2.6). Blandina, the last to be martyred,
is as a "noble mother who encourages her children
and sends them triumphant to the King, and then
herself repeating the struggles of her children
hastens to rejoin them" (Hist. eccl. 5.1.55). In
this image of the life-giving Mother the Church
and the martyr are brought into the most intimate
relationship, and in this relationship we reach
the depth of our letter's understanding of the
martyr. Delahaye in his book Ecclesia Mater has
admirably described this relationship:

> Dans ce premier récit, l'image de la femme,
> à la fois vierge et mère, a presque tous
> les traits qui font voir l'Eglise dans sa
> réalité vivante. Comme totalité des croyants
> elle est mère virginale dans sa relation à
> chacun individuellement pris, ses enfants.
> Le croyant est son enfant en tant qu'
> individu, mais en tant que membre de l'Église,
> il est lui-même mère. Par rapport au Christ,
> l'Église, et chaque individu en elle, a les
> traites de l'Épouse. L'Église, dans notre
> récit, est considereé comme l'unité de tous
> les croyants qui vivant et agissant dans la
> puissance de l'Esprit.[51]

> Dan notre récit des martyrs, la Mère Église
> apparaît dès lors dans ses enfants, à savoir
> les martyrs. "Par les martyrs, est-il dit,
> la plupart des apostats . . . furent une
> seconde fois reçus en son sein et ranimés",
> ce qui veut dire que les martyrs et les

confesseurs de la foi, qui sont des enfants
par rapport a l'ensemble de l'Église,
deviennent eux-mêmes la Mère Église par leur
témoignange et les peines qu'ils endurent
pour le salut de leurs frères menacés et
égarés.[52]

The martyr is the Church personified, the Church
in microcosm, and therefore the martyr does the
work of the Church (cf. Hist. eccl. 5.2.7).[53]

Certain passages in Irenaeus help to confirm
this conclusion. While our letter says that
Blandina "strengthened" Ponticus (στηρίζουσα
[Hist. eccl. 5.1.54]) and "sent her children forth
to the King" (προπέμψασα πρὸς τὸν βασιλέα [Hist.
eccl. 5.1.55]), Irenaeus writes that the Church
like the pillar of salt "strengthens and sends
forth her sons to their Father" (firmans et
praemittens filios ad Patrem ipsorum [Adv. haer.
4.31.3]).[54] Sanctus receives the "heavenly spring
of living water" (Hist. eccl. 5.1.22) which,
according to Irenaeus, is received by those who
participate in the Church (Adv. haer. 3.24.1).
Even the return of Blandina's youth in confession
(ἀνανεάζειν [Hist. eccl. 5.1.19]), which has a
certain parallel in 4 Macc 7:13, may be understood in this light. Irenaeus writes that the
Church is renewed and itself made to renew by the
faith deposited in it (Adv. haer. 3.24.1).[55]

There remains to discuss the episode of
Vettius Epagathus where the Spirit appears as the
Paraclete (Hist. eccl. 5.1.9-10). Vettius is
characterized as "full of love toward God and his
neighbor" and as one who, though young, was equal
to old Zacharias in that he "walked blamelessly in
all the commandments and precepts of the Lord and
was ever ready for any service to his neighbor"
(Hist. eccl. 5.1.9). Seeing the injustice being
done to his brethren, he attempted to speak on
their behalf. However, shouted down by the mob,
Vettius was forced to confess himself a Christian
and was taken up into the rank of the martyrs:

> Called the Paraclete of the Christians, he
> had the Paraclete within him, the Spirit of
> Zacharias, which was made manifest through
> the fullness of love. For he consented to
> lay down his own life on behalf of the
> defense of the brethren. For he was and is
> a genuine disciple of Christ, following the
> Lamb wherever he goes (Hist. eccl. 5.1.10).[56]

There are clear reminiscences of Johannine
language in this passage (cf. John 15:13; 1 John
3:16). However, a specific Johannine context may
be intended. Through the figure of Zacharias
the words concerning walking in the commandments
of the Lord, certainly taken from Luke 1:6, are
brought into connection with the figure of the
Paraclete. This reminds one of John 14:15-17
where "holding the commandments" and the sending
of the Paraclete are also combined. Other
similarities between this passage and the Vettius
episode exist. In both loving God and keeping
the commandments are connected (John 14:15; Hist.
eccl. 5.1.9). In both the Paraclete is "in" the
person (John 14:17; Hist. eccl. 5.1.10). The
Paraclete is the "Spirit of truth which the world
is not able to receive, for it does not see or
know the Paraclete" (John 14:17); Vettius, in
whom the Paraclete was, was shouted down by the
crowd and refused speech by the governor (Hist.
eccl. 5.1.10). The false accusations and the
persecution of the Christians is construed as
opposition to the Spirit himself, that is, as the
falling of divine judgment against the heathen.
Lods may be correct in believing that the Vettius
episode is an application of the heavenly court
motif in which διάβολος is the accuser.[57] Hist.
eccl. 5.1.14 does in fact mention Satan as the
prime mover in the false accusations (cf. Hist.
eccl. 5.1.25). By entering the lists on behalf
of his brethren, Vettius as paraclete is
encountering Satan as accuser.

Of interest, however, is the fact that
Vettius' work as paraclete does not only include
his willingness to speak on behalf of the brethren,

which he in fact is not able to do, but includes
as well his confession and his giving of his
life.[58] Through the totality of his action, up
to and including his death, Vettius acts as
paraclete.[59] In this action Satan, the accuser,
is himself accused and condemned. The letter
speaks similarly of Blandina: through her
several contests, she conquered the crooked
serpent "making inevitable his condemnation" (δια
πλειονων γυμνασματων νικησασα τῷ μεν σκολιῷ ὄφει
ἀπαραιτητον ποιηση την καταδικην [Hist. eccl.
5.1.42]). The Paraclete, whose presence in
Vettius is manifested by what Vettius did, is
here conceived as the judging presence of God,
who in exerting His love through the love of the
martyr, that is, the martyr's confession and
suffering, vindicates the Christian believer as
His own and condemns Satan and his followers as
His enemies.[60]

SUMMARY

The letter concerning the martyrs of Lyons
and Vienne presents Christian martyrdom as
confirmation of Rom 8:18: the sufferings of the
present age do not compare to the glory which
will be revealed. That glory is the glory of
Christ who conquered Satan and death and who is
now the resurrected Lord of the Church. The
glory of Christ, which is resurrection glory, is
present in the martyr, and for that reason the
martyr shows himself superior to the sufferings
of the present age.

The glory of Christ's victory, active in the
martyr, exhibits itself in five ways: 1) in
continued or renewed confession of the Name;
2) in the faithful endurance of suffering; 3) in
the overcoming of bodily weakness; 4) in various
experiences of glory--conversation with Christ,
insensibility to pain, healing; 5) in love for
the brethren which results in renewed confession
for apostate brethren and continued confession
for the weak brethren.

As bearers of the Spirit who experience the glory of the resurrected Lord, the martyrs are microcosms, icons of the Church itself. In their faithful confession of the Name even to the end, they show forth the Church for what it is, the locus of Christ's victorious reign over Satan and death.

NOTES OF CHAPTER FIVE

1 P. Nautin doubts the Eusebian dating and has suggested 174/175 (Lettres et écrivains chrétiens des IIe et IIIe siècles [His Patristica 2; Paris: Editions du Cerf, 1961] 62-64). The attempt of J. W. Thompson ("The Alleged Persecution of the Christians at Lyons in 177," AJT 16 [1912] 358-84; 17 [1913] 249-58) to prove the letter a later forgery was never taken seriously (see P. Allard, "Une nouvelle théorie sur le martyre des chrétiens de Lyon," RQH 93 [1913] 53-67; 95 [1914] 83-89). J. Colin has called into question the Gaulic provenance of these martyrdoms and has argued instead for Galatia (L'empire des Antonins et les martyrs gaulois de 177 [Bonn: R. Habelt, 1964]; "Martyrs grecs de Lyon ou martyrs galates? (Eusèbe, Hist. eccl. V.1)," L'antiquité classique 33 [1964] 108-15). This thesis has met strong opposition (see G. Jouassard, "Aux origines de l'église de Lyon," REAug 11 [1965] 1-8; A. Audin, "Les martyrs de 177," Cahiers d'Histoire 11 [1966] 343-67). For a good discussion of the problems presented by this letter, see W. H. C. Frend, Martyrdom and Persecution in the Early Church: A Study of a Conflict from the Maccabees to Donatus (Oxford: Basil Blackwell, 1965) 1-30.

2 Nautin, Lettres et écrivains, 55-59.

3 Mention may also be made of an Irenaean fragment concerning the events in Lyons preserved by Oecumenius (Migne, PG 7.1236).

4 P. Lanaro, "Temi del martiro nell' antichita cristiana. I martiri di Lione," Studia Patavina 14 (1967) 206: "la lettera denuncia un episodio della ostilita gigantesca contro Dio, la quale, divampata in cielo, si allarga fino ad incendiare anche i piccoli uomini. La persecuzione segna uno dei momenti in cui tale conflitto si rende transitoriamente visibile, fino a che esso esplodera in tutto il suo orrore nella catastrofe escatologica."

5 Eusebius, Hist. eccl. 5.1.5: παντὶ γὰρ σθένει
ἐνέσκηψεν ὁ ἀντικείμενος προοιμιαζόμενος ἤδη τὴν
ἀδεῶς μέλλουσαν ἔσεσθαι παρουσίαν αὐτοῦ. Cf.
Irenaeus, Adv. haer. 2.31.3, where the Gnostics
are called praecursores vero draconis eius.

6 The pagans are vicious (ἡ ὠμότης [Hist. eccl.
5.1.57]); wild (ἄγριος [5.1.57]; ἀγριωθῆναι
[5.1.53]); barbarous (βάρβαρος [5.1.57]); beastly
(ἀποθηριωθῆναι [5.1.15]; ἡ ὀργὴ θηρίου [5.1.58]);
mad (ἡ μανία [5.1.57]; ἐκμαίνεσθαι [5.1.39]).
They are no longer human (ἡ ἀπανθρωπία [5.1.37];
διὰ τὸ μὴ ἔχειν ἀνθρώπινον ἐπιλογισμόν [5.1.58]).
Cf. Lanaro, "I martiri di Lione," 212-27.

7 Who "the weak" are is never clearly defined.
Certainly included are those who apostatized
(Hist. eccl. 5.1.11). Probably to be included
are also those members of the Christian community
who in any way are strengthened or maintained in
their confession (Hist. eccl. 5.1.9,18,28,35,41).
Perhaps even the martyrs are to be included among
"the weak". Triumph despite bodily weakness is
an oft-recurring theme (Hist. eccl. 5.1.18,21-24,
28,29-31,42).

8 Eusebius, Hist. eccl. 5.1.6: ἀντεστρατήγει δὲ
ἡ χάρις τοῦ θεοῦ καὶ τοὺς μὲν ἀσθενεῖς ἐρρύετο,
ἀντιπαρέτασσε δὲ στύλους ἑδραίους δυναμένους διὰ
τῆς ὑπομονῆς πᾶσαν τὴν ὁρμὴν τοῦ πονηροῦ εἰς
ἑαυτοὺς ἑλκύσαι.

9 See below, pp. 199-203.

10 Eusebius, Hist. eccl. 5.1.6b: οἳ καὶ ὁμόσε
ἐχώρουν αὐτῷ πᾶν εἶδος ὀνειδισμοῦ καὶ κολάσεως
ἀνεχόμενοι· οἳ καὶ τὰ πολλὰ ὀλίγα ἡγούμενοι
ἔσπευδον πρὸς χριστόν, ὄντως ἐπιδεικνύμενοι ὅτι
οὐκ ἄξια τὸ παθήματα τοῦ νῦν καιροῦ πρὸς τὴν
μέλλουσαν δόξαν ἀποκαλυφθῆναι εἰς ἡμᾶς.

11 A. Brekelmans, Martyrerkranz: Eine symbolgeschichtliche Untersuchung im frühchristlichen
Schrifttum (AnGreg 150; Rome: Libreria Editrice

dell' Universita Gregoriana, 1965) 59: "Die--
sonst eschatologische--Glorie gilt hier als
sofortige Belohnung der Martyrer, denn als
Nachahmer Christi eilen sie zu ihrem himmlischen
Herrn."

12 Brekelmans correctly sees this in regard to
Hist. eccl. 5.1.23,27,35,41,48 (Martyrerkranz, 59).

13 It presents no problem that here the Father
and not Christ is mentioned. The letter often
refers to both as complementary subjects. In
Hist. eccl. 5.1.23 πατρὸς ἀγάπη is parallel to
χριστοῦ δόξα, and in Hist. eccl. 5.1.32 no
distinction is to be discerned between μεγάλη τις
οἰκονομία θεοῦ and ἔλεος ἀμέτρητον Ἰησοῦ.

14 To my knowledge this is the first occurrence
of the motif of martyrs presenting a crown to the
divinity. Cf. Cyprian, Ep. 10:4: (Dominus) . . .
ipse in certamine agonis nostri et coronat et
coronatur (CSEL 3/2.494). The theme of the martyr
presenting his victory crown to Christ occurs
early in Christian iconography, along with the
more common motif of Christ crowning the martyr.
Both motifs, of the divinity crowning and being
crowned, were common in imperial Roman art (cf.
A. Grabar, Martyrium: Recherches sur le culte
des reliques et l'art chrétien antique, 2 vols.
[Paris: Collège de France, 1946], 2:55-58).

15 The Father is parallel to Christ: πατρὸς
ἀγάπη is parallel to χριστοῦ δόξα (Hist. eccl.
5.1.23); μεγάλη τις οἰκονομία θεοῦ is parallel
to ἔλεος ἀμέτρητον Ἰησοῦ (Hist. eccl. 5.1.32);
the confession of those who once denied is seen
as the work of both Christ (τὸ ἀμέτρητον ἔλεος
χριστοῦ [Hist. eccl. 5.1.45]) and God
(ἐγγλυκαίνοντος . . . θεοῦ [Hist. eccl. 5.1.46]);
while it is to God that Alexander speaks at his
martyrdom (Hist. eccl. 5.1.51), Blandina speaks
to Christ (Hist. eccl. 5.1.56). Christ and the
Spirit are parallel: Vettius Epagathus, following
the Lamb wherever he goes, gave his own life,

thereby showing the presence of the Paraclete
(Hist. eccl. 5.1.10); Christ and the Spirit are
connected in the image of "the heavenly spring of
the water of life flowing from the side of Christ"
which keeps Sanctus firm in his confession (Hist.
eccl. 5.1.22). The heavenly spring of water is
the Spirit (cf. John 7:38-39; Irenaeus, Adv.
haer. 5.18.3; cf. H. Rahner, "Flumina de ventre
Christi: Die patristische Auslegung von Joh.
7.37,38," Biblica 22 [1941] 374-77); while the
Christians in prison are strengthened
(ἀναρρωννύμενοι) by the Lord (Hist. eccl. 5.1.28),
Pothinus is strengthened (ἀναρρωννύμενος) by the
Spirit (Hist. eccl. 5.1.29). Finally, the Father
and the Spirit stand closely allied: the
"fatherly Spirit" (τὸ πνεῦμα τὸ πατρικόν) supports
the confessors in prison (Hist. eccl. 5.1.34).
The assertion of von Campenhausen that the Spirit
plays no role during these martyrdoms is hard to
credit (Die Idee des Martyriums in der alten
Kirche, 2nd ed. [Göttingen: Vandenhoeck & Ruprecht,
1964] 90 n. 3).

16 The configuration of titles for Christ was
inspired, no doubt, by Rev 1:5 (cf. Rev 3:15;
Col 1:18). Cf. Irenaeus, Adv. haer. 4.24.1:
primogenitum mortuorum et principem vitae Dei.

17 The glory is the glory which Christ has
already won and which is now shown in the martyrs'
deaths. The same theme occurs in Acta Carpi 39;
42. Carpus and Agathonike see the glory of the
Lord. Usually this is interpreted as a heavenly
vision given to the two martyrs just before their
deaths. However, Carpus saw "the glory of the
Lord" when he witnessed the martyrdom of Papylus,
and Agathonike saw "the glory of the Lord" in
witnessing the death of Carpus (see above, p. 42).

18 Having defeated the Prince of death by his
death, the martyr lives unhindered by Satan. Life
and death by their nature exclude one another.
Cf. Irenaeus, Adv. haer. 3.23.7: victus autem
erat Adam, ablata ab eo omni vita; et propter

hoc victo rursus inimico recepit vitam Adam;
novissima autem inimica evacuatur mors, quae
primum possederat hominem.

19 For example, Blandina's confession is her
refreshment, rest and insensibility to her
sufferings (Hist. eccl. 5.1.19); the Name is
all-honorable, glorious, and life-giving (Hist.
eccl. 5.1.35).

20 "To confess" (ὁμολογεῖν), "to deny" (ἀρνεῖσθαι)
and their cognates appear no less than twenty-six
times in connection with the confession or denial
of the Name Christian: ὁμολογεῖν (10x), ὁμολογία
(8x), ὁμόλογοι (1x), ἀρνεῖσθαι (5x), ἐξάρνησις (1),
ἔξαρνοι (1x).

21 The words ὑπὲρ πάντα ἄνθρωπον 'beyond any
human resource' (Hist. eccl. 5.1.20) imply the
presence of divine power.

22 Those who have ὑπομονή are also οἱ ζῶντες
(Hist. eccl. 5.1.45), for the Name "Christian" is
life-giving (ζωοποιός [Hist. eccl. 5.1.35]).

23 Eusebius, Hist. eccl. 5.1.29: ὑπο δὲ
προθυμίας πνεύματος ἀναρρωννύμενος διὰ τὴν
ἐγκειμένην τῆς μαρτυρίας ἐπιθυμίαν. In Hist. eccl.
5.1.28 "strengthening" (ἀναρρωννύμενος) and
"giving power" (ἐνδυναμούμενος) are activities of
the Lord. Therefore, here πνεῦμα must be the
Holy Spirit, not the spirit of Pothinus.

24 Eusebius, Hist. eccl. 5.1.29: τηρουμένης δὲ
τῆς ψυχῆς ἐν αὐτῷ ἵνα δι᾽ αὐτῆς χριστὸς θριαμβεύσῃ.
H. Musurillo translates: "he still held on to
life that Christ might triumph in him" (The Acts
of the Christian Martyrs [OECT; Oxford: Clarendon,
1972] 71). However, τηρούμενος is better translated, "he was kept alive", thereby retaining
implicitly the divine subject which stands in the
background of this entire narrative.

25 μαρτυρία means the verbal confession of
allegiance to the Christian faith both in Hist.
eccl. 5.1.29 (see n. 23) and in Hist. eccl. 5.1.30.
Musurillo satisfactorily renders with "witness" in
Hist. eccl. 5.1.30, but wrongly translates with
"martyrdom" in Hist. eccl. 5.1.29 (Acts, 71).

26 Irenaeus, Adv. haer. 5.9.2: Sicut enim caro
infirma, sic spiritus promptus a Domino testimonium
accepit. Hic est potens perficere quaecunque in
promptu habet. Si igitur hoc, quod est promptum
Spiritus, admisceat aliquis velut stimulum
infirmitati carnis, necesse est omnimodo, ut id
quod est forte, superet infirmum, ita ut
absorbeatur infirmitas carnis a fortitudine
Spiritus; et esse eum qui sit talis, non iam
carnalem, sed spiritualem, propter Spiritus
communionem. Sic igitur martyres testantur et
contemnunt mortem, non secundum infirmitatem
carnis, sed secundum quod promptum est Spiritus.
Infirmitas enim carnis absorpta, potentem ostendit
Spiritum; Spiritus autem rursus absorbens
infirmitatem, hereditate possedit carnem in se;
et ex utrisque factus est vivens homo; vivens
quidem propter participationem Spiritus, homo
autem propter substantiam carnis (Stieren,
2:737-38; Migne, PG 7:1144-45). Cf. also Irenaeus,
Adv. haer. 5.3.1.

27 Eusebius, Hist. eccl. 5.1.17: δι' ἧς
ἐπέδειξεν ὁ χριστὸς ὅτι τὰ παρὰ ἀνθρώποις εὐτελῆ
καὶ ἀειδῆ καὶ εὐκαταφρόνητα φαινόμενα μεγάλης
καταξιοῦται παρὰ θεῷ δόξης, διὰ τὴν πρὸς αὐτὸν
ἀγάπην τὴν ἐν δυνάμει δεικνυμένη καὶ μὴ ἐν εἴδει
καυχωμένην.

28 Eusebius, Hist. eccl. 5.1.18: ἡ βλανδίνα
τοσαύτης ἐπληρώθη δυνάμεως ὥστε ἐκλυθῆναι καὶ
παρεθῆναι τοὺς . . . βασανίζοντας αὐτήν . . .
ὁμολογοῦντας ὅτι νενίκηνται. This passage shows
very nicely the eschatological perspective.
Mention of great power filling Blandina does not
lead to statements of the martyr's strength and
courage but to a statement of the enemy's defeat.

The letter's interest is in victory and defeat, not in the glorification of the martyr.

29 Irenaeus, Adv. haer. 5.3.1: Utrorumque autem experientia vera, quae est de Deo et homine, agnitionem indidit ei et auxit eius erga Deum dilectionem. Ubi autem augmentum est dilectionis, ibi maior gloria Dei virtute perficitur his qui diligunt eum (Stieren, 2:721; PG 7:1129).

30 Eusebius, Hist. eccl. 5.1.23: τὸ δὲ σωμάτιον μάρτυς ἦν τῶν συμβεβηκότων ὅλον τραῦμα καὶ μώλωψ καὶ συνεσπασμένον καὶ ἀποβεβληκὸς τὴν ἀνθρώπειον ἔξωθεν μορφήν, ἐν ᾧ πάσχων χριστὸς μεγάλας ἐπετέλει δόξας.

31 Grabar speaks of the theophany character of the martyr (Martyrium, 2:74): "Ainsi, de même que la passion du Christ est une manifestation de la gloire divine, donc une théophanie, de même les derniers épisodes de l'histoire de chaque martyr sont des manifestations du Saint-Esprit descendu sur eux et que les a rendus insensibles à la souffrance et indifférents à la mort."

32 Musurillo translates: "to the men's complete amazement" (Acts, 69). Similarly, Rufinus, the Latin translator of Eusebius: quod vix credi ab infidelibus potest. However, the δόξα of men is here contrasted with the δόξα χριστοῦ (Hist. eccl. 5.1.23). What happens to Sanctus is beyond any human act of power. Cf. Ad Diog. 7:9: ταῦτα ἀνθρώπου οὐ δοκεῖ τὰ ἔργα ταῦτα δύναμις ἐστι θεοῦ ταῦτα τῆς παρουσίας αὐτοῦ δείγματα.

33 See below, p. 197.

34 See M. Lods, Confesseurs et martyrs: Successeurs des prophètes dans l'eglise des trois premiers siècles (Cahiers Théologiques 41; Neuchâtel: Delachaux et Niestlè, 1958) 28-33.

35 Similarly, Tertullian states that the Christians' contempt for death is based on their

belief in the resurrection of the dead (Ad nat.
1.19.2).

36   Cf. Isa 30:19; 35:10; 51:11; 60:20; 65:19;
1 Enoch 5:7-9; 10:17; 25:6; 96:3;   Jub. 23:29-30;
Syr. Apoc. Bar. 73:1-74:1.   Cf. Str-B, 3:253-54;
4/2:810,892,965-66.

37   Irenaeus quotes Rev 21:1-4 to describe the
coming Kingdom (Adv. haer. 5.35.2).

38   Cf. Acts 6:15 (see above, pp. 38-40);   Mart.
Pol. 12:1;   Pass. Mont. et Luc. 4:2;   Pass. Mar.
et Jac. 8:4; 9:2.   According to Pass. Mar. et Jac.
9:2, one of the brethren had a shining countenance
quod iam per gratiam proxime passionis Christus in
eius ore et facie relucebat.   Christ, the victor
over death, shines on the martyr's face, for in
his coming death the martyr will be victor.

39   On the day of the Messiah the faces of the
righteous will shine (see Str-B, 4/2:887,891,941-42
1138-39.   Contrary to the confessors, those who
had denied their faith are "downcast, dejected,
ugly and devoid of all beauty" (Hist. eccl. 5.1.35).
A similar contrast appears in the Samaritan work,
Memar Marqah: on the Day of Vengeance, a light
will shine on the righteous, while the faces of
the evil will appear emaciated and it will be said
to them, "Why are your faces expressive of
affliction today?" (4:12).

40   Eusebius, Hist. eccl. 5.1.51: τοῦ μὲν
Ἀλεξάνδρου μήτε στενάξαντος μήτε γρύξαντός τι
ὅλως, ἀλλὰ κατὰ καρδίαν ὁμιλοῦντος τῷ θεῷ; Hist.
eccl. 5.1.56: καὶ ὁμιλίαν πρὸς χριστόν.   Cf. Mart.
Isa. 5:14 (see above, p. 10);   Mart. Pol. 2:2
(see above, p. 173).

41   Against Lods, Confesseurs et martyrs, 29:
"Nous comprenons aisément que les pressions
exerceés sur les confesseurs, c'est-à-dire les
tortures physiques qu'ils subissent, la crainte
continuelle dans laquelle ils vivent, comme aussi

l'exaltation que fait naître en eux la perspective de la gloire céleste, sont des éléments favorables à l'eclosion de phénomenes comme l'extase prophétique."

42 Irenaeus, Adv. haer. 5.36.1: praetereunte autem figura hac, et renovato homine, et vigente ad incorruptelam, ut non possit iam veterescere, erit caelum novum et terra nova, in quibus novus perseverabit homo, semper nova confabulans Deo (Stieren, 2:817; PG 7:1222). When he transgressed God's commandment, Adam became indignus venire in conspectum et colloquium Dei (Irenaeus, Adv. haer. 3.23.5 [Stieren, 2:549; PG 7:963]). Josephus used ὁμολία to express the communion between God and Adam in paradise (Ant. 1.45).

43 See Str-B, 4/2:888,945-46.

44 According to K. Holl, the idea of merit appears in this episode: "Jetzt gilt die Offenbarung als eine besondere Stufe der Begnadigung, zu der auch der Märtyrer nur emporgelangt, nachdem er sich vorher durch eine Leistung, durch ein erstes Bekenntnis vor der Obrigkeit oder durch einen Kampf ein Anrecht darauf erworben hat" ("Die Vorstellung vom Märtyrer und die Märtyrerakte in ihrer geschichtlichen Entwicklung," Gesammelte Aufsätze zur Kirchengeschichte, vol. 2: Der Osten [Tübingen: J. C. B. Mohr, 1928] 74). This goes far beyond the evidence. The phrase μετὰ τὸν πρῶτον ἀγῶνα (Hist. eccl. 5.3.2) ought not be pressed in this way. It is a mere chronological detail without particular theological importance.

45 The episode concerning Biblis forms an exception to this theme. Having once denied, she is again put on the rack in order that she might continue her slanders against the Christians. However, during the torture she awakens as from a deep sleep, reminded by the torture of the eternal punishment in Gehenna, and she begins to confess that she is a Christian (Hist. eccl.

5.1.25-26). Here the confessing martyr plays no role in the restoration of Biblis.

46 Against J. Hoh, who speaks of a "sofortiges 'Lösen'" on the part of "geistbegabten Märtyrern" (Die kirchlichen Busse im II Jahrhundert: eine Untersuchung der patristischen Busszeugnisse von Clemens Romanus bis Clemens Alexandrinus [Breslau: Müller & Seiffert, 1932]); and Lods, who speaks of the "right" or "privilege" (droit) of the confessors to forgive sin or bind sin (Confesseurs et martyrs, 67, 69-70).

47 Nautin believes that the letter intends to combat certain persons in Asia who represent a penitential rigorism and encratism (Lettres et écrivains, 33-36).

48 The phrase τῇ ἐκκλησίᾳ προσετέθησαν (Hist. eccl. 5.1.49) corresponds to ἀποπεσεῖν (Hist. eccl. 5.1.12) and to ἔμειναν δὲ ἔξω (Hist. eccl. 5.1.48). To deny the Name Christian is to show that one is outside the Church, for the Church is the community of those who confess.

49 Against B. Poschmann, who speaks of a "besondern Einfluss bei Gott"; "Als die bewährten Freunde Gottes vermitteln sie durch ihre Fürsprache dem Sünder Vergebung bei Gott" (Paenitentia secunda: Die kirchliche Busse im ältesten Christentum bis Cyprian und Origenes. Eine dogmengeschichtliche Untersuchung [Theophaneia 1; Bonn: Hanstein, 1940] 272). Hoh makes a stronger statement: "Sie verfügen offenbar als Märtyrer über eine besondere Fürbittmacht, ein besonderes Gnadenrecht bei Gott" (Die Busse, 102).

50 This is Irenaean thinking: victus autem erat Adam, ablata ab eo omni vita; et propter hoc victo rursus inimico recepit vitam Adam; novissima autem inimica evacuatur mors, quae primum possederat hominem (Adv. haer. 3.23.7 [Stieren, 2:551; PG 7:964]).

51 K. Delahaye, Ecclesia mater chez les pères des
trois premiers siècles: pour un renouvellement
de la Pastorale d'aujourd'hui (Unam Sanctam 46;
Paris: Editions du Cerf, 1964) 84. Also, Ecclesia
mater, 187: "Dans ce récit, la Mère ne vit plus
simplement avec ses enfants ou en face de ses
enfants. Le fait d'être enfant et le fait d'etre
mère à l'intérieur de l'ensemble de l'Eglise ne
sont plus attribués à deux personnes differentes,
mais les enfants de l'Église en tant que membres
de l'ensemble sont en même temps 'mere'; la Mère
vit dans ses enfants."

52 Delahaye, Ecclesia mater, 187. The Church
remains in and through her children "une mère qui
enfante sans cesse et transmet ainsi le salut.
L'Église est en ses enfants mater semper in partu".

53 Herein lies the true Spirit-possession of the
martyr. Cf. Irenaeus, Adv. haer. 3.24.1: hoc
enim ecclesiae creditum est Dei munus, quemadmodum
ad inspirationem plasmationi, ad hoc ut omnia
membra percipientia vivificentur; et in eo
deposita est communicatio Christi, id est Spiritus
sanctus, arrha incorruptelae et confirmatio fidei
nostrae et scala ascensionis ad Deum. . . . Ubi
enim ecclesia, ibi est Spiritus Dei; et ubi
Spiritus Dei, illic ecclesia et omnis gratia
(Stieren, 2:552-53; PG 7:966).

54 Cf. Irenaeus, Adv. haer. 4.33.9: quapropter
ecclesia omni in loco ob eam, quam habet erga
Deum dilectionem, multitudinem martyrum in omni
termpore praemittit ad Patrem (Stieren, 2:671;
PG 7:1078).

55 Irenaeus, Adv. haer. 3.24.1: Quam (the faith)
perceptam ab ecclesia custodimus, et quae semper
a Spiritu Dei, quasi in vaso bono eximium quoddam,
depositum iuvenescens, et iuvenescere faciens
ipsum vas in quo est (Stieren, 2:552; PG 7:966).
4 Macc 7:13-14 reads: (Eleazar) γέρων ὢν
λελυμένων μὲν ἤδη τῶν τοῦ σώματος τόνων,
περικεχαλασμένων δὲ τῶν σαρκῶν, κεκμηκότων δὲ καὶ
τῶν νεύρων ἀνενέασεν τῷ πνεύματι διὰ τοῦ λογισμοῦ.

Some scholars see in our letter great dependence
on the Maccabean literature. So Frend writes
that "it would be difficult to deny that the
writer of the Lyons letter was saturated in
Maccabean literature" (Martyrdom and Persecution,
20). Beyond mentioning similarities of ideas,
style, and vocabulary, Frend identifies Blandina
with the mother of the seven brothers (4 Macc
16:12-13; 2 Macc 7:20-23; Hist. eccl. 5.1.55),
parallels Pothinus with Eleazar (4 Macc 5:4-6:35;
2 Macc 6:18-31; Hist. eccl. 5.1.29-31), and
suggests that Vettius may be modelled on Razis
(2 Macc 14:37-46). O. Perler lists the verbal
similarities and tentively suggests that the
mention of nine martyrs in the Lyons letter may be
directly patterned after the Maccabean literature:
Pothinus would correspond to Eleazar, Blandina
to the mother, and the remaining seven to the
seven brothers ("Das vierte Makkabaeerbuch,
Ignatius von Antiochien und die Aeltesten
Martyrerberichte," RArchCr 25 [1949] 67-69). No
one can deny that similarities of style and
vocabulary do exist between our letter and the
literature of the Maccabees. Language of the
contest and the athlete is common to both, and
both render vivid descriptions of the tortures.
Yet, one must question the reality of some of
these alleged parallels. The fact that bishop
Pothinus was an old man hardly is cause to see a
literary dependence on the story of Eleazar. In
this context we must also say a word about
Blandina as the noble mother who encourages her
children and sends them on to the King (Hist.
eccl. 5.1.55). It is true that the Maccabean
mother "encourages" (προτρεπεῖσθαι) her sons
(4 Macc 16:13) just as Blandina "encourages"
Ponticus (Hist. eccl. 5.1.54). Also, the words
καὶ εἰς ἀθανασίαν ἀνατίκτουσα τὸν τῶν υἱῶν ἀριθμόν
(4 Macc 16:13) do remind one of the image of
giving birth (Hist. eccl. 5.1.11,54-55,49). But
precisely this last shows the questionability of
seeing in Blandina a conscious parallel to the
Maccabean mother. Not only Blandina but all the
martyrs perform the function of mother. Similarly,

218

as Blandina "encourages" (παρορμῆσαι) Ponticus
and her children (Hist. eccl. 5.1.54-55), so other
martyrs are said to have "encouraged" their
brothers (Hist. eccl. 5.1.28). All the martyrs
perform the activities that Blandina performs.
Blandina and the other martyrs are living images
of the Church. In support of this view, we add
one more passage from Irenaeus in addition to
those given above. That Blandina herself
duplicated all the agonies of her children
(ἀναμετρουμένη καὶ αὐτὴ πάντα τὰ τῶν παίδων
ἀγωνίσματα [Hist. eccl. 5.1.55]), while having no
parallel in the Maccabean story, does correspond
to Irenaeus' assertion that the Church endures
the opprobrium of those who suffer for righteousness sake and on account of their love toward God
and the confession of His Son (Adv. haer. 4.33.9:
opprobrium enim eorum qui persecutionem patiuntur
propter iustitiam et omnes poenas sustinent et
mortificantur propter eam quae est erga Deum
dilectionem et confessionem Filii eius, sola
Ecclesia pure sustinet [Stieren, 2:671; PG
7:1078]).

56 Eusebius, Hist. eccl. 5.1.10: παράκλητος
χριστιανῶν χρηματίσας, ἔχων δὲ τὸν παράκλητον
ἐν ἑαυτῷ, τὸ πνεῦμα τοῦ Ζαχαρίου, ὃ διὰ τοῦ
πληρώματος τῆς ἀγάπης ἐνεδείξατο, εὐδοκήσας ὑπὲρ
τῆς τῶν ἀδελφῶν ἀπολογίας καὶ τὴν ἑαυτοῦ θεῖναι
ψυχήν· ἣν γὰρ καὶ ἔστι γνήσιος χριστοῦ μαθητής,
ἀκολουθῶν τῷ ἀρνίῳ ὅπου ἂν ὑπάγῃ. Concerning the
mention of Zacharias, see H. von Campenhausen,
"Das Martyrium des Zacharias: Seine früheste
Bezeugung im zweiten Jahrhundert," Aus der Frühzeit
des Christentums. Studien zur Kirchengeschichte
des ersten und zweiten Jahrhunderts (Tübingen:
J. C. B. Mohr, 1963) 302-7. In his translation
Rufinus identifies the Paraclete as Jesus rather
than as the Spirit: ille vero habens in se
advocatum pro nobis Iesum (cf. 1 John 2:1).
Perhaps Rufinus was engaging in anti-Montanist
revision. However, the Paraclete's mention here
in no way is proof of Montanism in Lyons (cf.
Frend, Martyrdom and Persecution, 16-17). For

discussion of this question, see P. de Labriolle,
La crise montaniste (Paris: E. Leroux, 1913) 220ff;
U. Kahrstedt, "Die Märtyrerakte von Lugdunum 177,"
RheinMus n.s. 68 (1913) 398-99; E. Griffe, La
Gaule chrétienne a l'époque romaine, vol. 1: Des
origines chrétienne a la fin du IVe siècle (Paris:
Letouzey et Ané, 1964) 56-57; G. Bardy,
"Montanisme," DTC 10/2 (1929) 2360-61.

57 Lods, Confesseurs et martyrs, 49-50.

58 Confession of the Name and defense of the
Christians' innocence of evil doing are related
also in Hist. eccl. 5.1.19,26,52.

59 Elias Bickerman argues that παράκλητος
χριστιανῶν χρηματίσας does not mean "he was called
the Christians' paraclete" but that by his act
Vettius did style himself "comforter" ("The Name
of Christian," HTR 42 [1949] 113 n. 27).

60 Speaking against Holl, von Campenhausen writes
of the Lyons letter: "hier spielt der Geist
während des Martyriums keine Rolle (er gehört
schon längst vorher zu den Märtyrern: Eus. H.E.
V.1.10)" (Die Idee des Martyriums, 90 n.3). Such
a view supposes that martyrdom is in some way
qualitatively distinct from the rest of the
Christian life. Our presentation shows this to be
far from the view of the Lyons letter. Indeed,
rather than being "special", martyrdom is
conceived as an expression of the life of the
Church. For the same reason Brekelmans is in
error when he distinguishes between the
"Auferstehungsherrlichkeit" and the "jetzige
Martyrerglorie": "Mit dieser Doxa kann nicht die
Auferstehungsherrlichkeit gemeint sein. Da die
Martyrer schon in grosser Herrlichkeit sind,
handelt es sich hier um die jetzige Martyrerglorie"
(Martyrerkranz, 59). The glory which is shown in
the martyrs is nothing other than the future
glory, in which all those who confess participate.
Therefore, the letter can say that the "confessors"
(ὁμόλογοι) showed the power of martyrdom in deed

(καὶ τὴν μὲν δύναμιν τῆς μαρτυρίας ἔργῳ
ἐπεδείκνυντο [Hist. eccl. 5.2.4]) even as the
"martyrs" (μάρτυρες) themselves did.

Chapter 6

PASSION OF PERPETUA AND FELICITAS

In early 202 or 203 the city of Carthage witnessed the martyrdoms of six young Christians, four men and two women, who were victims of the Severan edict of 202 prohibiting conversion to Judaism or to Christianity. The Passio Perpetuae et Felicitatis recounts the sufferings of these martyrs and contains as well the autographical accounts of two of the martyrs, Perpetua and Saturus, of experiences and of visions granted to them while in prison (Pass. Perp. 3-10; 11-13).[1] The Passio itself is of very early date, being virtually contemporary with the events it narrates.[2] The evident literary and religio-historical importance of the Passio for an under-standing of the Christian community of North Africa in the early third century has made the Passio the object of considerable interest. A Latin and a Greek text, both of an early date, are extant. The question of priority continues to elicit special study, but there is a strong scholarly consensus in favor of the priority of the Latin text.[3]

1.

Tertullian's Relationship to the Passion of Perpetua

Of importance for our study is the much-debated question of Tertullian's relationship with the Passio. Is Tertullian the author or the redactor of the narrative portions of the Passio (Pass. Perp. 1-2; 14-21), or is he not? The question is of importance. For if Tertullian were the author of these passages, some insight would be gained into Tertullian's mind at that period of time when Montanism was beginning to exert an ever-increasing influence upon him.[4] On the basis

of verbal and stylistic similarities between
Tertullian and the Passio and certain correspondences of thought, a goodly number of scholars
have affirmed Tertullian's authorship of the
prologue and epilogue portions of the Passio.[5]
However, considerable reservation is in order.
Literary resemblances of themselves cannot con-
stitute proof. Tertullian and the redactor of
the Passio may both have drawn on a common verbal
environment, or the redactor, under the literary
influence of Tertullian, may have been imitating,
consciously or unconsciously, Tertullian's style
and terminology. Furthermore, one does not sense
in the redactor of the Passio the passion and the
intensity, the rhetorical flourish and the fiery
temper, which so characterize Tertullian's
writings.[6] A serious argument against Tertullian
as the redactor is the one explicit mention
Tertullian makes of the Carthaginian martyrs.
Arguing that only martyrs reach paradise before
the second coming of Christ, Tertullian writes
that Perpetua had a vision of paradise in which
she saw only martyrs (De anima 55:4).[7] However,
in none of Perpetua's visions is there mention of
martyrs in paradise.[8] Tertullian has confused a
vision of Saturus for one of Perpetua. Writing of
his vision Saturus recounts that in paradise he
saw both martyrs and many brothers (et coepimus
illic multos fratres cognoscere sed et martyras
[Pass. Perp. 13:8]). Hence, Tertullian not only
confused visions but misrepresented the vision as
well. It is not probable that the redactor of
the Passio would have made such an error.

While conceptual correspondences commonly
adduced in support of Tertullian as the redactor
of the Passio often rest on common hagiographical
accents, at least in one regard the narratives of
the Passio and Tertullian exhibit a distinct
difference of attitude and disposition. In both
his pre-Montanist and Montanist writings Tertullian
remarks of the encumbrances of married life as
opposed to the freedom of virginity and widowhood.
This theme appeared already in his pre-Christian

work, Liber ad amicum philosophum (see Jerome,
Ep. 22:22). In his pre-Montanist work, Ad uxorem,
Tertullian speaks of "the most bitter delight of
children" and then on the basis of Matt 24:19
speaks of the encumbrance of children in the
light of "imminent distresses". Widows, says
Tertullian, will have no such encumbrances but
"will bear freely any pressure and persecution,
there being no burden of marriage tossing in the
womb or on the bosom" (Ad uxorem 1.5.1-3).[9]
Tertullian sarcastically expresses the same
thought in In exhortatione castitatis 12:5 and in
De monogamia 16:5. Such a view, characteristic
of Tertullian throughout his Christian life, is
not that of the redactor of the Passio, who chose
to devote a full episode of his narrative to
Felicitas' giving of birth in prison (Pass. Perp.
15). There is no hint that Felicitas' pregnancy
is an encumbrance which impinges upon her pre-
paredness for or steadfastness in persecution.
Merely the timing of her pregnancy is inopportune.

At most the redactor of the Passio may be
said to reflect the general religious atmosphere
shared, and no doubt influenced by Tertullian.
But proof that Tertullian was the redactor of
the Passio has not been forthcoming. Indeed, the
evidence argues against Tertullian as the redactor
of the Passio.[10]

2.

Passion of Perpetua and Montanism

It is essential to our task that we answer
the question whether the Passio is Montanist or
bears Montanist imprint. The question is not an
easy one to answer. For one thing, Montanism
itself--its background, history, and essential
features--remains somewhat of an enigma.[11] This
is nowhere more true than for the Montanism of
North Africa. The writings of Tertullian are the
primary source for our knowledge of Montanism in
North Africa. However, it is not clear to what

extent they are faithful witnesses. A powerful
personality such as Tertullian could have shaped
the movement in Carthage as much as being shaped
by it. Yet, it is hardly probable that Tertullian
was unique in his Montanism, and his writings may
safely be regarded as offering an accurate
general picture of the attitudes and views of
Montanism in early third century North Africa.

The question whether Montanism exists in the
Passio is naturally divided into two parts: 1) Do
the autographical portions of Perpetua and Saturus
show Montanist features? 2) Does the narrative
of the redactor show Montanist features?
Concerning the first question most scholars either
deny any Montanist content in the reports of
Perpetua and Saturus or ascribe to them only a
tangential connection with Montanism.[12] Yet,
voices continue to be raised which assert the
outright Montanist character of the martyrs.
Campos asserts that the martyrs possess "un aire
montanista", and Barnes is of the opinion that
"the theological character of the Passio is Montanist through and through".[13]

The argument that Perpetua and Saturus betray
Montanist leanings rests on the prominent place
given to visions and on certain details which are
alleged to belie Montanist enthusiasm. That
visions have a prominent place is obvious, but
visions were hardly the monopoly of Montanists.
Visions appear in other martyrological literature
(Mart. Pol. 5:2; Pass. Mar. et Jac. 6:5; 7:2;
11:1-6; Pass. Mont. et Luc. 5; 7; 8; 11', in
apocalyptic literature such as the Shepherd of
Hermas,[14] and in major Catholic authors (Irenaeus,
Adv. haer. 2.32.4; Cyprian, Ep. 11:3,5; 39:1;
40:1; 66:10; Augustine, De div. quaest. ad
Simplicianum 2.1).

Barnes adduces three features which he
believes show that the martyrs were Montanists:
1) Perpetua's visions of Dinocrates imply that a
martyr can effect the release of a soul from hell
and secure its admittance to heaven (Pass. Perp.

7-8); 2) Saturus' dream manifests "a subversive attitude toward the clergy" and implies that the clergy's hope lies in the martyrs at whose feet they fall (Pass. Perp. 13); 3) The martyrs assist the persecutors. Saturus voluntarily gives himself up (Pass. Perp. 4:5), and Perpetua guides the executioner's hand to her throat (Pass. Perp. 21:9). In Barnes' eyes this is to come "near to suicide".[15]

Barnes' arguments are not convincing. Even if Perpetua's visions of Dinocrates did imply special petitionary powers of the martyr, this was not an uniquely Montanist viewpoint. In fact, however, the visions concerning Dinocrates may be explained quite apart from Montanist ideas. F. Dölger explained the visions on the basis of popular pagan conceptions concerning the condition of those who have died violently or prematurely.[16] More recently E. Corsini has argued that in these visions Perpetua is drawing upon a mystical-sacramental view of baptism whereby the beneficial effects of the two baptisms of Perpetua (water baptism and martyrdom) are efficaciously applied to Dinocrates.[17]

Secondly, rather than subverting the position of the clergy, the vision of Saturus tends to support and reinforce it. When the bishop Optatus and the presbyter Aspasius fall at the feet of Perpetua and Saturus, it is the martyrs who are surprised at this unexpected deference and disclaim any right to such honor: "Non tu es papa noster et tu presbyter, ut vos ad pedes nobis mittatis?" (Pass. Perp. 13:3). Note the deferential address, "papa", which implies that the martyrs recognize the bishop's authority. Furthermore, when the angels scold Optatus and Aspasius and tell them to let the martyrs alone and to settle their own disputes, the implication is that what had been asked of Perpetua and Saturus was beyond their competence. Reconciling quarreling parties was not the function and prerogative of martyrs. If there is an intended polemic in this scene, it is directed against a

growing tendency to ascribe to the martyr the
prerogatives of the local clergy, a development
which was to climax in North Africa fifty years
later.[18]

Concerning Barnes' third argument, it is
gratuitous to allege that Saturus' voluntary
surrender and Perpetua's action to facilitate her
death are manifestations of Montanist enthusiasm
for martyrdom. Only in passing does Perpetua
report that Saturus voluntarily surrendered
himself and even then she quickly explains why he
did so: quia ipse nos aedificaverat (Pass. Perp.
4:5). Not Montanist enthusiasm but a sense of
continuing responsibility toward the imprisoned
group motivated Saturus.[19] Perpetua's action to
quicken her death is no different from that of
Bishop Pionius, who placed himself on the gibbet
so that the nails could be driven in (Mart. Pion.
21:2). No Montanism need be imagined to
comprehend such a human action.

There are no features, therefore, in the
autographical accounts of Perpetua and Saturus
which reflect Montanism.[20] The martyrs were
orthodox, Catholic Christians. This conclusion
is supported by two considerations. Were Perpetua
a Montanist, it is most probable that Tertullian
would have noted that fact when he had occasion to
refer to the Passio (De anima 55:4). Earlier in
the same work, Tertullian expressly remarks that
a female visionary was a Montanist (est hodie
soror apud nos [De anima 9:4]). Secondly,
Perpetua and her comrades very early received
honor from the Catholic Church. By the fourth
century a church dedicated to their memory existed
in Carthage.[21] In Augustine's time the Passio
was regarded by some as canonical Scripture
(Augustine, De nat. et orig. animae 1.10.12 [PL
44:481]), and Augustine himself devoted sermons
in their honor (Serm. 280-282 [PL 38:1280-86]).
It is not likely that Catholic Christians would
have given such adoration to sectarian martyrs.[22]

Whether the redactor of the Passio was
Montanist is more difficult to answer. Pass. Perp.

20:8 is often given as evidence of Montanism. After being tossed by a wild heifer, Perpetua awakes "as from a sleep" and is not aware of her struggle with the beast. The redactor explains that she had been "in spirit and in ecstasy" (adeo in spiritu et in extasi fuerat).[23] This, however, is not the Montanist idea of ecstasy, which, as Tertullian often remarks, is closely associated with the giving of prophecy (De anima 11:4: ecstasy is "sancti Spiritus vis operatrix prophetiae"; De anima 21:2; De ieiun. 3:2; De anima 9:4; Adv. Marc. 4.22.4-5; 5.8.12). The ecstasy of Perpetua is simply that ecstasy which preserves the martyr from pain and which occurs in other martyrological documents as well (Mart. Isa. 5:14; Mart. Pol. 2:2; Eusebius, Hist. eccl. 5.1.51).

The general absence of a rigorist, austere attitude in the episodes chosen and narrated by the redactor argues against his being a Montanist. Mention has already been made of the disparity between Tertullian's severe attitude toward pregnancy and children in the light of "imminent distresses" and the simple, unconscious narrative of Felicitas' child-bearing in prison. This divergence of attitude evinces a lack of Montanist rigor on the part of the redactor of the Passio.[24] In De fuga 9:4 Tertullian quotes a Montanist oracle: "Do not desire to die on bridal beds, in miscarriages, or in soft fevers, but in martyrdoms that he might be glorified who suffered for you."[25] The antipathy between marital attachments, along with the concomitants of marriage, and martyrdom is here manifested. It may be doubted whether a Montanist redactor would have selected the pregnant, child-bearing Felicitas to grace his martyrological narrative.

The same may be said for another element in the Passio. On several occasions throughout the Passio there are notices that attempts were made to ameliorate the condition of the prisoners. One such instance is Pass. Perp. 16:2-4. Because of his excessively harsh treatment of the Christian

prisoners, the military tribune is rebuked by
Perpetua, and as a result he allows the prisoners
to receive visitors, food and drink. Compare this
with the attitude of Tertullian who verbally flogs
the "psychics" for making the condition of their
imprisoned brethren as comfortable as possible:
"It is clearly your practice to furnish kitchens
in the prisons for uncertain martyrs lest they
miss their accustomed habits, grow weary of life
and stumble on the new discipline of abstinence"
(De ieiun. 12:3). Or again: "Emaciation does
not displease us, for God does not bestow flesh
by weight just as he does not bestow the Spirit
by measure. Indeed, slender flesh will more
easily enter through the narrow gate of salvation;
light flesh will rise more swiftly; dry flesh
will endure longer in the tomb. . . . An over-fed
Christian shall be more necessary to bears and
lions than to God" (De ieiun. 17:6-9). In these
passages Tertullian is obviously using the full
force of his rhetorical sarcasm, and it would be
foolish to deduce from them that the Montanists
were apathetic toward the physical sufferings of
their fellow Christians. Yet, whether a Montanist
redactor, free to choose and select episodes for
his narrative, would have chosen the kind of
episodes just considered in the Passio is doubtful.
In a martyrological narrative one would expect
from a Montanist, with the heightened eschatological expectation persecution would have given
to him, more assertion of the martyrs' detachment
from the world. However, that is a motif to
which the Passio gives little, if any, attention.

Many scholars perceive Montanism especially
in the prologue and epilogue of the Passio.[26] The
pertinent passages are worthy of quotation:

> The deeds recounted about the faith in
> ancient times were a proof of God's favor
> and achieved the spiritual strengthening of
> men as well; and they were set forth in
> writing precisely that honor might be
> rendered to God and comfort to men by the
> recollection of the past through the written

word. Should not then more recent examples
be set down that contribute equally to both
ends? For indeed these too will one day
become ancient and needful for the ages to
come, even though in our own day they may
enjoy less prestige because of the prior
claim of antiquity. Let those then who would
restrict the power of the one Spirit to
times and seasons look to this: the more
recent events should be considered the
greater, being later than those of old, and
this is a consequence of the extraordinary
graces promised for the last stage of time
(cum maiora reputanda sunt novitiora quaeque
ut novissimiora secundum exuperationem
gratiae in ultima saeculi spatia decretam).
For in the last days, God declares, I will
pour out my Spirit upon all flesh and their
sons and daughters shall prophesy and on my
manservants and my maidservants I will pour
my Spirit, and the young men shall see
visions and the old men shall dream dreams.
So too we hold in honor and acknowledge not
only new prophecies but new visions as well,
according to the promise (prophetias ita et
visiones novas pariter repromissas). And we
consider all the other functions of the Holy
Spirit as intended for the good of the
Church; for the same Spirit has been sent to
distribute all his gifts to all, as the Lord
apportions to everyone. For this reason we
deem it imperative to set them forth and to
make them known through the word for the
glory of God. Thus no one of weak or
despairing faith may think that supernatural
grace was present only among men of ancient
times, either in the grace of martyrdom or of
visions, for God always achieves what he
promises, as a witness to the non-believer
and a blessing to the faithful (Pass. Perp.
1:1-5).27

Ah, most valiant and blessed martyrs! Truly
are you called and chosen for the glory of

231

Christ Jesus our Lord! And any man who
exalts, honors, and worships his glory should
read for the consolation of the Church these
new deeds of heroism which are no less
significant than the tales of old (utique et
haec non minora veteribus exempla). For
these new manifestations of virtue will bear
witness to one and the same Spirit who still
operates, and to God the Father almighty, to
his Son Jesus Christ our Lord, to whom is
splendor and immeasurable power for all the
ages. Amen. (Pass. Perp. 21:11).[28]

The major difficulty lies in the appearance of
Joel 3:1 (Acts 2:17), which speaks of God's outpouring of the Holy Spirit in the last days and
of such expressions as "cum maiora reputanda sunt
novitiora quaeque ut novissimiora" and "prophetias
ita et visiones novas pariter repromissas". At
first glance they seem Montanist. Only a close
examination of the redactor's flow of thought
will decide.

Did Joel 3:1 ever serve a Montanist function?
Tertullian quotes Joel 3:1 nine times, all of
which occur in writings from his Montanist period
(De anima 47:2; Adv. Marc. 5.4.2,4; 5.8.6; 5.11.4;
5.17.4; De resurr. carn. 10:2; 63:7; De fuga 6:4).
Of these, however, only one, De resurr. carn. 63:7,
is used in a distinctively Montanist way. Against
those who support their denial of the resurrection
of the flesh by mutilating or misrepresenting
Scripture, Tertullian writes that by pouring out
the Spirit, God has graciously "checked these
impostures of unbelief and perverseness, re-ani-
mated men's faith in the resurrection of the flesh,
and by the clear light of their words and meanings
purged the ancient Scriptures of all obscurity and
ambiguity". The Holy Spirit has illuminated the
Scriptures that the truth might be perceived with
no admixture of heresy and has given "an open and
clear explanation of the whole mystery through
the new prophecy which flows from the Paraclete"
(De resurr. carn. 63:7-9).[29] Tertullian here

enunciates the well-known Montanist principle
that the coming of the Paraclete gives a revelation which supplements and clarifies that which
had previously been given in the Gospel and which
introduces a more rigorous discipline. This view
repeatedly appears in Tertullian's writings (Adv.
Prax. 2:1; 13:5; De mono. 14:3-6; De ieiun. 12:2;
De virg. vel. 1; De mono. 2-3).[30]

Although John 16:13 usually provided the
proof text for this view (see Tertullian, Adv.
Prax. 2:1; 30:5; De mono. 2:2; De ieiun. 10:6;
De fuga 1:1; 14:3), as De resurr. carn. 63:7 shows,
Joel 3:1 could be used to lend support for this
Montanist belief. Is this likewise the case in
Pass. Perp. 1:3-4 where Joel 3:1 is quoted to
support the contention that "maiora reputanda sunt
novitiora quaeque ut novissimiora secundam
exuperationem gratiae in ultima saeculi spatia
decretam"? To answer this question, the following
questions must be answered: In what sense was the
activity of the Montanist Paraclete new or
superior? Is the redactor of the Passio reflecting
this Montanist sense when he speaks of "maiora"
and "novitiora"?

The Montanists were accused of introducing
novelty. Tertullian deals with this charge in De
mono. 2-3 and in De virg. vel. 1. The Paraclete
in no way has introduced anything "in opposition
to the Catholic tradition or contrary to the light
burden of the Lord" (De mono. 2:1).[31] Yet, argues
Tertullian, it is clear from John 16:12-13 that
the revelations of the Paraclete may be considered
"new", since they "have never been revealed before"
(ut nunquam retro edita [De mono. 2:2]) or since
they are "now being revealed" (quia nunc revelantur
[De mono. 2:4]). That which is now revealed
involves an advance over previously given revelation. This idea is best formulated in De virg.
vel. 1. While the law of faith remains constant,
that which concerns discipline admits the novelty
of correction, as the grace of God advances toward
the end (De virg. vel. 1:4). Discipline is being
led to perfection by the Vicar of the Lord, the

233

Holy Spirit (De virg. vel. 1:4). The work of the
Spirit is "to advance toward the better things"
(ad meliora proficitur [De virg. vel. 1:5]). As
a seed of grain passes through various stages of
growth before it is a ripe fruit, so righteousness
was first in a rudimentary stage, then with the
Law and the prophets it gained its infancy, then
with the Gospel it achieved its youth, and now
with the Paraclete it has arrived at maturity
(De virg. vel. 1:6-7). As Christ could abrogate
the counsel of Moses, so the Paraclete can repeal
that of Paul (De mono. 14:3). The activity of the
Paraclete is, therefore, new and superior because
it involves an extension and amplification of
God's prior revelations. It is new not only
because it is recent but also because--in the
sense of extension, clarification, and augmenta-
tion--it is different from what has gone before.
To be noted as well is the fact that the Paraclete
is now active due to the closeness of the end-time.
The time is "wound up" (cum magis nunc tempus in
collecto [De mono. 3:8; cf. De mono. 14:4]). The
time of the Paraclete is the last stage of God's
revelatory program.

The prologue and epilogue of the Passio do
not contain this Montanist argumentation. First
of all, the redactor does not display a heightened
sense of the nearness of the end-time. Almost
with nonchalance he declares that the events of
which he narrates will themselves one day be aged
(vetera) and necessary for coming generations (vel
quia proinde et haec vetera futura quandoque sunt
et necessaria posteris [Pass. Perp. 1:2]). This
itself should caution against placing too much
emphasis on the literal import of the phrase,
"maiora reputanda sunt novitiora quaeque". Were
this phrase interpreted in a strictly Montanist
sense, one would be forced to conclude that the
redactor looked forward to yet further stages of
revelation beyond that of the Paraclete. But
there are other elements which attentuate the
force of this phrase as well. In the epilogue the
redactor writes that the new examples of faith
"are no less significant" than the old examples

(haec non minora veteribus exempla [Pass. Perp.
21:11]). Clearly "maiora" is not to be taken in
an absolute sense. The argument is that the
events of which the redactor speaks are of equal
significance with earlier events, because the
events surrounding the martyrdoms of Perpetua and
her companions are the works of the same Spirit
and therefore equally bear the imprint of the last
days. Both, the more recent as well as the old
events, manifest "the superabundance of grace
promised for the last days". This is the sense of
the word "novissimiora". This form (the compara-
tive of a superlative), while not strange,[32] is
still somewhat infrequent and here appears to have
been used in view of the quotation of Joel 3:1
(in novissimis diebus). The "last days" began
with Pentecost, and the events of the Passio are
simply the most recent of those acts of the Spirit
which bear the imprint of the "last days". The
Spirit is working now in the Church in equal
measure and in the selfsame manner as in the
earliest days of the Church. That, and no more,
is the contention of the redactor. He could not
state it more clearly: "Assuredly also these
examples, which are no less than those of old,
ought to be read for the edification of the
Church, for also these new acts of power witness
that one and the same Holy Spirit is working even
to the present day" (Pass. Perp. 21:11). Unlike
Montanism, the redactor of the Passio perceives
no difference in the work of the Spirit in his
own time and in the time of the apostles. His
sole concern is that his Christian contemporaries
perceive that in the visions and martyrdoms of
Perpetua and her companions the Holy Spirit is
working among them in no less measure than among
the Christians of earlier days (ut ne qua aut
inbecillitas aut desperatio fidei apud veteres
tantum aestimet gratiam divinitatis conversatem
[Pass. Perp. 1:5]).

There is, therefore, no reason to assume
that the redactor of the Passio was a Montanist
or that he tended toward Montanism. What the
Passio shows is that within the Church at Carthage

235

there was a dispute concerning the continuance of
certain phenomena of the Spirit within the Church.
One party denied that the Spirit still worked in
the selfsame manner as in earlier periods (sed
viderint qui unam virtutem Spiritus unius Sancti
pro aetatibus iudicent temporum [Pass. Perp. 1:3]).
The other party--to which the redactor of the
Passio would have belonged--affirmed that the
Spirit continued to act in the Church as it had
always acted. The relationship of Montanism
with this conflict cannot be determined with any
precision. Possibly the introduction of Montanism
into Carthage elicited the conflict. If so, the
situation in Carthage was analogous to that in
Gaul. Irenaeus tells us that there were some who,
apparently in the face of Montanism, wished to
reject the Gospel of John because it contained
the promise of the Paraclete. These persons "set
at naught the gift poured out in the last times",
"set aside both the Gospel and the prophetic
Spirit", "expelled the gift of prophecy from the
Church" (Irenaeus, Adv. haer. 3.11.9; cf.
4.33.15).[33] In the light of Montanist enthusiasm
some reacted to the extent of denying the
continued activity of the Spirit. Such a situation appears to have existed in Carthage as well.

3.

Divine Activity in the
Passion of Perpetua

The Holy Spirit always works in the Church in
the same measure and in the selfsame manner. Of
this the revelations and martyrdoms of Perpetua
and her companions are proofs. Martyrdom is,
therefore, a work of the Spirit, and the martyrs
are bearers and instruments of the Spirit.
Perpetua reports that even the soldier in charge
of the prison, Pudens, recognized that "a great
power" resided in the martyrs (Pass. Perp. 9:1).
The martyrs, as bearers of the Spirit, are given
divine succor in the midst of their suffering.

236

Due to an ecstasy of the Spirit, Perpetua remains
unaware of her battle with a wild heifer until
she notices the wounds incurred by her in the
struggle (Pass. Perp. 20:8). Felicitas knows
that she shall be able to endure the pain of her
martyrdom, for then "another one will be in me who
shall suffer for me, because I also am about to
suffer for Him" (Pass. Perp. 15:6).

Dominating the Passio's view of martyrdom,
however, is the image of the gladiatorial contest.
The real opponents of the martyrs are not officials
or relatives who urge denial of the Christian
Name, nor the beasts which the martyrs must face.
The real opponent of the martyrs is Satan.
Perpetua's father used the arguments of the Devil
(argumenta diaboli) when he urged Perpetua to
apostatize (Pass. Perp. 3:3). It was the Devil
who chose for Perpetua and Felilitas a most
ferocious heifer as the beast against which they
must fight (Pass. Perp. 20:1). In her first
vision Perpetua saw a ladder reaching to heaven at
the foot of which lay an enormous dragon who would
attack those attempting to climb up (Pass. Perp.
4:4). The dragon symbolizes Satan as the real
obstacle to a successful martyrdom. Most graphic
is Perpetua's last vision in which she sees her
martyrdom as a hand-to-hand combat with an
Egyptian. Awakening from the vision, Perpetua
realizes that she was "going to fight not with
wild beasts but with the Devil" (Pass. Perp.
10:14).[34]

The motif of martyrdom as a gladiatorial
combat between Satan and the martyr determines
the role the divine subject plays in the actual
martyrdoms. Two features are to be noted. In the
vision of Perpetua's combat with the Egyptian,
there appears a figure described as "a man of
marvelous height so that he even exceeded the top
of the amphitheatre, clad in a loose tunic with a
purple stripe between two clamps running down
the middle of the breast and multiform sandals
made of gold and silver, and bearing a wand like
an athletic trainer (lanista) and a green branch

on which were golden apples" (Pass. Perp. 10:8).[35]
This figure determines the conditions of the
combat (Pass. Perp. 10:9) and upon the conclusion
of the contest gives the branch of golden apples
as prize to the winner (Pass. Perp. 10:12). The
Passio says that the figure was a lanista. A
lanista usually owned his own gladiatorial school
at which he supervised the drill of the gladiators.
During such drill he carried a rod or staff, to
which the Passio refers.[36] A lanista, therefore,
was a trainer of gladiators whose responsibility
it was to prepare his gladiators for combat.

However, the figure of Pass. Perp. 10 bears
resemblances to the agonothete as well. The
agonothete had responsibility for the orderly
proceeding of the games. Often a public official,
the agonothete would make all necessary prepara-
tions for the games--such as the registration of
the athletes, the dispersal of any public money
allocated for the games, and the exercise of
appropriate sacrifices. At the games themselves,
the agonothete was fully in charge. He gave the
signal for the contest to begin, was referee
concerning controverted situations arising from
the combat, levied penalties and fines, determined
the winner and loser, and gave the prize to the
victor. On the day of the contest, the agonothete
often appeared crowned and robed in a ceremonial
purple garb and carried in his hand a staff which
designated him as director of the games.[37] In
Pass. Perp. 10 the man of marvelous stature wears
a purple robe, referees the contest and gives the
prize to the victor of the contest. These features
comport with the agonothete better than with the
lanista.

Clearly the figure is symbolic of a divine
being. However, to what divine person the figure
corresponds is not completely clear. Corsini has
argued that the figure represents the risen Christ
who has triumphed over death and who now is
present as judge. The figure's dress, a tunic
with purple stripe, is symbolic of the victory
won by Christ through his bloody death.[38] Yet,

features suggest that God the Father may rather be meant. First of all, the figure generally performs the functions of an agonothete to which the Father is compared by Tertullian on several occasions (Ad mart. 3:3; Scorp. 6:4,5,6; De fuga 1:5). Secondly, when Perpetua takes the victor's prize from the figure's hand, he kisses her and calls her "daughter". Whomever the figure may represent, he does not take an active role in the fight itself. The martyr receives no aid or exhortation from him. He is there to state the conditions of combat, to referee the combat, to award the victor.

Certainly the Passio does not wish to imply that the martyr struggles against Satan alone (see Pass. Perp. 15:6). In the vision of her contest with the Egyptian, the deacon Pomponius accompanies Perpetua to the center of the arena and there says to her: "Do not be afraid. I am here with you and I shall struggle with you" (Pass. Perp. 10:4). Pomponius may here be representative of Christ who, according to Tertullian, leads the martyr to the place of combat (Ad mart. 3:4).[39] During the contest itself Perpetua is raised into the air and beats at the Egyptian without touching the ground (Pass. Perp. 10:11). Obviously, Perpetua is fighting a fight with divine dimensions. Finally, the oil with which Perpetua is rubbed before the contest may well indicate an anointing with the Holy Spirit (see Tertullian, Ad mart. 3:4).

Nevertheless, while recognizing these hints of the divine presence at Perpetua's martyrdom, the vision of Perpetua's gladiatorial combat with Satan tends to place any divine actor at the edge of the struggle rather than in the struggle as a direct participant. Even if Pomponius does represent Christ who struggles with the martyr, the thrust of this is attenuated by the remark that Pomponius left Perpetua alone in the arena (et abiit). Similarly, the man of marvelous size is explicitly said to have withdrawn from the place of combat (et recessit [Pass. Perp. 10:10]).

Obviously, he has no active role in the contest itself. In like manner, the remark that a rubdown with oil before a contest is common practice (quomodo solent in agone [Pass. Perp. 10:7]) tends to empty the image of anointing of any intended spiritual meaning.

When no divine figure plays a central part in martyrdom, the understanding of martyrdom is affected. An ethical, heroic dimension comes to the fore. Such a dimension is in danger of gaining primacy in the Passio. The significance of Perpetua's encounter with Satan is given in the words of the man of wondrous height: "If the Egyptian should conquer her, he shall kill her with the sword; if she should defeat the Egyptian, she shall receive this branch" (Pass. Perp. 10:9). The story of Perpetua's martyrdom is essentially the story of Perpetua's fate. She either dies or she wins. Since Christian martyrdom is essentially the struggle of the martyr against Satan, victory over Satan is regarded as essentially the feat of the martyr. Therefore, the glory won is also the glory of the martyr. Upon receiving the victory branch, Perpetua began to walk "with glory" towards the Gate of Life (et coepi ire cum gloria ad portam sanavivarium [Pass. Perp. 10:13]). Perpetua, dishevelled by the wild heifer, tidied her dress and hair lest she should appear to be mourning "in her glory" (Pass. Perp. 20:5). The struggle against Satan and the subsequent glory is essentially the struggle and glory of the martyr.

This is a considerably different perspective from that offered in the letter concerning the martyrs of Lyons. There Christ himself is so centrally active in the martyr's suffering and death that he is envisioned as the mighty and invincible athlete who fights Satan (Eusebius, Hist. eccl. 5.1.42). For the Lyons martyrs, Christian martyrdom is essentially a locus of Christ's eschatological struggle against Satan. The martyr's suffering and death are the manifestation of the resurrection victory of Christ over

240

Satan and, therefore, the manifestation of Christ's glory. While the Passio can speak of Christian martyrdom as "glory" (Pass. Perp. 16:1) and as a power of the Holy Spirit (Pass. Perp. 21:11), the eschatological character of Christian martyrdom as a revelation of Christ's resurrection glory gives way to an ethical perspective in which the martyr strives through martyrdom to attain glory for himself. The same perspective dominates Tertullian's presentation as well.

SUMMARY

Although the Passion of Perpetua and Tertullian share common conceptions concerning martyrdom and although similar images and language appear in both the Passio and Tertullian, it is very doubtful that Tertullian was in any way responsible for the writing of the Passio. The erroneous comments made by Tertullian in De anima 55.4 concerning a vision of Perpetua, and the disparate attitudes of the Passio and Tertullian toward the effect of marriage and human attachments on a Christian's readiness for martyrdom make it unlikely that Tertullian was either the author or the redactor of the Passio.

The Passio is often regarded as a Montanist or at least as an incipiently Montanist document. However, neither in the autographical accounts of Perpetua and Saturus nor in the narrative portions of the redactor can explicitly Montanist features be discerned. Visions were not the special prerogative of Montanist Christians, and the content of the visions do not reflect Montanist attitudes. There is no derogation of local clergy, no untoward desire for martyrdom, as is sometimes asserted. Likewise, the narrative portions of the Passio are devoid of Montanist elements. The austere, rigorist attitude reflected in Tertullian's Montanist writings is absent in the Passio. The prologue and the epilogue of the Passio simply maintain that the

241

visions and martyrdoms narrated show that the
Holy Spirit continues to work in the selfsame
manner as in the age of the apostles. They do
not wish to assert the Montanist view that the
martyrdoms and visions were new and superior
revelations of the Spirit. The Passio appears to
be directed against some within the Christian
community at Carthage who, perhaps in view of
Montanist enthusiasm, were denying the continuance
of certain manifestations of the Spirit.

According to the Passio, Christian martyrdom
is a clear manifestation of the Spirit's continuing activity in the Church. Martyrdom is of the
Spirit and therefore is a sign that the Church is
living in the last days. The martyr possesses
great power and is aware that he shall be given
divine assistance in his struggle. Yet, an
ethical perspective generally dominates the
Passio's account. The martyr is like a gladiator
who, while perhaps trained and schooled for
combat, is nevertheless essentially on his own
before his adversary. Divine activity is
basically restricted to the instituting of
persecution and to the awarding of the victor's
prize. Martyrdom itself is the martyr's heroic
deed, and the glory won the martyr's glory.

1 Pass. Perp. 2:3: haec ordinem totum martyrii
sui iam hinc ipsa narravit sicut conscriptum manu
sua et suo sensu reliquit; Pass. Perp. 11:1: sed
et Saturus benedictus hanc visionem suam ededit,
quam ipse conscripsit; Pass. Perp. 14:1: hae
visiones insigniores ipsorum martyrum beatissimorum
Saturi et Perpetuae, quas ipsi conscripserunt.
Doubts expressed by E. Schwartz (De Pionio et
Polycarpo [Göttingen: W. F. Kaestner, 1905] 23)
and J. Geffken ("Die christlichen Martyrien,"
Hermes 45 [1910] 502) concerning the authenticity
of the reports of Perpetua and Saturus have long
been resolved in favor of authenticity. The
reports differ markedly in style and language from
the rest of the Passio and from each other; see
H. Delehaye, Les passions des martyrs et les
genres littéraires (Bruxelles: Societe des
Bollandistes, 1921) 64-65; J. Armitage Robinson,
The Passion of S. Perpetua (Texts and Studies 1/2;
Cambridge: Cambridge University, 1891) 43-58;
W. H. Shewring, "Prose Rhythm in the Passio S.
Perpetuae," JTS 30 (1929) 56-57; "En marge de la
Passion des Saintes Perpétue et Félicité," Revue
Benedictine 43 (1931) 15-22.

2 The redactor recognizes that his reading
audience will include eyewitnesses of the events
he narrates (Pass. Perp. 1:6). Tertullian refers
to Perpetua in De anmina 55:4, which is to be
dated around 207. See T. D. Barnes, Tertullian:
A Historical and Literary Study (Oxford:
Clarendon, 1971) 263-65.

3 J. Rendel Harris discovered the Greek text in
Jerusalem in 1889. In the following year Harris,
along with Seth K. Gifford, published the Greek
text and defended its priority (The Acts of the
Martyrdom of Perpetua and Felicitas: The Original
Greek Text now first edited from a ms. in the
library of the Convent of the Holy Sepuchre at
Jerusalem [London: C. J. Clay, 1890]). J.
Armitage Robinson (Passion of S. Perpetua, 2-9)

and especially Pio Franchi de' Cavalieri (La
Passio S.S. Perpetuae et Felicitatis [RQ,
Supplementheft 5; Roma: Spithöver, 1896]) replied
with arguments for the Latin text which still
demand assent. Latin priority is affirmed also
by E. Rupprecht, "Bemerkungen zur Passio SS.
Perpetuae et Felicitatis," RheinMus n.s. 90 (1941)
177-80; V. Reichmann, Römische Literatur in
griechischer Übersetzung (Philologus,
Supplementband 34/3; Leipzig: Dieterich, 1943)
101-30; J. Campos, "El autor de la 'Passio SS.
Perpetuae et Felicitatis'," Helmantica 10 (1959)
362-67. See also C. J. M. J. van Beek, Passio
Sanctarum Perpetuae et Felicitatis, vol. 1:
Textus Graecus et Latinus ad fidem codicum mss.
(Nijmegen: 1936) 84-91. Most recently Å. Fridh
has adduced arguments showing that while the parts
attributed to the redactor and to Perpetua were
originally Latin, the report of Saturus was
probably originally in Greek (Le probleme de la
passion des saintes Perpetue et Felicite [Studia
graeca et latina Gothoburgensia 26; Göteborg:
Almquist & Wiksell, 1968] 46-82).

4 Indeed, P. de Labriolle entitles the chapter in
which he discusses the Passio "Les premiers phases
de l'evolution de Tertullien vers le Montanisme"
(La crise montaniste [Paris: E. Leroux, 1913] 338).

5 For the verbal similarities, see de Labriolle,
La crise montaniste, 345-51; de Labriolle,
"Tertullien, auteur du prologue et de la
conclusion de la passion de Perpetue et de
Felicite," Bulletin d'ancienne litteraire et
d'archeologie chretienne 3 (1913) 126-32; Campos,
"El autor de la 'Passio'," 377-80. Among those
who assert Tertullian's authorship are Robinson,
Passion of S. Perpetua, 47-58; Th. Zahn, "Die
Passio Perpetuae," Theologisches Literaturblatt
13 (1892) 42; Delehaye, Passions des martyrs, 67;
Campos, "El autor de la 'Passio'," 367-81; H.
von Campenhausen, Die Idee des Martyriums in der
alten Kirche, 2nd ed. (Göttingen: Vandenhoeck &
Ruprecht, 1964) 117 n. 2.

6 Cf. Rupprecht, "Bemerkungen," 180-81; R. Braun, "Tertullien est-il le rédacteur de la Passio Perpetuae?" Revue des Études Latines 33 (1955) 81.

7 Tertullian, De anima 55:4: Quomodo Perpetua, fortissima martyr, sub die passionis in revelatione paradisi solos illic martyras vidit, nisi quia nullis romphaea paradisi ianitrix cedit nisi qui in Christo decesserint, non in Adam (CChr 2:862).

8 In Perpetua's first vision there is a short narration of her reception into paradise by a tall, grey-haired man in shepherd's dress, milking sheep, and "surrounded by many thousands in white garments" (Pass. Perp. 4:8). The text gives no cause to restrict the "many thousands" to martyrs. A scene similar to that of Rev 4 and 5 is probably meant.

9 Tertullian, Ad uxorem 1.5.3: ad primam angeli tubam expeditae prosilient, quamcunque pressuram persecutionemque libere perferent, nulla in utero, nulla in uberibus aestuante sarcina nuptiarum (CChr 1:379).

10 Among those who argue against Tertullian as redactor of the Passio are P. Monceaux, Histoire littéraire de l'Afrique chrétienne depuis les origines jusqu'à l'invasion arabe, 7 vols. (Paris: E. Leroux, 1901-23), 1:83-84; Rupprecht, "Bemerkungen," 180-82; and Braun, who argues in favor of the deacon Pomponius ("Tertullien," 80-81). Fridh comes to a balanced conclusion: "Tout au plus on oserait affirmer qu'il est très vraisemblable que l'auteur est à chercher dans le même milieu et dans la meme génération que Tertullian. . . . Nous ignorons jusqu'aux noms de la plupart des contemporains de Perpétue. Il est plus que probable que nous ne saurons jamais celui de notre auteur" (Probleme de la passion, 9-11). See also Barnes, Tertullian, 265. In a recent article R. Braun returned to the question of Tertullian's authorship. With detailed and

convincing linguistic and stylistic arguments, Braun again argues that Tertullian was not the redactor of the Passio ("Nouvelles observations linguistiques sur le rédacteur de la 'Passio Perpetuae'," VigChr 33 [1979] 105-17).

11 For literature, see G. Nathanael Bonwetsch, Die Geschichte des Montanismus (Erlangen: Andreas Deichert, 1881); de Labriolle, La crise montaniste; W. Scheperlern, Der Montanismus und die phrygischen Kulte: eine religions-geschichtliche Untersuchung (Tübingen: J. C. B. Mohr, 1929); K. Aland, "Der Montanismus und die kleinasiatische Theologie," ZNW 46 (1955) 109-16; "Bemerkungen zum Montanismus und zur früh-christlichen Eschatologie," Kirchengeschichtliche Entwürfe (Gütersloh: Gerd Mohn, 1960) 105-48; K. Froehlich, "Montanism and Gnosis," The Heritage of the Early Church. Essays in honor of Georges Vasilievich Florovsky (Orientalia Christiana Analecta 195; Rome: Pont. Institutum Studiorum Orientalium, 1973) 91-111.

12 The orthodoxy of the martyrs was defended at length by Cardinal Joseph Augustine Orsi, Dissertatio apologetica pro SS. Perpetuae, Felicitatis et sociorum orthodoxia (Florentiae: 1728; printed in PL 3:61-170). In this century their orthodoxy has been defended by A. d'Alès ("L'auteur de la Passio Perpetuae," RHE 8 [1907] 14-18) and de Labriolle (La crise montaniste, 341-44). On the other hand, Bonwetsch speaks of "eine Verwandtschaft mit dem Montanismus" (Montanismus, 185); A. von Harnack writes of "der neuen Prophetie nahestehenden Katholiken" (Geschichte der altchristlichen Literatur bis Eusebius, Part 2: Die Chronologie, 2nd ed. [Leipzig: J. C. Hinrichs, 1958], 2:321 n. 1); P. Carrington writes that if the martyrs reflect Montanism, it was "a liberal-minded, unreflective Montanism of the second degree" (The Early Christian Church, vol. 1: The Second Christian Century [Cambridge: Cambridge University, 1957] 427-28).

13 Campos, "El autor de la 'Passio'," 376-77;
Barnes, Tertullian, 77-79. Cf. also J. de Soyres,
Montanism and the Privitive Church: A Study in
the Ecclesiastical History of the Second Century
(Cambridge: Bell, 1878) 44-45.

14 The Shepherd of Hermas was read by the
Catholics of North Africa (cf. Tertullian, De
orat. 16:1; De Pud. 10:12; 20:2).

15 Barnes, Tertullian, 77-79.

16 F. J. Dölger, "Antike Parallelen zum leidenden
Dinocrates in der Passio Perpetuae," Antike und
Christentum: Kultur- und religionsgeschichtliche
Studien, 6 vols. (Münster: Aschendorff, 1929-50),
2:1-40. See also A. de Waal, "Der leidende
Dinokrates in der Vision der heiligen Perpetua,"
RQ 17 (1903) 839-47.

17 Eugenio Corsini, "Proposte per una Lettera
della 'Passio Perpetuae'," Forma Futuri. Studi
in onore del Cardinale Michele Pellegrino (Torino:
Bottega d'Erasmo, 1975) 499-505.

18 Cf. Corsini, "Proposte," 511-12.

19 Apparently Saturus had been the teacher of
these catechumens before their arrest. Possibly
Perpetua felt constrained to add the clarifying
comment to preclude a Montanist interpretation
from being placed on Saturus' action.

20 The argument that the eating of cheese (Pass.
Perp. 4:9) might refer to a Montanist eucharistic
practice has been amply refuted by d'Alès
("L'auteur de la Passio Perpetuae," 16-18) and
H. Leclercq ("Perpetue et Felicite," DACL 14
[1939] 403-4).

21 Leclercq, "Perpetue et Felicite," 432-39.

22 The assertion by Barnes (Tertullian, 79) and
H. Musurillo (The Acts of the Christian Martyrs

[OECT; Oxford: Clarendon, 1972] xxvi) that the Montanist character of the martyrs was either ignored or not perceived by Augustine is not credible in view of the fact that Augustine was an active and diligent opponent of Donatism, which was a recurrence of the spiritualistic rigor characteristic of Montanism.

23 Robinson, Passion of S. Perpetua, 52: "the technical phraseology of Montanism"; de Labriolle, La crise montaniste, 351: "il est impossible de ne pas apercevoir derrière cette remarque la préoccupation d'un montanisant".

24 Likewise the idea that Perpetua was Montanist is controverted by her concern for her baby, a concern which actually dictated her attitude toward her imprisonment (Pass. Perp. 3:9).

25 Tertullian, De fuga 9:4: Nolite in lectulis nec in aborsibus et febribus mollibus optare exire, sed in martyriis, uti glorificetur qui est passus pro vobis (CChr 2:1147). Tertullian quotes the same oracle in slightly different form in De anima 55:5.

26 Concerning the prologue: W. Gass, "Das christliche Märtyrerthum in den ersten Jahrhunderten und dessen Idee," Zeitschrift für historische Theologie 30 (1860) 323-24: "Der montanistische Sinn dieser Einleitung ist unzweifelhaft und wird durch den Schluss der Erzählung bestätigt"; de Soyres, Montanism, 140: "the Redaktor's language is precisely that of the Montanist, whose cardinal passage of Scripture he puts forth, as it were, as his text (viz. Joel ii.28)"; Monceaux, Histoire littéraire, 80: "c'est la toute la these montaniste". P. de Labriolle lists Pass. Perp. 1 as a Montanist source (Les sources de l'histoire du Montanisme [Collectanea Friburgensia 24; Fribourg: Librairie de l'université, 1913] 9-11). Concerning the epilogue: de Soyres, Montanism, 141: "another outburst of Montanism".

27 Pass. Perp. 1:1-5: Si vetera fidei exempla et
Dei gratiam testificantia et aedificationem
hominis operantia propterea in litteris sunt
digesta ut lectione eorum quasi repraesentatione
rerum et Deus honoretur et homo confortetur, cur
non et nova documenta aeque utrique causae
convenientia et digerantur? vel quia proinde et
haec vetera futura quandoque sunt et necessaria
posteris, si in praesenti suo tempore minori
deputantur auctoritati propter praesumptam
venerationem antiquitatis. sed viderint qui unam
virtutem Spiritus unius Sancti pro aetatibus
iudicent temporum, cum maiora reputanda sunt
novitiora quaeque ut novissimiora secundum
exuperationem gratiae in ultima saeculi spatia
decretam. In novissimis enim diebus, dicit
dominus, effundam de Spiritu meo super omnem
carnem, et prophetabunt filii filiaeque eorum; et
super servos et ancillas meas de meo Spiritu
effundam; et iuvenes visiones videbunt, et senes
somnia somniabunt. itaque et nos qui sicut
prophetias ita et visiones novas pariter
repromissas et agnoscimus et honoramus ceterasque
virtutes Spiritus Sancti ad instrumentum Ecclesiae
deputamus (cui et missus est idem omnia donativa
administraturus in omnibus, prout unicuique
distribuit dominus) necessario et digerimus et ad
gloriam Dei lectione celebramus, ut ne qua aut
inbecillitas aut desperatio fidei apud veteres
tantum aestimet gratiam divinitatis conversatam,
sive in martyrum sive in revelationum dignatione,
cum semper Deus operetur quae repromisit, non
credentibus in testimonium, credentibus in
beneficium. The English translation in the text
is taken from Musurillo, Acts, 107.

28 Pass. Perp. 21:11: O fortissimi ac beatissimi
martyres! o vere vocati et electi in gloriam
domini nostri Iesu Christi! quam qui magnificat
et honorificat et adorat, utique et haec non
minora veteribus exempla in aedificationem
Ecclesiae legere debet, ut novae quoque virtutes
unum et eundem semper Spiritum Sanctum usque
adhuc operari testificentur, et omnipotentem

Deum Patrem et Filium eius Iesum Christum dominum nostrum, cui est claritas et inmensa potestas in saecula saeculorum. Amen. The English translation in the text is taken from Musurillo, _Acts_, 131.

29 Tertullian, _De resurr. carn._ 63:7-9: Atenim deus omnipotens adversus haec incredulitatis et perversitatis ingenia providentissima gratia sua effundens in novissimis diebus de suo spiritu in omnem carnem, in servos suos et ancillas, et fidem laborantem resurrectionis carnalis animavit et pristina instrumenta manifestis verborum et sensuum luminibus ab omni ambiguitatis obscuritate purgavit. Nam quia haereses esse oportuerat, ut probabiles quique manifestentur, hae autem sine aliquibus occasionibus scripturarum audere non poterant, idcirco pristina instrumenta quasdam materias illis videntur subministrasse, et ipsas quidem isdem litteris revincibiles. Sed quoniam nec dissimulare spiritum sanctum oportebat, quominus et huiusmodi eloquiis superinundaret, quae nullis haereticorum versutiis semina sumspargerent, immo et veteres eorum cespites vellerent, idcirco iam omnes retro ambiguitates et quantas volunt parabolas aperta atque perspicua totius sacramenti praedicatione discussit per novam prophetiam de paraclito inundantem (CChr 2:1012).

30 Cf. V. Morel, "Le développement de la 'Disciplina' sous l'action du Saint-Esprit chez Tertullien," _RHE_ 35 (1939) 243-65.

31 Tertullian was insistent that Montanism agreed with the Church's Rule of Faith (_De virg. vel._ 1; _De pud._ 1; _Adv. Prax._ 2).

32 Such a formulation appears several times in Tertullian (see de Labriolle, _La crise montaniste_, 346-47).

33 It is interesting that in this context Irenaeus quotes Joel 3:1 (_Adv. haer._ 3.12.1): those who react in such an extreme manner against

Montanism fight against the Spirit which has been poured out upon the Church in the last days. Corsini argues that the dispute was not concerning the continuity of revelation but concerning the multiplicity of continued revelation, that is, whether martyrdoms could be reckoned as a way in which the Spirit continues to manifest itself ("Proposte," 485-87). If this were so, the prominent place given to visions would be difficult to understand.

34 See F. J. Dölger, "Der Kampf mit dem Ägypter in der Perpetua-Vision: Das Martyrium als Kampf mit dem Teufel," Antike und Christentum: Kultur- und religionsgeschichtliche Studien, 6 vols. (Münster: Aschendorff, 1929-50), 3:177-88.

35 Pass. Perp. 10:8: et exivit vir quidam mirae magnitudinis ut etiam excederet fastigium amphitheatri, discinctatus, purpuram inter duos clavos per medium pectus habens, et galliculas multiformes ex auro et argento factas, et ferens virgam quasi lanista, et ramum viridem in quo erant mala aurea. I have adopted Corsini's interpretation of inter duos clavos ("Proposte," 505-6).

36 See s.v. "lanista," PW 12/1 (1924) 690-91.

37 See s.v. "agonothetes," PW 1 (1893) 870-77; H. A. Harris, Greek Athletes and Athletics (Bloomington: Indiana University, 1967) 151-69. Agonothetes were often individuals who gave and organized games from their private wealth.

38 Corsini, "Proposte," 506.

39 According to Corsini, Pomponius is a figure of the Christ "who lives in the Church and who suffers in the Church"; he is the assistance which Christ offers to his martyrs through the medium of the Church ("Proposte," 505,514).

Chapter 7

TERTULLIAN

The Church in which Tertullian lived and worked was pre-eminently a Church of martyrs. The first account of the African Church is that of the Scillitan martyrs whose faith was tested in persecution but victorious in martyrdom. Tertullian himself waxes eloquent in describing the impact the steadfastness of the Christian martyr could have on the pagan world. The ready submission of the Christian martyr to suffering and death for his cause elicited investigation and inquiry into the reason for this noble behavior. Such inquiry often led to the adoption of the Christian faith (Apol. 50:13-16; Ad Scap. 5:4). "The blood of Christians is seed" (Apol. 50:13). Very likely the sight of Christian martyrs played a role in Tertullian's own conversion to the Christian faith. Be that as it may, Christian martyrdom was a theme to which Tertullian alluded in virtually all his writings and to which he devoted several works in their entirety. Tertullian came to regard Christian martyrdom as the very form and figure of the Christian life. Every Christian is a miles Christi by virtue of the oath of allegiance to God which he gave at baptism (Ad mart. 3:1).[1] Persecution comes to the Christian like war comes to the soldier (Scorp. 4:5). Tertullian likens the imprisonment of the Christian to the ardor of military life by which the soldier becomes inured for the rigor of war (Ad mart. 3:1). On several occasions Tertullian views the whole of the Christian life as preparation for martyrdom. Christian women ought to refrain from bedecking themselves with finery lest the strength of their faith be enervated and they become unable to face hardship (De cultu fem. 2.13.3-7). The increased rigor which the Paraclete enjoins allows the Christian to become familiarized with prison (carcer ediscendus) so that he "may enter prison

253

in like condition as though he had just come out of prison" (De ieiun. 12:2).[2] The life of the Christian, like that of the soldier, is one of obedience or disobedience to the terms of his oath. Like the good soldier the Christian obeys in the hope of obtaining promised rewards for duty well done and in fear of the master's wrath should he shrink from his obligation (Ad Scap. 1:1).

At times of persecution, therefore, the Christian is under obligation to God.[3] Martyrdom is above all a duty (debitum) and a necessity (Scorp. 2:1; De fuga 1:3; 4:1). This is so, for prior to all other considerations concerning persecution and martyrdom is the fact that God is their author. He wills and commands them. Behind all persecution and Christian martyrdom lies God's auctoritas (Scorp. 2:1: auctoritas divina praecedit). Tertullian comes to this conclusion through two distinct though closely related arguments. In Scorpiace Tertullian argues that since God has repeatedly forbidden idolatry (Scorp. 2:2-14) and has repeatedly punished those who transgressed this command (Scorp. 3), He has given occasion for persecution and martyrdoms and therefore wills them. For these events elicit obedience to His command (Scorp. 4:2-5).[4] In De fuga in persecutione Tertullian argues that persecution is "worthy" (dignus) of God, for through the fire of persecution judgment takes place. God executes His judgment, the sifting of His people, by calling forth persecutions. Persecution has to do, therefore, with God's glory, and what pertains to God's glory comes from His will (De fuga 1).[5]

In persecution, therefore, the Christian is confronted by God who in willing and commanding worship and obedience to Himself alone brings about a judgment either to glory and honor or to dishonor and reprobation. The image most commonly employed by Tertullian to speak of God as the author of persecution is that of the athletic contest in which God is the agonothete.[6] As the agonothete institutes athletic and gladiatorial

254

contests and proclaims victory to the one combatant and the dishonor of defeat to the other, so God authors persecutions through which He judges some to be approved and judges others to be rejected. In De fuga 1:3-4, Tertullian writes: "For what is the outcome of persecution, what other result does it have, other than the approving and rejecting of faith by which the Lord tests His people. Persecution is a judgment through which one is adjudged either approved or rejected."[7] Thereupon Tertullian likens persecution to a winnowing-shovel which separates the "grain of the martyrs" from the "chaff of the deniers", to the ladder of Jacob by which some ascend and others descend, and to a contest in which God is the agonothete who both initiates the contest and awards the prizes (cf. also Ad mart. 3:3; Scorp. 6:4-6). God as the sovereign Judge is the prime actor in the drama of martyrdom. At times of persecution God calls His people to account. He demands from them an unflinching offering of worship to Him alone. Throughout He is sifting, approving and rejecting. Martyrdom, on the other hand, is the opposite of idolatry (Scorp. 5:3-4; 8:4). It is the pursuit of true religion and the exercise of righteousness (Scorp. 8:1). It is perfect obedience.[8]

God in active judgment and man's obligation to respond in absolute obedience to God's command are the two prominent elements in Tertullian's thinking concerning persecution and martyrdom. Dominating the whole is the tension between God and man.[9] Persecution is God's testing of man. Nowhere is this clearer than in the role which Satan plays. While God wills persecution in order that there might be a testing of faith, Satan supplies the injustice necessary for this testing (De fuga 2:1).[10] Satan thus becomes a minister of God in the execution of the divine judgment. Persecution is "from God" (a Deo) but "through Satan" (per diabolem)(De fuga 2:2; 3:2; 4:1). Satan confronts the Christian with his injustice not of his own free will but because he is in the service of God (De fuga 2:2).[11] Satan is not at liberty to do everything to the servants of God but only that which God allows him to do (De fuga 2:3-4). Tertullian concludes: "Therefore it is manifest that both things belong to God, the shaking of faith and its protection--the shaking by Satan and the protection by the Son" (De fuga 2:4).[12]

To be sure, the idea that Satan is an enemy to be defeated in martyrdom is present in Tertullian. According to De fuga 2:2, God gives Satan leave to afflict His servants so that God might destroy Satan "through the faith of the elect which is victorious in trial". Expressed from the human perspective, persecution is man's God-given opportunity to trample Satan through the steadfastness of faith (Ad mart. 1:4; Scorp. 6:1). Yet, in persecution Satan is fundamentally God's servant and minister of judgment. Satan is God's instrument of reprobation. This is a considerably different perspective than that of Ignatius of Antioch and the martyrs of Lyons. For these the enmity was fully between God (Christ) and Satan. In Christian martyrdom Satan was condemned, for Christ's victory over him was therein enacted. For Tertullian, however, Satan is first of all God's instrument for testing faith. The tension is between God who judges and man who is judged. Martyrdom is not Christ's victory but evidence that man was obedient to God's command even unto death.

As Tertullian conceives Satan to be God's instrument for the shaking of faith, so does he conceive Christ or the Holy Spirit to be God's ministers for the preservation of faith. The Christian, argues Tertullian, ought not despair of God's power. He ought refrain from flight in the trust that "God, if He wills, will Himself protect me" (De fuga 5:3). Thus, De fuga 2:4-5 states that the Son has the protection of faith committed to him.[13] On the other hand, if God hands a person over to Satan, this signifies that God has taken His Spirit away. This was the case with Saul, whom God handed over to Satan as to

256

"an executioner for punishment" (De fuga 2:7).
From this perspective Tertullian discusses the
Old Testament martyrs. The holy men and prophets
were witnesses to true religion. They worshipped
God alone and for that reason were persecuted and
killed. Yet, they were guided by the Spirit of
God who always directed them to martyrdoms (Scorp.
8:3-4).[14] As men under the guidance of the Spirit,
the prophets remained true to the worship of God.
So also, argues Tertullian, Christians are subject
to "the discipline of enduring persecution".
Martyrdoms are commanded in the new covenant as
they were in the old, for the Holy Spirit has been
transmitted to the apostles and through them to
the Christians of Tertullian's day (Scorp. 9:3).[15]
Similarly in Ad martyras Tertullian writes that
the Holy Spirit entered prison with the martyrs.
Indeed, had the Spirit not entered prison with
them, the martyrs would not be in prison (Ad mart.
1:3). Implied in this passage is that the Spirit
is the divine agent for the executing of the
divine will. The martyrs are not in prison of
their own accord, nor do they remain there on
their own. Rather, the Spirit's active presence
is the requisite for their innocent suffering. He
is the Why and the How of their suffering.

As would be expected, the divine aid of the
Spirit plays an important role in Tertullian's
Montanist writings. Tertullian writes in Adv.
Prax. 29:7: "We are not able to suffer for God
unless the Spirit of God is in us, who even speaks
through us those things which pertain to confession. Not that He Himself suffers, but He sees to
it that we are capable of suffering."[16] A similar
statement concludes De fuga. The Paraclete, who
guides into all truth and exhorts to every
endurance, is said to be "necessary" for obedience
to God's will that there be no flight from persecution. Those who have received the Paraclete
will neither flee from persecution nor will they
attempt to purchase their safety, for they have
Him who will speak for them during interrogation
and will aid them in suffering (De fuga 14:3).[17]

In this way Tertullian concludes De fuga as he commenced it, with a reference to the Paraclete. Barnes has argued that De fuga is in fact a Montanist protrepticus in which it is maintained that what is obligatory for the Christian is possible only for those who accept the guidance of the Paraclete.[18] In his exhorting to perseverance, the Paraclete, the "exhortator omnium tolerantiarum" (De fuga 14:3), makes perseverance possible. Tertullian quotes Montanist oracles which contain such exhortation. Climaxing a long argument that his contemporary Christian brethren have no injunction to flee from persecution, Tertullian relates two Montanist oracles of the Spirit who "virtually exhorts everyone to martyrdom, not to flee from it":

> If you are exposed to the public, it is good for you. For he who is not exposed to dishonor among men will be before the Lord. Do not be ashamed. Righteousness brings you before the public gaze. Why should you be ashamed when you are gaining honor? The opportunity is yours when you are before the eyes of men.
>
> Seek not to die on bridal beds, nor in miscarriages, nor in soft fevers, but to die the martyr's death, that he may be glorified who has suffered for you (De fuga 9:4; cf. De anima 55:5).[19]

The Paraclete who exhorts to martyrdom also brings to martyrdom and makes possible endurance in martyrdom.

On five different occasions Tertullian discusses the words of Jesus, "the spirit is willing but the flesh is weak" (Matt 26:41; Mark 14:38). Tertullian's non-Montanist writings contain three of these occasions; his Montanist writings contain two. In his non-Montanist writings Tertullian understands "spirit" to mean the spirit of man, man's higher faculty which motivates the flesh (Ad mart. 4:1; De pat. 13:7;

Ad uxorem 1.4.1ff.). However, in the two occurrences in his Montanist writings, Tertullian
interprets "spirit" to mean the divine Spirit, the
Spirit of God, who gives aid during martyrdom
(De fuga 8:1-2; De mono. 14:6). In De fuga 8:1-2
Tertullian argues that Jesus' example indicates
that Christians ought not flee from persecution.
Jesus did not flee, although he acknowledged that
"his soul was anxious unto death and his flesh was
weak". Jesus admitted of this weakness so that
there might be no doubt that he was truly human
and that we might know that soul and body can do
nothing of themselves without the Spirit.[20] Left
to themselves, the soul and flesh would have been
unable to sustain the anxiety and fear of
approaching death. But with the strength of the
Spirit, Jesus could and did place himself in submission to the Father's will: "not however what
I will but what You will". So also the Christian
ought recognize that he has the Spirit's strength
as well as the flesh's weakness. There is thus
no excuse for failing to do God's will.

A similar argument occurs in De mono. 14:6.
Here "spirit" is understood to be the Paraclete
whose strength enables one to follow the more
rigorous requirements of the last days. Thus, no
one can excuse himself from performing the
precepts of the Montanist ethic on the basis of
the infirmity of the flesh. The Spirit is
"prompt", that is, the Spirit conquers the flesh,
placing that which is weaker in subjection to that
which is stronger.

According to Tertullian, therefore, the Holy
Spirit is the divine instrument by whose aid the
Christian perseveres in the worship of the one,
true God and in obedience to God's commands. By
enabling the Christian to persevere, the Spirit
in effect guides and exhorts to martyrdom, for
unrighteousness always attacks righteousness.
While this view occurs in the non-Montanist works
of Tertullian (Ad mart. 1:3; Scorp. 8:3; 9:3),
it is most prevalent in the Montanist work, De
fuga in persecutione, where the activity of the

Spirit is especially viewed as the strength
required to overcome the weakness of the flesh.[21]
Yet, while Tertullian insists on the necessity of
the Spirit's presence if the Christian is to
remain obedient, the principal thrust of
Tertullian's martyrological thinking is ethical.
God wills persecution for the testing of faith,
but it is still man's faith which must manifest
itself as man's obedience. Therefore, Tertullian
often presents his views and exhortations from a
decidedly anthropological perspective.[22]

For example, the hardships of prison themselves offer assistance for the enduring of martyrdom. Tertullian likens imprisonment to the
training of a soldier for the battle (Ad mart.
3:1-2). As in peacetime the soldiers are inured
to war by undergoing toil and inconveniences, so
the hardships of prison help to prepare the
Christian for the endurance of martyrdom.
Similarly, prison is likened to a palaestra where
athletes prepare themselves for the contest through
rigorous exercise (Ad mart. 3:3-5). The rigors of
prison have as their purpose "the exercise of the
powers of mind and body" (ad exercitationem
virtutum animi et corporis [Ad mart. 3:3]). Like
a trainer (epistates) who leads a wrestler to the
wrestling circle, Christ leads the Christian to
prison in order that there the Christian's powers
may be strengthened through harsh treatment (Ad
mart. 3:4).[23] Tertullian allows his reflections
on the role of the divine subject to be confined
to this image of martyrdom as an athletic contest.
Just as an epistates may supervise an athlete and
bring him to the place of contest but yet in no
way is himself a source of strength for the
athlete, so Christ is not understood here as a
source of strength. Rather, Tertullian conceives
the martyr's preparation quite physically. The
exercise, the hardship and deprivation of prison
prepare the martyr, for they accustom the mind and
the body of the martyr to hardship and pain
(virtus duritia exstruitur [Ad mart. 3:5]).
Clearly implied is that in the actual contest of

martyrdom the virtus of the martyr, hardened and strengthened by exercise, will enable the martyr to remain steadfast and faithful.[24]

Tertullian, to be sure, does mention the Spirit twice in Ad mart. 3:3-4. The Spirit is said to be the xystarches in the good fight which the martyr shall undergo, and the Spirit is likened to the oil which Christ, the epistates, rubs on the athlete. A xystarches was a president of an athletic organization or the manager of a place of athletic exercise. With this image Tertullian at most implies that martyrdom is under divine aegis; no significant activity by the Spirit is indicated. On the other hand, the image of Christ's anointing the martyr with the Spirit refers to baptism, at which time the martyr had been granted the Spirit and had taken the baptismal oath (see Ad mart. 1:3; 3:1). The Spirit works to guarantee the Christian's fidelity to that oath in which the things of the world have been renounced.[25]

Within martyrological contexts Tertullian at times understands the "spirit" of Matt 26:41; Mark 14:38 to be man's spirit (Ad mart. 4:1-2; De pat. 13:7; cf. Ad uxorem 1.4.1ff.). Also in these passages Tertullian reveals the anthropological perspective of his martyrological reflections. The martyr may find no excuse in the fact that the flesh is weak, for Christ taught that the spirit is willing in order to show that the flesh ought to be subject to the spirit and receive its strength from the spirit (Ad mart. 4:1).[26] How does the spirit give the flesh the fortitude necessary to withstand the pain of martyrdom? It recalls to mind the many examples of heroic suffering among the pagans. These examples, male and female alike, willingly took on pain and torture for temporal glory (Ad mart. 4:3-9; cf. Apol. 50:4-11; Ad nat. 1.18). Ought not the Christian then willingly undergo pain and torture for eternal glory? For Tertullian the martyrdom of Christians is primarily an ethical activity. The principle underlying both Christian suffering and pagan heroism is the same: suffering for a just cause is heroic and is rewarded with fame and glory. For this reason pagan examples will serve as exhortatory models just as well as Christian examples or even Christ himself.

Such a view completely dissolves any eschato-logical significance in Christian martyrdom. The martyr's death is a show of the martyr's strength and virtue of spirit and mind, and such a display of courage deserves the reward of glory. Should the martyr refuse to suffer, he does not so much deny Christ as shirk his duty and obligation toward God's command. Thus, even pagan examples will serve as witnesses against the unfaithful on the day of judgment. That pagans willingly assumed pain for vainglory will remove all room for excuse for a Christian who refused to suffer for eternal glory (Ad mart. 5:2).

Tertullian's anthropological, ethical perspective is retained even when the Spirit is present. In the wellknown passage, Ad mart. 1:3, Tertullian writes: "First, then, O blessed, do not grieve the Holy Spirit (Eph 4:30) who entered prison with you. For if he had not entered with you, you would not be there today. Therefore, exert every effort in order that he may persevere with you and so lead you from prison to the Lord."27 In this way Tertullian exhorts the imprisoned Christians not to lament the loss of the world's enjoyments, since they have gained spiritual advantage. They have gone out of a prison rather than into one: "The world has the greater darkness, blinding men's hearts. The world imposes the more grievous fetters, binding men's very souls. The world breathes out the worst impurities, human lusts. The world contains the larger number of criminals, even the whole human race" (Ad mart. 2:1-3). Apart from the world the Christians are free from idolatrous images and ceremonies, free from the sight of brothels and fleshly temptations: "The prison does the same service for the Christian which the desert did for the prophet" (Ad mart. 2:8).

In Ad mart. 1:3 Tertullian makes reference to
Eph 4:30: "Do not grieve the Holy Spirit of God
by whom you have been sealed for the day of
redemption."[28] The imprisoned Christians whom
Tertullian is addressing are on the way between
their baptism and the day of their martyrdom. We
have seen that the Christian is a miles Christi
serving under his baptismal oath of allegiance to
God which he gave at his baptism. When faced
with persecution, the Christian recognizes that
the conditions of his baptismal oath are being
realized, and by standing firm in persecution he
lives out the terms of his oath.[29] Tertullian
briefly intimates of what the terms of the
baptismal oath consisted: it involved the renunciation of the Devil and of all his pomp and his
angels (De corona 3:2). Obedience to the oath
given at baptism to forswear the Devil and the
things of this world leads the Christian to a life
of renunciation: "We have been called to the
warfare of the living God at that very time when
we responded to the words of the sacrament" (Ad
mart. 3:1). The imprisoned Christian is like the
soldier who does not go into battle laden with
luxuries or from a comfortable chamber but who
goes into the fight from the field tent where he
lives in hardship and unpleasantness (Ad mart.
3:1b). Like soldiers who live between their
military oath of allegiance and the battefield,
the Christian in prison is living between the
oath made at baptism and the day of battle in
martyrdom. Martyrdom is the outcome of the
Christian's baptismal oath, for martyrdom is total
renunciation of Satan and of the world.

Through the imperative, "Do not wish to
grieve the Holy Spirit" (nolite contristare
Spiritum sanctum), Tertullian exhorts the martyrs
to remain true to their baptismal oath which they
gave at their baptisms, when the Holy Spirit was
bestowed upon them. Not to do so would be to
grieve the Spirit who works as the guarantor of
the Christian's fidelity to his oath and thereby
leads him to that fate wherein the baptismal oath

is realized. Therefore, it was the Holy Spirit
who entered prison with the martyrs, bringing on
them the renunciation of worldly things which
necessarily accompanies imprisonment.

Tertullian discusses the theme of willing
acceptance of the loss of worldly goods at length
in De patientia. This work offers, as it were, a
commentary on Ad mart. 1:3. In De pat. 7:5-7
Tertullian writes that since all things belong to
God, the Christian ought patiently to accept any
loss lest he covet what is in fact not his,
namely, that which is God's. He who through loss
becomes impatient gives earthly goods precedence
over heavenly things and so sins against God, for
on behalf of worldly goods he shocks the Spirit
which he had received from God.[30] This passage
is a good commentary on the imperative, nolite
contristare. The martyr is not to deplore the
loss of his worldly pleasures and freedoms. To
do so would be to love the world more than the
spiritual good which prison and martyrdom offer
to the Christian. It would be to distress the
Spirit who brings humble acceptance of the God-
given fate and thus is present to see the martyr
through. Such acceptance of loss and trial, that
is, patience, is the indivisible companion of the
Spirit: "When the Spirit of God descends,
patience accompanies him indivisibly" (De pat.
15:7).[31] Thus, the Christian martyr cannot and
will not endure without the presence of the
Spirit.

Yet, the martyr may resist this presence and
give occasion for the Spirit to leave him.
Tertullian, therefore, exhorts the Christians in
prison: "exert every effort that the Spirit may
persevere with you" (date operam ut illic vobiscum
perseveret [Ad mart. 1:3]). De pat. 15:7 provides
commentary. He to whom the Spirit comes must also
accept patience or else the Spirit may not, indeed,
cannot remain: "If we do not admit patience with
the Spirit, will he (the Spirit) always remain
with us? Indeed, I do not know whether he would
persevere any longer. Without his companion and

handmaid it is necessary that he be distressed in
every time and place. Whatever his enemy inflicts
he shall be unable to sustain it, since he lacks
the instrument of sustaining" (De pat. 15:7).[32]
The Christian must give way to the gifts of the
Spirit or the Spirit shall depart. The Christian
must accept the loss of worldly goods with
patience or he rejects the work of the Spirit,
forcing the Spirit to leave. Thus, the imperative,
date operam, exhorts the martyrs to submit to the
hardships of prison and to stand steadfast in
them and thereby to allow the Spirit to prompt
them. For only should they do so shall the
martyrs allow the Spirit to lead them to the Lord,
that is, to the day of their martyrdom, to the day
of their redemption.

In this one passage, Ad mart. 1:3, the two
aspects of Tertullian's martyrological thinking
are combined. The Christian is martyr, since God
wills it and through the gift of the Spirit
executes His will. The Spirit guides the Christian
to martyrdom and accompanies the Christian to
martyrdom. Without the Spirit there is no renunciation of the world, no steadfastness in prison,
no Christian martyrdom. Yet, on the other hand,
martyrdom is an ethical act of the martyr which
he performs by virtue of the strength of his
spirit and of his body, which have been trained
through the hardships of prison. The martyr's
steadfast obedience and allegiance to his
baptismal oath--and therefore to the God to whom
he swore his oath--is a human, courageous work of
the martyr the faithful completion of which brings
the martyr successfully to his appointed end and
makes him worthy of reward. As an human act of
courage, the martyr's death itself loses all
specifically Christian characteristics. It is not
a divinely ordained locus for the confession of
Christ. It is not, as in Paul, Ignatius, and the
martyrs of Lyons, an epiphany of the crucified
Lord. It is an heroic deed, similar to that of
pagan heroes, springing out of the inner recesses
of human courage, human virtue, and human loyalty
to a valued cause. Such a view can make Christ

or the Holy Spirit merely circumstantial. For example, in De fuga 10:2 Tertullian speaks of the martyr's having put on Christ and of Christ being in the martyr. Yet, Tertullian does not mean by this that Christ is present as fighter and victor on behalf of the martyr. "Christ in you" is a circumstance which makes the cowardice of flight all the more reprehensible.[33] Tertullian nowhere attempts to reconcile the apparent contradiction: martyrdom as a divine ordination and martyrdom as a human act. He only knows that in the reality of Christian martyrdom both, God's will effective in the Spirit and man's active obedience, are present.

SUMMARY

Tertullian's discussion of Christian martyrdom is dominated by an ethical perspective which conceives of martyrdom as primarily an act of human obedience to the divine will. Primary is the divine will which desires to test the mettle of Christian faith and allegiance through persecution. Christian martyrdom is, therefore, essentially the Christian's obedience to the divine command to have no other god before the Creator. In this view, Satan is not the adversary of God and for that reason the adversary of the Christian. Satan is a minister of God through whose agency the Christian is tested. On the other hand, Christ or the Holy Spirit are ministers of divine exhortation and support who help and aid the Christian to remain faithfully steadfast. But Christ and the Spirit are not themselves actively engaged in conflict. The martyr is by and large alone in his martyrdom, required to exercise his virtue and courage lest he prove himself unworthy and become subject to God's condemnation. As an ethical struggle for a right cause, Christian suffering is no different than that of the suffering of pagans who remain loyal to their beliefs. Indeed, martyrdom is only one form of adverse fate which can come upon the Christian to test him (Ad mart. 6).

1 Tertullian, Ad mart. 3:1: vocati sumus ad
militiam Dei vivi iam tunc, cum in sacramenti
verba respondimus (CChr 1:5). The Christian life
as that of a soldier is a common theme in
Tertullian (see A. von Harnack, Militia Christi:
Die christliche Religion und der Soldatenstand
in den ersten drei Jahrhunderten [Tübingen:
J. C. B. Mohr, 1905] 32-40, 104-9).

2 Tertullian, De ieiun. 12:2: cum carcer
ediscendus et fames ac sitis exercendae et tam
inediae quam anxii victus tolerantia usurpanda
sit, ut in carcerem talis introeat Christianus,
qualis inde prodisset, non poenam illic passurus,
sed disciplinam, nec saeculi tormenta, sed sua
officia (CChr 2:1270).

3 The basic outline of Tertullian's thinking
concerning martyrdom was not affected by his
conversion to Montanism. W. Gass writes correctly:
"Hinsichtlich des Märtyrerthums aber verschärfte
er . . . lediglich seinen frühern Standpunkt"
("Das christliche Märtyrerthum in den ersten
Jahrhunderten und dessen Idee," Zeitschrift für
historische Theologie 30 [1860] 321).

4 Tertullian, Scorp. 4:3-4: si enim praeceptum
observando vim patior, hoc erit quodammodo
observandi praecepti praeceptum, ut id patiar per
quod potero observare praeceptum, vim scilicet,
quaecumque mihi imminet cavenda ab idololatria.
Et utique qui inponit praeceptum, extorquet
obsequium. Non potuit ergo noluisse ea evenire
per quae constabit obsequium (CChr 2:1076).

5 Tertullian, De fuga 1:5: totum, quod agitur in
persecutione, gloria Dei est, probantis et
reprobantis, imponentis et deponentis. Quod
autem ad gloriam Dei pertinet, utique ex voluntate
illius eveniet (CChr 2:1136).

6 For discussion of the agonothete, see above, p. 238.

7 Tertullian, De fuga 1:3-4: quis est enim exitus persecutionis, quis effectus alius, nisi probatio et reprobatio fidei, qua suos utique Dominus examinavit? Hoc nomine iudicium est persecutio, per quam quis aut probatus aut reprobatus iudicatur (CChr 2:1135-36).

8 The three young men in the fiery furnace underwent perfect martyrdoms, although they did not suffer: O martyrium et sine passione perfectum! (Scorp. 8:7). They were martyrs precisely because they totally refused to capitulate to idolatry.

9 So correctly H. von Campenhausen, Die Idee des Martyriums in der alten Kirche, 2nd ed. (Göttingen: Vandenhoeck & Ruprecht, 1964) 118: "Die Spannung zwischen Gott und Mensch . . . beherrscht die Situation und gibt der Bekenntnisforderung ihre Schärfe und ihre Wucht."

10 Tertullian, De fuga 2:1: scire debemus, quatenus nec persecutio potest sine iniquitate diaboli nec probatio fidei sine persecutione, propter probationem fidei necessariam iniquitatem non patrocinium praestare persecutioni, sed ministerium (CChr 2:1136-37).

11 Tertullian, De fuga 2:2: Igitur quod ministerium non est arbitrii, sed servitii-- arbitrium enim Domini persecutio propter fidei probationem, ministerium autem iniquitas diaboli propter persecutionis instructionem--, ita eam per diabolum, si forte, non a diabolo evenire credimus (CChr 2:1137).

12 Tertullian, De fuga 2:4: Per quod ostenditur utrumque apud Deum esse, et concussionem fidei et protectionem, cum utrumque ab eo petitur, concussio a diabolo, protectio a filio (CChr 2:1137).

13 Tertullian, De fuga 2:5 (continuing from De fuga 2:4, n. 12): Et utique cum filius Dei protectionem fidei habet in sua potestate, quam a patre postulat, a quo omnem accepit potestatem in caelis et in terris (CChr 2:1138).

14 Tertullian, Scorp. 8:4: Et utique qui spiritu dei agebantur, ab ipso in martyria dirigebantur etiam patiendo quae et praedicassent (CChr 2:1083). The imperfects (agebantur, dirigebantur) show that holy men were commonly led by the Spirit to martyrdom. Agere is used in the Rule of Faith to describe the work of the Spirit (De prae. haer. 13:5: misisse vicarium vim spiritus sancti qui credentes agat).

15 T. D. Barnes uses this passage to argue for the non-Montanist character of Scorpiace ("Tertullian's Scorpiace," JTS n.s. 20 [1969] 115-16). According to Barnes, this passage leaves no room for the New Prophecy. Barnes dates Scorpiace to late 203 or early 204.

16 Tertullian, Adv. Prax. 29:7: nec nos pati pro Deo possumus nisi Spiritus Dei sit in nobis qui et loquitur de nobis quae sunt confessionis, non ipse tamen patiens sed pati posse praestans (CChr 2:1203).

17 Tertullian, De fuga 14:3: Et ideo Paracletus necessarius, deductor omnium veritatum, exhortator omnium tolerantiarum. Quem qui receperunt, neque fugere persecutionem neque redimere noverunt, habentes ipsum, qui pro nobis erit, sicut locuturus in interrogatione, ita iuvaturus in passione (CChr 2:1155). Matt 10:19 is implied. In De fuga 6:1-3, Tertullian explicitly argues that Matthew 10 refers not just to the apostles but to his contemporaries as well.

18 Barnes, "Tertullian's Scorpiace," 118.

19 Tertullian, De fuga 9:4: Publicaris inquit, bonum tibi est; qui enim non publicatur in

hominibus, publicatur in Domino. Ne confundaris;
iustitia te producit in medium. Quid confunderis
laudem ferens? Potestas fit, cum conspiceris ab
hominibus. Sic et alibi: Nolite in lectulis nec
in aborsibus et febribus mollibus optare exire,
sed in martyriis, uti glorificetur qui est passus
pro vobis (CChr 2:1147).

20 Tertullian, De fuga 8:1: Professus quidem et
ipse est animam anxiam usque ad mortem et carnem
infirmam, ut tibi ostenderet primo in se utramque
substantiam humanam fuisse ex proprietate
anxietatis animae et imbecillitatis carnis, ne
aliam, ut quidam nunc induxerunt, aut carnem aut
animam Christi interpretareris, dehinc ut,
demonstratis condicionibus earum, scires illas
nihil valere per semetipsas sine Spiritu (CChr
2:1145).

21 Cf. W. Bender, Die Lehre über den Heiligen
Geist bei Tertullian (Münchener Theologische
Studien II, Systematische Abteilung 18; München:
M. Heuber, 1961) 156.

22 The remarks of von Campenhausen are to the
point (Die Idee des Martyriums, 123): "Vielmehr
geht Tertullian, paulinisch gesprochen, noch
durchaus den Weg des 'Gesetzes', idem er im
Gehorsam gegen die Gebote und im Vertrauen auf
Gottes Allmacht und wunderbaren Beistand sich
zuletzt doch selbst zu bewahren und zu erretten
hofft. Dadurch wird aber wie bei jeder
gesetzlichen Lösung des sittlichen Problems
alsbald inmitten seiner theozentrisch angesetzten
Martyrologie nun doch wieder ein Spielraum frei
für eine ganz anders gerichtete, anthropologische
Betrachtung des Geschehens."

23 Tertullian, Ad mart. 3:4: Itaque epistates
vester Christus Iesus, qui vos Spiritu unxit, et
ad hoc scamma produxit, voluit vos ante diem
agonis ad duriorem tractationem a liberiore
condicione seponere, ut vires corroborarentur in
vobis (CChr 1:5).

24 A. Brekelmans can with justice approach
Tertullian's martyrology from the aspect of the
martyr's glory (Martyrerkranz: Eine symbolgeschichtliche Untersuchung im frühchristlichen
Schrifttum [AnGreg 150; Rome: Libreria Editrice
dell' Università Gregoriana, 1965] 72-76). He
shows that Tertullian conceives the martyr's glory
in terms analogous to the glory in agonistic
games: "Wie der römische Ruhm aus der praktischen
und sozial-ethischen Tat hervorgeht, so hängt auch
die christliche Glorie bei Tertullian eng mit der
virtus zusammen."

25 The oil rubbed on the wrestler prior to a bout
served only the hygenic function of keeping the
pores of the wrestler's skin free from soot. It
was not used to prevent the opponent from gaining
a firm grasp, which would destroy the very nature
of wrestling as a contest of strength and skill.
Therefore, this image of Christ's rubbing the
wrestler with the oil of the Spirit does not imply
that the Spirit was a sort of prophylactic,
keeping the martyr from the grasp of Satan. The
martyr must still be exhorted not to grieve the
Spirit (Ad mart. 1:3).

26 Tertullian, Ad mart. 4:1: Propterea enim
praedixit spiritum promptum, ut ostenderet, quid
cui debeat esse subiectum, scilicet, ut caro
serviat spiritui, infirmior fortiori, ut ab eo
etiam ipsa fortitudinem assumat (CChr 1:6). That
"spirit" is man's spirit is clear from Ad mart.
4:2, which speaks of the "common salvation" of
the spirit and of the flesh.

27 Tertullian, Ad mart. 1:3: Inprimis ergo,
benedicti, nolite contristare Spiritum sanctum,
qui vobiscum introiit carcerem. Si enim non
vobiscum nunc introisset, nec vos illic hodie
fuissetis. Et ideo date operam ut illic vobiscum
perseveret et ita vos inde perducat ad Dominum
(CChr 1:3). The martyres designati are called
benedicti (Ad mart. 1:1,3; 2:4; 3:1,3; 5:2). This
is to be understood in the light of De pat. 6:2

where Abraham is called "blessed" because through his patience he showed himself to be faithful.

28 Tertullian quotes only the first part of the passage: Nolite contristare Spiritum sanctum. The entire verse in the Old Latin Bible read: Nolite contristare Spiritum Sanctum Dei in quo signati estis in diem redemptionis (cf. Cyprian, De bono pat. 16; Ad Quir. 3:7; Augustine, De pecc. mer. et remis. et de bapt. parv. 1:46).

29 Tertullian, Ad Scap. 1:1: Nos quidem neque expavescimus, neque pertimescimus ea quae ab ignorantibus patimur, cum ad hanc sectam, utique suscepta condicione eius pacti, venerimus, ut etiam animas nostras exauctorati in has pugnas accedamus, ea quae Deus repromittit consequi optantes, et ea quae diversae vitae comminatur pati timentes (CChr 2:1127).

30 Tertullian, De pat. 7:7: Qui damni inpatientia concitatur terrena caelestibus anteponendo, de proximo in deum peccat: spiritum enim quem a domino sumpsit saecularis rei gratia concutit (CChr 1:307).

31 Tertullian, De pat. 15:7: Cum ergo spiritus dei descendit, individua patientia comitatur eum (CChr 1:316).

32 Tertullian, De pat. 15:7: Si non cum spiritu admiserimus, in nobis morabitur semper? Immo nescio an diutius perseveret: sine sua comite ac ministra omni loco ac tempore angatur necesse est, quodcumque inimicus eius inflixerit solus sustinere non poterit carens instrumento sustinendi (CChr 1:316).

33 Cf. von Campenhausen, Die Idee des Martyriums, 122-25.

CONCLUSION

Writing about the motivating ideal in the martyrological literature of Judaism, Hans von Campenhausen says the following:

> Es ist aber auch, sachlich gesehen, tatsächlich nicht der Gedanke des Zeugnisses vor dem Volk und unter den Völkern, an dem sich die jüdische Idee eines "Martyriums" orientiert. Es ist vielmehr die Treue gegenüber dem Gesetz und der Gehorsam unter Gottes Gebot, die den Frommen auch in der äussersten Todesqual zum Durchhalten bestimmen und ihm jedes Murren verbieten. . . . Ein Jude, der lieber willig in den Tod geht, statt das Gesetz zu brechen, hat in dieser Haltung Gott gegenüber die rechte "Liebe" bewährt, und das macht seine religiöse Grösse aus. Aber das Martyrium selbst ist normalerweise ein reines Unglück, dessen grundsätzliche Beurteilung unsicher bleibt.[1]

The last sentence especially raises the question of the significance of suffering and death for and in the name of a religious cause. Our discussion of the literature of Judaism, especially that of the Maccabees, tends to confirm von Campenhausen's evaluation of it. Faithful obedience to the commands of the Law was of the essence of martyrdom. However, suffering and death themselves were an embarrassment which raised an acute theodicy problem and issued into an idea of resurrection as an other-worldly reward for a this-worldly meritorious deed.

The situation was fundamentally different for the early Christians. Suffering and death for the Name were accompanied with rejoicing and hymn singing (cf. Acts 5:41). Where believers were startled by persecution and reacted fearfully to it, the exhortation came to be glad, for their suffering was a participation in the sufferings of Christ (cf. 1 Pet 4:13).[2] The question which this

273

conjunction of suffering and rejoicing raises is that concerning the relationship between the cross and the resurrection, between the cross and the new age, between the cross and the Holy Spirit. Some early Christians had apparently answered this question by denying that any inner connection between cross and resurrection existed. Paul speaks of a certain Hymenaeus and a certain Philetus who were perverting the truth with the assertion that the resurrection had already occurred (2 Tim 2:17-18). The opponents of Paul in Corinth perceived the power of the Kingdom in their deeds of strength and wonder. The view of these persons was apparently that since Christ was risen from the dead, lowliness and suffering were of the old, defeated aeon and the Spiritual man was free to exist in untrammeled resurrection glory.

The New Testament and the central, "orthodox" tradition of the Christian community rejected such a separation of cross and resurrection. The words of Jesus that to be his disciple one must take up the cross were remembered, and Jesus' foretelling of future persecutions, imprisonments, and even deaths had become reality for the Church. Clearly, the resurrection of Jesus did not have prophylactic character, preserving the Christian from all suffering. How was this to be reconciled with the belief that the Christian believer was a participant in the new age?

Determinative for the answer to this question was the Christian conviction that in the earthly life of Jesus the Kingdom of God had broken in. In Jesus' life of lowly servanthood, especially in his suffering and death on the cross (cf. Mark 10:35-45), the telos of God's plan had arrived, the fulfillment of God's promises. Jesus' ministry and his suffering and death, therefore, had eschatological significance, and that meant that the Spirit--the pre-eminent gift and sign of the endtime--was connected indivisibly and inseparably with Jesus' life, his suffering and his death.

However, the suffering and death of Jesus could be perceived from two perspectives. Both perspectives are incorporated in Jesus' words that "it is necessary that the Son of Man suffer many things and be rejected by the elders, the chiefpriests and the scribes and be killed and after three days to rise again" (Mark 8:31). On the one hand, Jesus' suffering and death were the necessary--and paradoxical--form in which God accomplished His purposes. Christ on the cross was not in defeat, but rather Christ on the cross was the very manner in which God's eschatological power was bringing about God's victory over His foes. Christ crucified, writes Paul, is the "power of God and the wisdom of God" which is wiser and stronger than that of men (1 Cor 1:23-25). Perceived from this perspective, the cross of Jesus can never be viewed apart from his resurrection. The resurrection of Jesus did not put an end to the cross in the sense that Jesus' death receded into the past as a dead, historical act. The resurrection was rather the victory of the cross in which the cross was manifested as the eschatological power of God over the Satanic powers of sin and death. Resurrection meant that the risen and exalted Lord remained the Crucified One who exercises his rule through the cross, for it was in the cross that he victored over Satan. Through the resurrection, the cross of Jesus continues to be the very <u>locus</u> and the very form of Jesus' victory over death.

On the other hand, Jesus' suffering and death also can be perceived as the form in which the forces opposed to God attacked God's Son and messenger and attempted to thwart and destroy God's plan in him. Suffering and death were threats to the successful completion of Jesus' ministry and were the hostile context within which he had to carry out his task. Jesus' suffering and death were the hostile acts of hostile men who hated him and wished to do away with him. Perceived from this perspective, the cross of Jesus is the <u>locus</u> of Satan's most

275

concerted attack upon Jesus; it is the most savage attempt to bring Jesus to disobedience. As the attack of death and the temptation to disobedience, the cross is that which itself is broken and conquered in the resurrection. Jesus' resurrection was Jesus' victory over death and the cross and his victory over the temptation which they brought. Resurrection meant that the risen and exalted Lord remained he who in obedience had gone into death and whose rule now finds expression in the steadfast obedience of his disciples.

Jesus' resurrection, therefore, was Jesus' victory <u>over</u> <u>death</u>, but this victory was <u>in</u> <u>the</u> <u>cross</u>. The new age, the age of the Spirit, was to be characterized by victory over death, but this victory was to be won in obedience which may involve suffering and death. The way of Jesus, who is the Lord, through the Spirit was also to be the way of Jesus' disciples. The Christians understood that their way would be one of conflict which would call for steadfast obedience and faithfulness and that this obedience and faithfulness might take the form of their dying for the Name. However, since the way of the Christian believer was the way of the Lord Jesus, the way of the Christian itself possessed eschatological significance. It was of the Spirit and therefore full of faith and hope and joy. The way of the Christian was full of Life, for the way of obedience, even unto death, was the exercise and expression of the rule of the Resurrected One who in death conquered death.

The persecution and martyrdom of Christians, therefore, did not raise an acute theodicy problem for the Church. They were rather indications that the community of believers was living in the new age whose Lord was the Crucified Christ and whose power was that of the Spirit. They were manifestations of the eschatological presence of the risen and victorious Jesus among the believers. However, as the cross of Jesus could be perceived from two perspectives--as the very form of God's eschatological power and as

276

the result of opposition to Jesus' ministry--so also the persecution and martyrdom of Jesus' disciples could be perceived from these two perspectives. On the one hand, Christian suffering and martyrdom were the very form in which Jesus' victory over death in the cross manifested itself in the Christian believer. On the other hand, Christian suffering and martyrdom were the concerted attack of Satanic forces against the Christian believer through whom the risen Jesus continued his ministry. Persecution and martyrdom were the hostile context within which Christian proclamation and confession had to be made, and to the extent that this proclamation and confession were obediently made, Jesus victory over death in the cross was manifested.

The martyrological equivalent to the statement, "in the cross Jesus victored over death", is the statement, "in persecution and martyrdom the martyr proclaims and confesses Jesus". Corresponding to this statement, the role of the Holy Spirit could also be understood in a two-fold manner. The Spirit could be seen as the agency of Jesus' victorious reign over death in that the Spirit effected the continued proclamation and confession of Jesus in the face of persecution and martyrdom. Or, the Spirit could be seen as the agency of Jesus' victory in the cross in that the Spirit continually brought Christians to martyrdom in order that therein Jesus' victory over death might be manifested.

Within the New Testament and the early Christian writings which we have considered in this study, both views of the Spirit's work are represented. Jesus' promise of the Spirit in Matt 10:17-20 assured the disciples that they did not shoulder the responsibility of proclamation alone. The Holy Spirit would see to it that even within the most threatening of environments the proclamation of God's Kingdom would continue. Similarly, the "willing Spirit" would enable the disciples to remain obedient in times of trouble just as Jesus remained obedient in the Garden

(Matt 26:41). The Acts of the Apostles relate
the repeated fulfillment of Jesus' promise concerning the Spirit's aid. The Spirit is the constant companion of the apostles as they proclaim
the message of Christ before hostile audiences.
The Spirit enables the apostles to "speak boldly"
of Jesus as the Christ (Acts 4:1ff.; 5:12ff.;
6:8ff.; 7:55-56; 13:46ff.). Within the Gospel of
John the Paraclete is he who brings to the
disciples' remembrance the words of Jesus and
gives witness concerning Jesus in the face of
opposition (John 15:18-16:4a). Within the
Revelation of John the "Spirit of prophecy" is the
instrument of Jesus' rule over the Christian
community. Through the "Spirit of prophecy" Jesus
"witnesses" to the community and brings about the
community's witness concerning Jesus. In 1 Peter
the Spirit enables the Christian to follow the
pattern of Jesus not only in proclamation and
confession but also in the constant exercise of
good works within situations of unjust suffering.

The Martyrdom of Polycarp and the letter
concerning the martyrs of Lyons continue the theme
of the Spirit's effecting confession and proclamation in persecution. The wonders of the Spirit
surrounding Polycarp's martyrdom give witness to
the presence of God's divine assistance to those
who are instrument of His will. Polycarp is
obedient to God's will, since God enables him to
be so. According to the martyrs of Lyons, the
steadfast confession of the Name and the unbending
endurance of suffering are manifestations of
Christ's victory over death. They are proofs that
the future glory is mightier than present woes.
As epiphanies of Christ's victory over death,
confession and endurance are accompanied by signs
of resurrection life: the martyrs experience
healing; the martyrs overcome their bodily weaknesses; the martyrs love the brethren.

The most complete representative of the view
that the Spirit works in the form of the cross is
the apostle Paul. Against the claim of certain
"super apostles" that his weaknesses disqualified

278

him from being an apostle of the risen Lord, Paul asserted that it was precisely his weakness that proved his apostleship. In his apostolic suffering the life of the risen Lord was manifested. As he would preach no other gospel than that of Christ crucified, so the very form of his apostolic existence would be none other than that of the cross. The Gospel of John shares this view. Through the Paraclete the messianic community continues Jesus' ministry in word and deed. Love is shown in giving one's life for the brethren. 1 John 5:6-8 stands within the purview of this motif.

Outside the New Testament, Ignatius of Antioch best represents the understanding of the Christian life as cross and suffering. He viewed his impending martyrdom solely in terms of the "cross character" of the resurrection life. Christ died in the flesh, was raised in the flesh, and as the "sarkophoros" still works in the flesh. Only for that reason was Ignatius' death in the flesh to be an expression of Christ's Lordship over him. Since Christ in passion was united with the Father and in passion unites his people with himself, in his martyrdom Ignatius shall be united with God.

For the writings just reviewed, the thought of resurrection from the dead is integral to reflection on Christian suffering and martyrdom. It was integral because martyrdom was Christologically founded and oriented. Christian suffering and martyrdom were a sign of Christ's reign in the Church and, therefore, were inherently of the Spirit. The Christian martyr who in faith and hope entered into death for the Name showed precisely therein that death had no power over him. That is, the martyr manifested the final defeat of death. He showed forth the victory of resurrection to life.

However, this essentially Christological and eschatological perspective rather early began to be lost. Martyrdom began to be viewed as a

courageous exercise of the human will on behalf
of a religious truth, and as such Christian martyrdom began to take one tragic proportions. It
was the evil end of righteous men who now deserved
reward and honor for their bravery and courage.
The Martyrdom of Polycarp gives an early instance
of this tendency (Mart. Pol. 2:2). Tertullian,
and to a lesser extent the Passion of Perpetua and
Felicitas, represent this ethical view. Martyrdom
is essentially the struggle of the martyr to
remain faithful to the divine will. However,
God need be in no way directly involved in the
struggle itself. The image of the gladiatorial
contest, to which Tertullian's thinking is largely
confined, relegates the Father, Christ, and the
Spirit to the sidelines. They may exhort, but
they do not fight. Christian reflection on
martyrdom has reverted to the Jewish view represented by the Maccabean literature. Christian
suffering and death possess no significance in
themselves. Indeed, Tertullian even feels free to
compare Christian martyrdom to any contingency of
accidental or sudden death. Death in the arena
is no different than death at the hand of a high-
way robber, or by a sudden fire, or by a beast met
by chance in the forest (Ad mart. 6). Resurrection from the dead has no place in such martyrological thinking, for the battle of the martyr is
the martyr's battle for life. It is not Christ
the Risen One doing battle through the Spirit for
and in the martyr.

NOTES TO THE CONCLUSION

1 Hans von Campenhausen, Die Idee des Martyriums in der alten Kirche, 2nd ed. (Göttingen: Vandenhoeck & Ruprecht, 1964) 3-4.

2 In his study on the motif of suffering in 1 Peter, Helmut Millauer concludes that while Judaism had the concept of a future joy after suffering and of a joy in spite of suffering, the concept of rejoicing because of suffering was typically early Christian (Leiden als Gnade: Eine traditionsgeschichtliche Untersuchung zur Leidenstheologie des ersten Petrusbriefe [Europäische Hochschulschriften, series 23, Theologie 56; Bern: Herbert Lang, 1976] 165-85).

BIBLIOGRAPHY

1. Books

Asting, Ragnar Kristian. Die Heiligkeit im
Urchristentum. Forschungen zur Religion und
Literatur des Alten und Neuen Testaments,
edited by Rudolf Bultmann and Hermann
Gunkel, vol. 46 (new series, vol. 29).
Göttingen: Vandenhoeck & Ruprecht, 1930.

Aune, David Edward. The Cultic Setting of Realized
Eschatology in Early Christianity. Supple-
ments to Novum Testamentum, vol. 28. Leiden:
E. J. Brill, 1972.

Baer, Heinrich von. Der Heilige Geist in den
Lukasschriften. Beiträge zur Wissenschaft
vom Alten und Neuen Testament, edited by
Rudolf Kittel, vol. 39 (3rd series, vol. 3).
Stuttgart: W. Kohlhammer, 1926.

Barnes, Timothy David. Tertullian: A Historical
and Literary Study. Oxford: Clarendon, 1971.

Barrett, Charles Kingsley. The Holy Spirit and
the Gospel Tradition. London: SPCK, 1947.

Bartsch, Hans-Werner. Gnostisches Gut und
Gemeindetradition bei Ignatius von Antiochien.
Beiträge zur Förderung christlicher Theologie,
edited by Paul Althaus, vol. 44. Gütersloh:
C. Bertelsman, 1940.

Bauer, Walter. Die Briefe des Ignatius von
Antiochia. In Die Apostolischen Väter.
Handbuch zum Neuen Testament, edited by Hans
Lietzmann, Ergänzungsband, pp. 185-281.
Tübingen: J. C. B. Mohr, 1923.

Beek, C. J. M. J. van. Passio Sanctarum Perpetuae
et Felicitatis. Disputatio inauguralis, quam
. . . publico examini submittet C. I. M. I.
van Beek, vol. I: Textus Graecus et Latinus
ad fidem codicum mss. Accedunt acta breva
SS. Perpetuae et Felicitatis. Nijmegen: 1936.

283

Bender, Wolfgang. Die Lehre über den Heiligen
  Geist bei Tertullian. Münchener Theologische
  Studien II. Systematische Abteilung, vol. 18.
  München: M. Heuber, 1961.

Bihlmeyer, Karl. Die Apostolischen Väter.
  Neubearbeitung der Funkschen Ausgabe. 3rd ed.
  Reprint of the 2nd ed. by Wilhelm
  Schneemelcher. Sammlung ausgewählter kirchen-
  und dogmengeschichtlicher Quellenschriften,
  edited by Gustav Krüger. Tübingen: J. C. B.
  Mohr, 1970.

de Boer, Willis Peter. The Imitation of Paul: An
  Exegetical Study. Kampen: J. H. Kok, 1962.

Bommes, Karin. Weizen Gottes: Untersuchungen zur
  Theologie des Martyriums bei Ignatius von
  Antiochien. Theophaneia. Beiträge zur
  Religions- und Kirchengeschichte des Altertums,
  edited by Theodor Klauser and Ernst Dassmann,
  vol. 27. Köln/Bonn: Peter Hanstein, 1976.

Brekelmans, Antonius J. Martyrerkranz: Eine
  symbolgeschichtliche Untersuchung im frühchristlichen Schrifttum. Analecta Gregoriana,
  vol. 150. Rome: Libreria Editrice dell'
  Università Gregoriana, 1965.

Brown, Schuyler. Apostasy and Perseverance in the
  Theology of Luke. Analecta Biblica, vol. 36.
  Rome: Pontifical Biblical Institute, 1969.

Brox, Norbert. Zeuge und Märtyrer: Untersuchungen
  zur frühchristlichen Zeugnis-Terminologie.
  Studien zum Alten und Neuen Testament, edited
  by Vinzenz Hamp and Josef Schmid, vol. 5.
  München: Kösel, 1961.

Büchsel, Friedrich. Der Geist Gottes im Neuen
  Testament. Gütersloh: C. Bertelsmann, 1926.

Campenhausen, Hans Freiherr von. Die Idee des
  Martyriums in der alten Kirche. 2nd rev. ed.
  Göttingen: Vandenhoeck & Ruprecht, 1964.

Charles, Robert Henry, ed. The Apocrypha and
  Pseudepigrapha of the Old Testament in

English with Introductions and Critical and
Explanatory Notes to the Several Books.
2 vols. Oxford: At the Clarendon Press, 1913.
Reprint. Oxford: At the University Press,
1963.

Corwin, Virginia. St. Ignatius and Christianity
in Antioch. Yale Publications in Religion,
edited by David Horne, vol. 1. New Haven:
Yale University, 1960.

Delahaye, Karl. Ecclesia mater chez les pères des
trois premiers siècles: pour un renouvellement
de la Pastorale d'aujourd'hui. Translated
by P. Vergriete and E. Bouis. Unam Sanctam,
vol. 46. Paris: Éditions du Cerf, 1964.

Delehaye, Hippolyte. Les passions des martyrs et
les genres littéraires. Bruxelles: Société
des Bollandistes, 1921.

Delehaye, Hippolyte. Sanctus: Essai sur le culte
des saints dans l'antiquité. Subsidia
hagiographica, vol. 17. Bruxelles: Société
des Bollandistes, 1927.

Frend, William Hugh Clifford. Martyrdom and
Persecution in the Early Church: A Study of
a Conflict from the Maccabees to Donatus.
Oxford: Basil Blackwell, 1965. Anchor Books
edition, Garden City, New York: Doubleday,
1967.

Fridh, Åke. Le problème de la passion des saintes
Perpétue et Félicité. Studia graeca et
latina Gothoburgensia, vol. 26. Göteborg:
Almquist & Wiksell, 1968.

von der Goltz, Eduard Alexander. Ignatius von
Antiochien als Christ und Theologe: eine
dogmengeschichtliche Untersuchung. Texte
und Untersuchungen zur Geschichte der
altchristlichen Literatur, vol. 12/3.
Leipzig: J. C. Hinrichs, 1894.

Grabar, André. Martyrium: Recherches sur le culte
des reliques et l'art chrétien antique.
2 vols. Paris: Collège de France, 1946.

Grundmann, Walter. Der Begriff der Kraft in der
neutestamentlichen Gedankenwelt. Beiträge
zur Wissenschaft vom Alten und Neuen
Testament, edited by Albrecht Alt and Gerhard
Kittel, vol. 60 (4th series, vol. 8).
Stuttgart: W. Kohlhammer, 1932.

Güttgemanns, Erhardt. Der leidende Apostel und
sein Herr: Studien zur paulinischen
Christologie. Forschungen zur Religion und
Literatur des Alten und Neuen Testaments,
edited by Ernst Käsemann and Ernst Würthwein,
vol. 90. Göttingen: Vandenhoeck & Ruprecht,
1966.

Gunkel, Hermann. Die Wirkungen des heiligen
Geistes nach der populären Anschauung der
apostolischen Zeit und der Lehre des Apostel
Paulus. Göttingen: Vandenhoeck & Ruprecht,
1899.

Hellmanns, Wilhelm. "Wertschätzung des Martyriums
als eines Rechtfertigungsmittels in der
altchristlichen Kirche bis zu Anfänge des
vierten Jahrhunderts." Dissertation,
University of Breslau, 1912.

Knopf, Rudolf, ed. Ausgewählte Märtyrerakten.
3rd rev. ed. by Gustav Krüger. Sammlung
Ausgewählter Kirchen- und Dogmen-
geschichtlicher Quellenschriften, edited by
Gustav Krüger, vol. 3. Tübingen: J. C. B.
Mohr, 1929.

Kuhl, Curt. Die drei Männer im Feuer (Daniel
Kapitel 3 und seine Zusätze): Ein Beitrag zur
israelitisch-jüdischen Literaturgeschichte.
Beihefte zur Zeitschrift für die
alttestamentliche Wissenschaft, vol. 55.
Giessen: Alfred Töpelmann, 1930.

Lods, Marc. Confesseurs et martyrs: Successeurs
des prophetes dans l'eglise des trois
premiers siecles. Cahiers Théologiques,
vol. 41. Neuchâtel: Delachaux et Niestlé,
1958.

Lohse, Eduard. Märtyrer und Gottesknecht: Untersuchungen zur urchristlichen Verkündigung vom Sühntod Jesu Christi. Forschungen zur Religion und Literatur des Alten und Neuen Testaments, edited by Rudolf Bultmann, vol. 64 (new series, vol. 46). Göttingen: Vandenhoeck & Ruprecht, 1955.

Lucius, Ernst. Die Anfänge des Heiligenkults in der christlichen Kirche. Edited by Gustav Anrich. Tübingen: J. C. B. Mohr, 1904; reprint Frankfurt/Main: Minerva, 1966.

Martín, José Pablo. El Espiritu Santo en los Origenes del Cristianismo: Estudio sobre I Clemente, Ignacio, II Clemente y Justino Martir. Biblioteca di Scienze Religiose, vol. 2. Zürich: Pas, 1971.

Maurer, Christian. Ignatius von Antiochien und das Johannesevangelium. Abhandlungen zur Theologie des Alten und Neuen Testaments, edited by Walther Eichrodt and Oscar Cullmann, vol. 18. Zürich: Zwingli, 1949.

Michel, Otto. Prophet und Märtyrer. Beiträge zur Förderung christlicher Theologie, vol. 37/2. Gütersloh: C. Bertelsmann, 1932.

Millauer, Helmut. Leiden als Gnade: Eine traditionsgeschichtliche Untersuchung zur Leidenstheologie des ersten Petrusbriefes. Europäische Hochschulschriften, 23rd series, Theologie, vol. 56. Bern: Herbert Lang; Frankfurt/Main: Peter Lang, 1976.

Musurillo, Herbert. The Acts of the Christian Martyrs: Introduction, Texts and Translations. Oxford Early Christian Texts, edited by Henry Chadwick. Oxford: At the Clarendon, 1972.

Nautin, Pierre. Lettres et écrivains chrétiens des IIe et IIIe siècles. His Patristica, vol. 2. Paris: Éditions du Cerf, 1961.

Nirschl, Joseph. Die Theologie des heiligen Ignatius, des Apostelschülers und Bischofs

von Antiochien, aus seinen Briefen dargestellt
Mainz: Franz Kirchheim, 1880.

Paulsen, Henning. Studien zur Theologie des
Ignatius von Antiochien. Forschungen zur
Kirchen- und Dogmengeschichte, vol. 29.
Göttingen: Vandenhoeck & Ruprecht, 1978.

Peterson, Erik. Zeuge der Wahrheit. Leipzig:
J. Hegner, 1937.

Quacquarelli, Antonio. Q. S. F. Tertulliani "Ad
martyras": Prolegomeni, testo critico,
traduzione e commento. Opuscula patrum,
vol. 2. Roma/Paris: Desclée, 1963.

Rackl, Michael. Die Christologie des heiligen
Ignatius von Antiochien. Nebst einer
Voruntersuchung: Die Echtheit der sieben
ignatianischen Briefe verteidigt gegen
Daniel Völter. Freiburger theologische
Studien 14. Freiburg: Herder, 1914.

Rathke, Heinrich. Ignatius von Antiochien und die
Paulusbriefe. Texte und Untersuchungen zur
Geschichte der altchristlichen Literatur,
vol. 99. Berlin: Akademie, 1967.

Reuning, W. Zur Erklärung des Polykarp-Martyriums.
Darmstadt: 1917.

Robinson, Joseph Armitage. The Passion of S.
Perpetua: Newly Edited from the MSS. with an
Introduction and Notes. Texts and Studies.
Contributions to Biblical and Patristic
Literature, vol. 1, no. 2. Cambridge: At the
University Press, 1891.

Rüsch, Theodor. Die Entstehung der Lehre vom
Heiligen Geist bei Ignatius von Antiochia,
Theophilus von Antiochia und Irenäus von Lyon.
Studien zur Dogmengeschichte und
systematischen Theologie, vol. 2. Zürich:
Zwingli, 1952.

Schilling, Frederick Augustus. The Mysticism of
Ignatius of Antioch. Philadelphia: 1932.

Schlatter, Adolf von. Der Märtyrer in den Anfängen der Kirche. Beiträge zur Förderung christlicher Theologie, vol. 19/3. Gütersloh: C. Bertelsmann, 1915.

Schlier, Heinrich. Religionsgeschichtliche Untersuchungen zu den Ignatiusbriefen. Beihefte zur Zeitschrift für die neutestamentliche Wissenschaft und die Kunde der älteren Kirche, edited by Hans Lietzmann, vol. 8. Giessen: Alfred Töpelmann, 1929.

Schneider, Johannes. Die Passionsmystik des Paulus: ihr Wesen, ihr Hintergrund und ihre Nachwirkungen. Untersuchungen zum Neuen Testament, vol. 15. Leipzig: J. C. Hinrichs, 1929.

Schoeps, Hans Joachim. Die jüdische Prophetenmorde Symbolae Biblicae Upsalienses, vol. 2. Uppsala: Wretmans, 1943.

Schweizer, Eduard. Erniedrigung und Erhöhung bei Jesus und seinen Nachfolgern. 2nd rev. ed. Abhandlungen zur Theologie des Alten und Neuen Testaments, edited by Walter Eichrodt and Oscar Cullmann, vol. 28. Zürich: Zwingli, 1962.

Surkau, Hans-Werner. Martyrien in jüdischer und frühchristlicher Zeit. Forschungen zur Religion und Literatur des Alten und Neuen Testaments, edited by Rudolf Bultmann, vol. 54 (new series, vol. 36). Göttingen: Vandenhoeck & Ruprecht, 1938.

Swete, Henry Barclay. The Holy Spirit in the New Testament: A Study of Primitive Christian Teaching. London: Macmillan, 1909.

Trites, Allison A. The New Testament Concept of Witness. Society for New Testament Studies Monograph Series, edited by Matthew Black and R. McL. Wilson, vol. 31. Cambridge: Cambridge University, 1977.

Weinel, Heinrich. Die Wirkungen des Geistes und der Geister im nachapostolischen Zeitalter

bis auf Irenäus. Freiburg/Leipzig/Tübingen:
J. C. B. Mohr, 1899.

Wichmann, Wolfgang. Die Leidenstheologie: Eine
Form der Leidensdeutung im Spätjudentum.
Beiträge zur Wissenschaft vom Alten und Neuen
Testament, 4th series, vol. 2. Stuttgart:
W. Kohlhammer, 1930.

Wustmann, Georg. Die Heilsbedeutung Christi bei
den apostolischen Vätern. Beiträge zur
Förderung christlicher Theologie, vol. 9/2-3.
Gütersloh: C. Bertelsmann, 1905.

Zahn, Theodor. Ignatius von Antiochien. Gotha:
1873.

2. Articles

d'Alès, Adhémar. "L'auteur de la Passio Perpetuae."
Revue d'Histoire Ecclésiastique 8 (1907):
5-18.

Alfonsi, Luigi. "Sull' Ad Martyras di Tertulliano."
In In memoriam Achillis Beltrami: Miscellanea
Philologica. Pubblicazioni dell' Instituto
di filologia classica, vol. 3, pp. 39-49.
Genova: Universita di Genova, Facoltà di
lettere, 1954.

Audin, A. "Les martyrs de 177." Cahiers
d'Histoire 11 (1966): 343-67.

Baden, H. "Der Nachahmungsgedanke im Polykarpmartyrium." Theologie und Glaube 3 (1911):
115-22.

Barnard, Leslie William. "The Background of St.
Ignatius of Antioch." Vigiliae Christianae
17 (1963): 193-206.

Barnard, Leslie William. "In Defense of Pseudo-
Pionius' Account of Polycarp's Martyrdom."
In Kyriakon: Festschrift Johannes Quasten,
vol. 1, edited by Patrick Granfield and
Josef A. Jungmann, pp. 192-204. Münster:
Aschendorff, 1970.

Barnes, Timothy David. "Tertullian's Scorpiace." The Journal of Theological Studies, n.s. 20 (1969): 105-32.

Benz, Ernst. "Christus und Sokrates in der alten Kirche: Ein Beitrag zum altkirchlichen Verständnis des Märtyrers und des Martyriums." Zeitschrift für die neutestamentliche Wissenschaft 43 (1950/51): 195-224.

Berthouzoz, Rogers. "Le Père, le Fils et le Saint-Esprit d'après les Lettres d'Ignace d'Antioche." Freiburger Zeitschrift für Philosophie und Theologie 18 (1971): 397-418.

Bertram, Georg. "Paulus Christophorus: Ein anthropologisches Problem des Neuen Testaments." In Stromata: Festgabe des Akademisch-theologischen Vereins zu Giessen, edited by Georg Bertram, pp. 26-38. Leipzig: J. C. Hinrichs, 1930.

Bower, Richard A. "The Meaning of ΕΠΙΤΥΓΧΑΝΩ in the Epistles of St. Ignatius of Antioch." Vigiliae Christianae 28 (1974): 1-14.

Braun, René. "Tertullien est-il le rédacteur de la Passio Perpetuae?" Revue des Études Latines 33 (1955): 79-81.

Braun, René. "Nouvelles observations linguistiques sur le rédacteur de la 'Passio Perpetuae'." Vigiliae Christianae 33 (1979): 105-17.

Brox, Norbert. "'Zeuge seiner Leiden'. Zum Verständnis der Interpolation Ign. Rom. II.2." Zeitschrift für katholische Theologie 85 (1963): 218-20.

Bultmann, Rudolf. "Ignatius und Paulus." In Studia Paulina: In honorem Johannis de Zwaan Septuagenarii, pp. 37-51. Haarlem: De Erven F. Bohn, 1953.

Cambier, J. "Le critère paulinien de l'apostolat en 2 Cor. 12,6s." Biblica 43 (1962): 481-518.

Camelot, P. Th. "L'engagement chrétien: du Baptême au Martyre." Nova et Vetera 24 (1949): 326-48.

Campenhausen, Hans Freiherr von. "Bearbeitungen und Interpolationen des Polykarpmartyriums." In Aus der Frühzeit des Christentums: Studien zur Kirchengeschichte des ersten und zweiten Jahrhunderts, pp. 253-301. Tübingen: J. C. B. Mohr, 1963.

Campos, J. "El autor de la 'Passio SS. Perpetuae et Felicitatis'." Helmántica 10 (1959): 357-81.

Carrez, Maurice. "Souffrance et gloire dans les epîtres pauliniennes." Revue d'Histoire et de Philosophie Religieuse 31 (1951): 343-53.

Cerfaux, Lucien. "L'Antinomie paulinienne de la vie apostolique." Recherches de Science Religieuse 39 (1951): 221-35.

Colson, J. "Agapè chez Saint-Ignace d'Antioche." Texte und Untersuchungen zur Geschichte der altchristlichen Literatur, vol. 78 (=Studia Patristica, vol. 3), pp. 341-53. Berlin: Akademie, 1961.

Corsini, Eugenio. "Proposte per una lettera della 'Passio Perpetuae'." In Forma futuri: Studi in onore del Cardinale Michele Pellegrino, pp. 481-541. Torino: Bottega d'Erasmo, 1975.

Cristiani, Leon. "Saint Ignace d'Antioche: sa vie d'intimité avec Jesus-Christ." Revue d'Ascetique et de Mystique 25 (1949): 109-16.

Davies, Paul E. "Did Jesus die as a Martyr-Prophet." Biblical Research 2 (1957): 19-30.

Davies, Stevan L. "The Predicament of Ignatius of Antioch." Vigiliae Christianae 30 (1976): 175-80.

Delehaye, Hippolyte. "Martyr et Confesseur." Analecta Bollandiana 39 (1921): 20-49.

Donahue, Paul J. "Jewish Christianity in the Letters of Ignatius of Antioch." Vigiliae Christianae 32 (1978): 81-93.

Dölger, Franz Josef. "Antike Parallelen zum leidenden Dinocrates in der Passio Perpetuae." In Antike und Christentum: Kultur- und religionsgeschichtliche Studien, vol. 2, pp. 1-40. Münster: Aschendorff, 1930.

Dölger, Franz Josef. "Gladiatorenblut und Märtyrerblut: eine Szene der Passio Perpetuae in kultur- und religionsgeschichtlicher Beleuchtung." In Vorträge der Bibliothek Warburg, 1923-1924, pp. 196-214. Leipzig: 1926.

Dölger, Franz Josef. "Der Kampf mit dem Ägypter in der Perpetua-Vision: Das Martyrium als Kampf mit dem Teufel." In Antike und Christentum: Kultur- und religions-geschichtliche Studien, vol. 3, pp. 177-88. Münster: Aschendorff, 1932.

Dölger, Franz Josef. "Tertullian über die Bluttaufe." In Antike und Christentum: Kultur- und religionsgeschichtliche Studien, vol. 2, pp. 117-41. Münster: Aschendorff, 1930.

Feuillet, André. "Mort du Christ et mort du chrétien d'après les épitres pauliniennes." Revue Biblique 66 (1959): 481-513.

Fischel, H. A. "Martyr and Prophet: A Study in Jewish Literature." The Jewish Quarterly Review, n.s. 37 (1946/47): 265-80, 363-86.

Gass, Wilhelm. "Das christliche Märtyrerthum in den ersten Jahrhunderten und dessen Idee." Zeitschrift für historische Theologie 29 (1859): 323-92; 30 (1860): 315-81.

Gatti, I. "La 'Passio SS. Perpetuae et Felicitatis'." Didaskaleion 1 (1923): 31-43.

Geffcken, Johannes. "Die christlichen Martyrien." Hermes 45 (1910): 481-505.

Guillaumin, Marie-Louise. "En marge du 'Martyre de Polycarpe' le discernement des allusions scripturaires." In Forma futuri: Studi in onore del Cardinale Michele Pellegrino, pp. 462-69. Torino: Bottega d'Erasmo, 1975.

Hamman, Adalbert. "Signification doctrinale des Actes des martyrs." Nouvelle Revue Theologique 75 (1953): 739-45.

Hedde, R. "Martyre." Dictionnaire de Théologique Catholique, vol. 10, coll. 220-54. Paris: Librairie Letouzey et Ané, 1928.

Holl, Karl. "Die Vorstellung vom Märtyrer und die Märtyrerakte in ihrer geschichtliche Entwicklung." In Gesammelte Aufsätze zur Kirchengeschichte, vol. 2: Der Osten, pp. 68-102. Tübingen: J. C. B. Mohr, 1928.

Hörmann, Karl. "Das Geistreden des Heiligen Ignatius von Antiochia." In Mystische Theologie, Jahrbuch 2, pp. 39-53. Wien: 1956.

Jouassard, G. "Aux origines de culte des martyrs dans le Christianisme. Saint Ignace d'Antioche, Rom. II.2." Recherches de Science Religieuse 39 (1951): 362-67.

Jouassard, G. "Le rôle des Chrétiens comme intercesseurs auprès de Dieu dans la Chrétienté lyonnaise au second siècle." Revue des Sciences Religieuses 30 (1956): 217-29.

Kahrstedt, U. "Die Märtyrerakte von Lugdunum 177." Rheinisches Museum, N.F. 68 (1913): 395-412.

Kamlah, Ehrhard. "Wie Beurteilt Paulus sein Leiden?: Ein Beitrag zur Untersuchung seiner Denkstruktur." Zeitschrift für die neutestamentliche Wissenschaft 54 (1963): 217-32.

Kattenbusch, Ferdinand. "Der Märtyrertitel." Zeitschrift für die neutestamentliche Wissenschaft 4 (1903): 111-27.

Keresztes, Paul. "The Massacre at Lugdunum in 177 A.D." Historia 16 (1967): 75-86.

Klauser, Theodor. "Christlicher Märtyrerkult, heidnischer Heroenkult und spätjüdische Heiligenverehrung: Neue Einsichten und neue Probleme." Arbeitsgemeinschaft für Forschung des Landes Nordrhein-Westfalen, Geistes- wissenschaften, Heft 91, pp. 27-38. Köln: Westdeutscher Verlag, 1960.

Kraft, Heinrich. "Zur Entstehung des altchristlichen Märtyrertitels." In Ecclesia und Res Publica, edited by Georg Kretschmar und Bernhard Lohse, pp. 64-75. Göttingen: Vandenhoeck & Ruprecht, 1961.

Kuhn, Heinz-Wolfgang. "Jesus als Gekreuzigter in der frühchristlichen Verkündigung bis zur Mitte des 2. Jahrhunderts." Zeitschrift für Theologie und Kirche 72 (1975): 1-46.

Kuhn, Karl Georg. "Jesus in Gethsemane." Evangelische Theologie 12 (1952/53): 260-85.

Kuhn, Karl Georg. "Πειρασμός-ἁμαρτία-σάρξ im Neuen Testament und die damit zusammen- hängenden Vorstellungen." Zeitschrift für Theologie und Kirche 49 (1952): 200-22.

Labriolle, Pierre de. "Tertullien, auteur du prologue et de la conclusion de la passion de Perpétue et de Félicité." Bulletin d'ancienne litterature et d'archéologie chrétienne 3 (1913): 126-32.

Lanaro, P. "Temi del martiro nell' antichita cristiana. I martiri di Lione." Studia Patavina. Rivista di filosofia e teologia Padova 14 (1967): 204-35, 325-59.

Leclercq, Henri. "Perpétue et Félicité." Dictionnaire d'archéologie chrétienne et le liturgie, vol. 14, coll. 393-444. Paris: Librairie Letouzey et Ané, 1939.

Lefkowitz, Mary R. "The Motivations for St. Perpetua's Martyrdom." Journal of the American Academy of Religion 44 (1976): 417-21.

295

Lods, Marc. "Le rôle public et la position politique des confesseurs et des martyrs dans l'église ancienne." Positions luthériennes 26 (1978): 211-33.

Lohmeyer, Ernst. "Die Idee des Martyriums in Judentum und Urchristentum." Zeitschrift für systematische Theologie 5 (1928): 232-49.

Lomanto, Valeria. "Rapporti fra la 'Passio Perpetuae' e 'Passiones' Africane." In Forma futuri: Studi in onore del Cardinale Michele Pellegrino, pp. 566-86. Torino: Bottega d'Erasmo, 1975.

Mazzucco, Clementina. "Il Significato Cristiano della 'Libertas' proclamata dai Martiri della 'Passio Perpetuae'." In Forma futuri: Studi in onore del Cardinale Michele Pellegrino, pp. 542-65. Torino: Bottega d'Erasmo, 1975.

Meinhold, Peter. "Episkope--Pneumatiker--Märtyrer: Zur Deutung der Selbstaussagen des Ignatius von Antiochien." Saeculum 14 (1963): 308-24.

Moffatt, James. "An Approach to Ignatius." The Harvard Theological Review 29 (1936): 1-38.

Moffatt, James. "Ignatius of Antioch: A Study in Personal Religion." The Journal of Religion 10 (1930): 169-86.

Müller, Hermann. "Das Martyrium Polycarpi: Ein Beitrag zur altchristlichen Heiligen-geschichte." Römische Quartelschrift 22 (1908): 1-16.

Müller, Ulrich B. "Die Bedeutung des Kreuzestodes Jesu im Johannesevangelium: Erwägungen zur Kreuzestheologie im Neuen Testament." Kerygma und Dogma 21 (1975): 49-71.

Mundle, Wilhelm. "Die Stephanusrede Apg. 7: eine Märtyrerapologie." Zeitschrift für die neutestamentliche Wissenschaft 20 (1921): 133-47.

Nauck, Wolfgang. "Freude im Leiden: Zum Problem einer urchristlichen Verfolgungstradition." Zeitschrift für die neutestamentliche Wissenschaft 46 (1955): 68-80.

Nestle, Eberhard. "Joh 7,38 im Brief der gallischen Christen." Zeitschrift für die neutestamentliche Wissenschaft 10 (1909): 323.

Paciorkowske, R. "L'héroisme religieux d'après la Passion des saintes Perpétue et Félicité." Revue des Études Augustiniennes 5 (1959): 367-89.

Pellegrino, Michele. "L'imitation du Christ dans les Actes des Martyrs." La vie spirituelle 98 (1958): 38-54.

Pellegrino, Michele. "Le sens ecclesial du martyre." Revue des Sciences Religieuses 35 (1961): 151-75.

Perler, Othmar. "Das vierte Makkabaeerbuch, Ignatius von Antiochien und die Aeltesten Martyrerberichte." Rivista di Archeologia Cristiana 25 (1949): 47-72.

Peterson, Erik. "Le Martyr et l'Eglise." Dieu vivant 5 (1947): 19-31.

Pizzolato, Luigi Franco. "Note alla 'Passio Perpetuae et Felicitatis'." Vigiliae Christianae 34 (1980): 105-19.

Preiss, Theodor. "La mystique de l'imitation du Christ et de l'unité chez Ignace d'Antioche." Revue d'Histoire et de Philosophie Religieuse 18 (1938): 197-241.

Quacquarelli, Antonio. "La persecuzione secondo Tertulliano." Gregorianum 31 (1950): 562-89.

Reitzenstein, Richard. "Bemerkungen zur Martyrienliteratur. I. Die Bezeichnung Märtyrer." In Nachrichten von der königlichen Gesellschaft der Wissenschaften zu Göttingen, pp. 417-67. Berlin: Weidmann, 1916.

Richardson, Cyril C. "The Church in Ignatius of Antioch." The Journal of Religion 17 (1937): 428-43.

Riddle, Donald W. "The Martyr Motif in the Gospel According to Mark." The Journal of Religion 4 (1924): 397-410.

Riddle, Donald W. "Die Verfolgungslogien in formgeschichtlicher und soziologischer Beleuchtung." Zeitschrift für die neutestamentliche Wissenschaft 33 (1934): 271-89.

Romanides, J. S. "The Ecclesiology of St. Ignatius of Antioch." Greek Orthodox Theological Review 7 (1961): 53-77.

Rordorf, Willy. "Zur Entstehung der christlichen Märtyrerverehrung." In Aspekte früh-christlicher Heiligenverehrung. Oikonomia. Quellen und Studien zur orthodoxen Theologie, vol. 6, pp. 35-53. Erlangen: 1977.

Rordorf, Willy. "L'espérance des martyrs chrétiens." In Forma futuri: Studi in onore del Cardinale Michele Pellegrino, pp. 445-61. Torino: Bottega d'Erasmo, 1975.

Rordorf, Willy. "Martirio e Testimonianza." Rivista di Storia e Letteratura Religiosa 8 (1972): 239-58.

Rordorf, Willy. "Aux origines du culte des martyrs." Irénikon 46 (1972): 316-31.

Rupprecht, E. "Bemerkungen zur Passio SS. Perpetuae et Felicitatis." Rheinisches Museum, N.F. 90 (1941): 177-92.

Schlegel, G. D. "The Ad Martyras of Tertullian and the Circumstances of its Composition." Downside Review 63 (1945): 125-28.

Schrage, Wolfgang. "Leid, Kreuz und Eschaton: Die Peristasenkataloge als Merkmale paulinischer theologia crucis und Eschatologie." Evangelische Theologie 34 (1974): 141-75.

Schwartz, J. "Note sur le martyre de Polycarpo de Smyrne." Revue d'Histoire et de Philosophie Religieuses 52 (1972): 331-35.

Shewring, W. H. "En marge de la Passion des Saintes Perpétue et Félicité." Revue Benedictine 43 (1931): 15-22.

Shewring, W. H. "Prose Rhythm in the Passio S. Perpetuae." The Journal of Theological Studies 30 (1929): 56-57.

Sieben, Hermann Josef. "Die Ignatianen als Briefe: Einige formkritische Bemerkungen." Vigiliae Christianae 32 (1978): 1-18.

Simonetti, Manlio. "Alcune osservazioni sul martirio di S. Policarpo." Giornale Italiano di Filologia 9 (1956): 328-44.

Simonetti, Manlio. "Qualche osservazione sui luoghi comuni negli atti dei martiri." Giornale Italiano di Filologia 10 (1957): 147-55.

Snyder, Graydon F. "The Historical Jesus in the Letters of Ignatius of Antioch." Biblical Research 8 (1963): 3-12.

Spicq, Ceslaus. "L'imitation de Jésus-Christ durant des derniers jours de l'apôtre Paul." In Mélanges Bibliques en hommage au R. P. Béda Rigaux, edited by Albert Descamps and R. P. André de Halleux, pp. 313-22. Gembloux: Ducolot, 1970.

Stanley, David Michael. "'Become Imitators of Me': The Pauline Conception of Apostolic Tradition." Biblica 40 (1959): 859-77.

Strathmann, Hermann. "μάρτυς." Theologisches Wörterbuch zum Neuen Testament, vol. 4, edited by Gerhard Kittel, pp. 477-520. Stuttgart: W. Kohlhammer, 1942.

Swartley, Willard M. "The Imitatio Christi in the Ignatian Letters." Vigiliae Christianae 27 (1973): 81-103.

Tinsley, E. J. "The imitatio Christi in the Mysticism of St. Ignatius of Antioch." Texte und Untersuchungen zur Geschichte der altchristlichen Literatur (=Studia Patristica, vol. 2), pp. 553-560. Berlin: Akademie, 1957.

Viller, Marcel. "Les Martyrs et l'Esprit." Recherches de Science Religieuse 14 (1924): 544-51.

Viller, Marcel. "Martyre et Perfection." Revue d'Ascetique et de Mystique 6 (1925): 3-25.

Waal, A. de. "Der leidende Dinokrates in der Vision der heiligen Perpetua." Römische Quartelschrift 17 (1903): 839-47.

Walaskay, Paul W. "Ignatius of Antioch: The Synthesis of Astral Mysticism, Rational Theology and Christian Witness." Religion in Life 58 (1979): 309-22.

Walter, E. "Die Kraft wird in der Schwachheit vollendet: Zur paulinischen Theologie der Schwachheit." Geist und Leben 28 (1955): 248-55.

Winslow, Donald F. "The Idea of Redemption in the Epistles of St. Ignatius of Antioch." Greek Orthodox Theological Review 11 (1965): 119-31.

Zahn, Theodor. "Die Passio Perpetuae." Theologische Literaturblatt 13 (1892): coll. 41-45.

INDEX OF REFERENCES

1. OLD TESTAMENT

2. APOCRYPHA AND PSEUDOPIGRAPHA

302

3. DEAD SEA SCROLLS

305

5. IGNATIUS OF ANTIOCH

6. MARTYRDOM OF POLYCARP

7. LETTER OF THE LYONS MARTYRS

8. PASSION OF PERPETUA

9. TERTULLIAN

10. OTHER CHRISTIAN LITERATURE

CURRICULUM VITAE

I was born on 1 March 1945 to Carl and Erna Weinrich in Ponca City, Oklahoma, and I spent my entire youth in that city. From 1960 to 1963 I attended Ponca City Senior High School, and I received its Diploma in 1963.

In the fall of 1963 I entered the University of Oklahoma, Norman, Oklahoma, and four years later the University awarded me the degree of Bachelor of Arts in history and philosophy (1967). At the same time I was elected to the scholastic honor society, Phi Beta Kappa.

In the fall of 1967 I entered Concordia Theological Seminary, St. Louis, Missouri. After one year at Concordia Seminary, I made use of a Rotary International Fellowship to study theology at the University of Basel, Basel, Switzerland (1968-69). During this year I had the privilege of hearing O. Cullmann, B. Reicke, H. Ott, M. A. Schmidt, and G. Müller. Returning to the United States, I completed my basic theological training at Concordia Theological Seminary, receiving the Master of Divinity degree from that institution in May, 1972.

A graduate fellowship from the Lutheran World Federation made it possible for me to return to the University of Basel for study towards the Doctor of Theology degree (1972-1975). During this period of study I had the privilege of studying under B. Reicke, M. A. Schmidt, J. M. Lochman, W. Bieder, M. Barth, F. Buri, and H. Ott.

I submitted my dissertation to the Faculty of Theology, Basel, in February, 1977, and it was accepted by it in June of that year. On 20 October 1977 I passed my oral examination and was thereupon awarded the degree of Doctor of Theology, Insigni cum laude.

On 30 November 1975 I was ordained into the ministry of the Lutheran Church-Missouri Synod.

Since December, 1975, I have served as Assistant Professor of Early Church History and Patristic Studies at Concordia Theological Seminary, Fort Wayne, Indiana (formerly located in Springfield, Illinois).